75 Years on 4 Strings

75 Years on 4 Strings

The Life and Music of François Rabbath

Hans Sturm

avant bass

Published 2022 by Avant Bass LLC, Lincoln, Nebraska.
avant-bass.com

Seventy-Five Years on Four Strings was supported by generous grants from the Hixson-Lied College of Fine and Performing Arts and the Glenn Korff School of Music at the University of Nebraska–Lincoln.

Printed in the United States of America

ISBN   979-8-9853057-0-8 (paperback)
ISBN   979-8-9853057-3-9 (hardcover)
ISBN   979-8-9853057-1-5 (cloth commemorative edition)
ISBN   979-8-9853057-2-2 (ebook)

Publisher's Cataloging-in-Publication Data
(provided by Five Rainbows Cataloging Services)

Names: Sturm, Hans, author.
Title: 75 years on 4 strings : the life and music of François Rabbath / Hans Sturm.
Description: Lincoln, NE : Avant Bass, 2022. | Includes index.
Identifiers: LCCN 2022900342 (print) | ISBN 979-8-9853057-0-8 (paperback) |
    ISBN 979-8-9853057-3-9 (case laminate) | ISBN 979-8-9853057-1-5 (cloth) |
    ISBN 979-8-9853057-2-2 (ebook)
Subjects: LCSH: Double bassists—Biography. | Jazz musicians—Biography. |
    Musicians—France. | Double bass—Methods. | Music—20th century—History
    and criticism. | BISAC: BIOGRAPHY & AUTOBIOGRAPHY / Music. | MUSIC /
    Individual Composer & Musician. | MUSIC / Musical Instruments / Strings.
Classification: LCC ML410.R33 S78 2022 (print) | LCC ML410.R33 (ebook) |
    DDC 780.92—dc23.

Library of Congress Control Number: 2022900342

Cover artwork by Marco Pascolini, derived from a portrait of François Rabbath by Ruthie Ingram. Used by special permission and arrangement with the artists and the KC Bass Workshop, for whom the works were created, Johnny Hamil, director.

Cover design by Marianne Jankowski

Interior design by THINK Book Works

To François Rabbath, whose boundless artistry,

generosity, and love inspires everyone he touches

———————

To Jackie & Wolfgang, my nearest and dearest

Contents

Photographs follow page 129.

Preface

first became aware of François Rabbath in the early 1980s. After transferring between three universities within four years, I had finally settled on a path in music and landed at the University of Wisconsin–Madison in 1981 as a student of NEA Jazz Master Richard Davis. I took a course in string pedagogy, team-taught by Lowell Creitz and Tyrone Grieve, where I was introduced to the world of bass pedagogy. Fascinated, I joined the International Society of Bassists (ISB) and, through their journal, learned about François's *Nouvelle technique* and his recordings. Like others before me, I excitedly plowed into his books without truly understanding what he intended. Over a decade later I heard one of my former students, Sandor Ostlund, give an exceptional performance of Bach's Cello Suite No. 4 at the 1999 ISB convention in Iowa City. He told me that he had been studying with François in Paris and suggested that I do the same. I was intimidated by the thought, especially after witnessing François's masterclass and performance of Frank Proto's *Four Scenes after Picasso* two years earlier at the ISB convention in Houston. But learning that François would be teaching at the George Vance Summer Bass Workshop in Washington, DC, I signed up as a student. After I played my transcription of Astor Piazzolla's *Le grand tango*, he asked his classic question, "Why you play like that, exactly?," followed immediately by, "You must come to Paris to study with me." Hard to believe that moment was over twenty years ago.

Born in 1931 in Aleppo, Syria, François would become an internationally renowned soloist, composer, and pedagogue who would completely revolutionize the world of one of the least celebrated instruments, the double bass. Along the way, his life path would intersect with some of the most intriguing figures of the twentieth century. Some years ago, François was inspired to pen a brief unpublished autobiography, a series of stories that shaped his life. He had no reservations about sharing many of his most intimate moments and emotions in the hope that others may benefit from his experiences, yet he was hesitant to share his successes for fear of being perceived as pretentious. His desire was to explain how he developed his technique in less than seven years and why he created his seminal method, the *Nouvelle technique de la contrebasse*. François's autobiographical stories were intriguing and inspiring, and yet they shared only a brief glimpse into the fascinating and complex tapestry of his life's story.

So, I find myself in a rather awkward position. I, too, am a bassist and have been greatly influenced by François's innovations—to the point of authoring and producing two state-of-the-art DVDs of his pedagogy featuring biomechanics animations and user-selectable camera angles. As the great biographer Nigel Hamilton points out in his noteworthy text *How to Do Biography*, I am therefore the least qualified person to write this book. (Should politicians write biographies of other politicians, or scientists write about scientists?)

Of course, the world of the double bass is quite small. You can find us in virtually every acoustic musical setting imaginable—orchestras, chamber music, jazz bands, folk music, new music, early music ensembles, and more—but on only the rarest of occasions will you hear the bass on top (apologies to Paul Chambers). The majority of bassists make their livelihoods supporting others (and you *will* miss us if we aren't there). Despite the fundamental necessity of the instrument's deep, rich, sonorous presence to establish a musical foundation, few major composers have embraced the instrument and its unique qualities as a solo voice. For instance, the two most famous Romantic concertos composed for double bass were written by Giovanni Bottesini and Serge Koussevitzky, both bassists. The two also happened to be celebrated conductors. Bottesini is best known for his work with the Italian National Opera, and Koussevitzky, with the Boston Symphony Orchestra. Our instrument's largest organization, the International Society of Bassists (ISB), hosts a biennial composition competition and has sought to commission major living composers to write major works for the instrument, the most recent being Pulitzer Prize winner John Harbison's Concerto for Bass Viol and Orchestra (2006). The moral of the story: despite being the underdogs (apologies to Charles Mingus), we bassists do for ourselves.

As François entered his ninth decade, it seemed clear to me that his was a story well worth telling, not just for the bassists who wish to know more about this intriguing personality, but also for the general public, who might come to embrace the love of a bass. He has been gracious enough to sit for many hours of interviews over a handful of years. Through the process of reviewing his earlier text with him, our discussions would often lead to the recollection of additional details, which in turn would often lead to another story. François also shared a great variety of documents (reviews, calendars, and lengthy documents related to performances and recordings), highlights of which are included in this book. I have also had the opportunity to interview many of the bassists and other musicians who have interacted with him over the years.

François's career can be viewed as evolving through five stages:

1. The Early Years (1943–1956): Covers the period from his introduction to the bass, through the Hotel Normandy residence in Beirut, until he moves to Paris.
2. Charles Aznavour (1956–1962): Marks the period when François tours internationally with Charles Aznavour and begins to become established in the French recording industry.
3. Solo Career (1962–1980): Extends from the release of *The Sound of a Bass* on Philips, which propels François's solo and freelance career, until he auditions for the Paris Opera Orchestra after the birth of his second son, Cyril.
4. The Paris Opera Years (1980–1995): Supported by the stability of a well-paying job, François continues to tour, teach, and inspire. He retires at age sixty-five.
5. Later Career (1995–present): Retiring from the opera allows François time to add volumes to his *Nouvelle technique de la contrebasse* and expand his musical explorations and collaborations.

At the time of my writing, in 2021, François recently celebrated his ninetieth birthday with a forty-five-minute live-streamed recital. He cannot believe that he has lived in such good health for so long, except to say that he has been lucky. He still practices one to two hours daily—a scale routine, a few new ideas, always a few movements of a Bach suite, and a variety of miscellaneous works. The sixth volume of his method is now in the hands of his publisher. He is working on composing a new concerto, his fourth, with Sylvain, his youngest son, collaborator, and pianist for many years. There is also the pending release of another CD, *Rabbath and Friends*, and his list of friends is formidable: Benny Golson, Michel Legrand, Paco Ibáñez, Ron Carter, and Rufus Reid, among others.

François is grateful for his health and has always been aware that learning never stops. He has often said in masterclasses that it would take him another lifetime or more to master what he dreams to play. In 1999 he received a phone call from an elderly gentleman who said that he would like to meet François and take a few lessons. He said he had heard great things about the new technique and wanted to have the opportunity to explore these concepts. François welcomed him into his home and learned that the man was ninety years old and had retired from the Paris Opera some years before François had been hired. At the time of their meeting, François himself had only just retired from the opera. Intrigued by the man's story, but not expecting much, François was impressed by the man's ability to learn and apply his *Nouvelle technique* after having played for a lifetime using traditional methods.

François has chosen to perform less frequently. The gradually decreasing frequency of solo recitals comes for a variety of reasons. The act of traveling has become very tiring, and while it has always been a challenge to fly with a double bass, the security issues and visa requirements have made the whole process much more complicated and exhausting, especially at his advanced age. Bassists must acquire a kind of sarcophagus to place the instrument in the hold of the plane—it's awkward and difficult to maneuver—and then there is the worry for the safety of the instrument when handled by the baggage crew. Complicating matters, François will only perform with his son Sylvain. Sylvain's reputation as a record producer, recording engineer, and keyboard artist has grown exponentially, and he has been working with a variety of artists on major labels. Consequently, Sylvain's schedule must align with his father's in order to make travel possible.

Despite all these challenges, François's endurance, energy, and focus remain unflagging. His recitals are filled with demanding repertoire, over seventy minutes in length without intermission, and performed from memory—a monumental feat for an artist at any age. He continues to perform many of the works that he created early in his career, pieces he wrote for his earliest albums dating from the 1960s and '70s, inspired by people, places, and events. He pairs these with movements from works written for him by Frank Proto, movements from the Bach suites or Vivaldi, and an occasional jazz standard. Nevertheless, his repertoire continues to expand, as he introduces new works for unaccompanied bass and works composed in collaboration with his son.

When asked about the major themes running through his life, what the threads were that held everything together, François's response was simple: "La basse au centre de tout" (The bass is the center of everything).

The thousands of bassists and other musicians whose lives François has touched know him as gentle and generous to a fault. For those lucky enough to have passed through his door on the sixth floor of 26 rue de Clichy and spent some real time with him, they were likely invited to sip a Turkish coffee and nibble on homemade hummus. As George Vance remarked in 2002, at the end of his interview about François with Henry Peyrebrune, "You know he has this weakness in his nature, and that is he wants you to love him. That's it. That's all he wants from you. If you love him, you can have anything. He's a sucker for that. And he has the childlike nature that is spoken about in the Gospels for instance. Unless you become like little children, you can't enter the kingdom of heaven. Well, those aren't just clichés, there are people like that walking around and he's one of them."[1]

Acknowledgments

I am deeply indebted to the dozens of people who have generously and graciously shared their time and stories to help me complete a portrait of this gentle and generous musical genius. Many bassists who have encountered François have been unsparing in their openness and hospitality.

First and foremost, my most profound thanks go to François Rabbath, whose teaching has always been an inspiration and whose life story exemplifies his spirit and humanity. I had initially intended to write a book focused on the ways in which his philosophy shaped his pedagogy, a uniquely powerful combination that has completely changed the arc of double bass history. However, after a year of writing, it became clear that the lessons learned from his life's story were critical to the development of his philosophy and needed to be told. Many of the earlier stories are based on François's short unpublished autobiography, written in French, and they have been greatly enhanced and expanded through interviews I conducted with him over several years. This has been an emotionally moving journey, and I greatly cherish the many hours we spent together. I am also deeply indebted to François's immediate family, particularly his wife, Martine, and his son Sylvain. They have always welcomed me warmly into their home, and they graciously took time from their busy schedules to share many personal insights and stories.

François has several champions in the United States who shared innumerable stories from their early experiences and those that continued over a forty-year period. Frank Proto invited me into his home and spent three days sharing historic recordings, scores, and fascinating stories from their collaborative life. Paul Ellison also welcomed me into his home and was happy to share his experiences with François, not only from decades of teaching together, but also from his personal journal kept during his studies in Paris. The directness of these personal reflections speaks to the earliest experiences many bassists had when they stepped into François's living room for the first time. Barry Green shared a very emotional interview about his journey with François. Honest and direct, he expressed how those experiences continue to affect his musical life to this day.

Special thanks to Henry Peyrebrune for sharing his marvelous interview with George Vance, and to Henry's wife, Tracy Rowell, for helping to arrange access to the complete unedited version; to Martha Vance, for giving her permission to include excerpts from the interview; to Johnny Hamil and Christian Chesanek for helping to transcribe the document; and to Hal Robinson for helping to illuminate the genesis of the *Progressive Repertoire* project. And, of course, my deepest thanks to George Vance, who was a brilliant, inspiring bass pedagogue whose work continues to have a major impact on beginning bassists.

Many bassists who were instrumental in helping François's early international career in Europe were happy to share their experiences and thoughts. Johnny Sølvberg (Copenhagen) was kind enough to share stories of his early encounters with François in Paris and his efforts to bring François to Scandinavia multiple times, along with programs, reviews, and stories about the early premiere of Proto's Concerto No. 2 and the Michel Legrand concerto, *Contrebande pour contrebasse*. Special thanks to Kristen Korb, with assistance from Morten Korb Støve, for translating the Danish reviews of François's performances. Jack Goldzweig (London) was very frank about his relationship and work with François, which included negotiating contracts for film soundtracks and arranging formal concerts in London, as well as attending several of François's summer workshops. Thanks to Caroline Emery (London) for sharing her stories about hearing François for the first time and subsequently bringing him to London to teach at the Menuhin School and the Royal College of Music. Tom Martin (London) was kind enough to share his story of performing with François on the movie soundtrack for *The Temptation of Isabelle*, finding a second Quenoil bass for him, and spending time studying his method.

Several bassists shared extraordinary stories from François's time in the Paris Opera Orchestra. Thierry Barbé, one of the two super soloists in the Paris Opera Orchestra and a professor at the Paris Conservatory, shared numerous stories of studying and working with François over the ten years they spent together in the Paris Opera. His frank, unvarnished perspective breathed life into those years. He also helped identify Paris Opera members in historic photographs. Likewise, Louis Guilbert, one of François's closest friends, was both a member of the Paris Opera bass section and the orchestra's personnel manager for many years. He confirmed many of the stories from the opera and shared several of his own. Michael Greenberg was an invaluable help in researching François's early career. He was unstinting in his assistance, helping with interview translations and identifying people in historic photographs. His master's thesis at the Sorbonne is an exceptional academic study of François's career in documents through the mid-1990s.

I could not have completed the section on François's brilliant recording of all six Cello Suites by J. S. Bach without the unflinchingly honest interviews with GP Cremonini and Minas Lourian. GP not only shared very personal stories from his experiences and his extensive notes taken during François's Bach recording, but also welcomed me into his home for several days and hosted extraordinary meals at his world-class restaurant, Riviera, in Venice. Minas, the director of the Center for Studies and Documentation of Armenian Culture (Centro Studi e Documentazione della Cultura Armena) in Venice, spent several hours with me, hosting a tour of the Palazzo Zenobio, where the Bach recording was made, and discussing the recording process at length.

François made several tours of Australia through the efforts of several bassists. Thanks to Ken Poggioli for chatting at length about François's trips Down Under and for sharing several programs and reviews. Also, thanks to Peter McLachlan, Nick Tsiavos, and Michael Fortescue, each of whom shared their own experiences with François in addition to programs and reviews.

American bassists who have worked extensively with François more recently were also very generous with their time and stories. They include Nicholas Walker, who, among many other things, shared valuable insights into François's *In a Sentimental Mood* recording and his workshop in Venice hosted by GP Cremonini. Johnny Hamil has been one of the greatest proponents of the work of both

George Vance and François Rabbath and shared a beautiful testimonial about their work together. I am also deeply indebted to Johnny, a close friend and collaborator for many years, for arranging permissions for the cover artwork. Lloyd Goldstein, a certified practitioner at the Moffitt Cancer Center, shared a very moving testimonial about François's inspirational teaching. Lloyd uses François's philosophy and teaching as he performs daily at the bedside of cancer patients. Ted Botsford, now a member of the Los Angeles Philharmonic, shared stories about his studies with George Vance, François Rabbath, and Paul Ellison.

Other international bassists who shared their stories include Michael Schneider, Silvio Dalla Torre, and Szymon Marciniak (Germany); Renaud Garcia-Fons and Joe Carver (France); and Etienne Lafrance (Canada).

Jazz bassists have long embraced François's pedagogy, finding it freeing from more traditional methods. Thanks to Ray Brown for producing the film *The Art of Playing the Bass*, featuring François. John Clayton shared a beautiful statement about how he has embraced and shared François's positive approach to teaching. Rufus Reid also wrote about François as an inspiring guru and shared how he uses François's techniques in his performing. Lynn Seaton, professor of jazz bass at the University of North Texas, sent a testimonial about how he continues to use François's teaching methods in working with advanced jazz bassists.

French luthiers, including bass makers Horst Grunert and Christian Laborie and bow makers Jean Grunberger, Gilles Duhaut, and Boris Fritsch, have shared how their work was inspired and shaped by François.

The celebrated French educational filmmaker Thierry Le Nouvel shared his films and accompanying stories over an afternoon meeting and in emails about the making of *Bass Ball*, *La Carte Blanche*, and *François Rabbath: The Double Bass* CD-ROM.

Additional thanks to Guillermo Benavides for his insights into the making of *In a Sentimental Mood*, Philippe Petit for his contributions to the story about the first Palais des Sports concerts, Gerald Fischbach for introducing bassists to the Rabbath method with his heterogeneous method, David Walter for encouraging François and spreading the word in the bass community in the United States,

Myung-Whun Chung for his work with the Paris Opera, Dennis Trembly for his statements about François, Jacques Dubois for seeking ways to apply the *Nouvelle technique* to the violin, and finally, Paco Ibáñez and Michel Legrand, both of whom made magical music with François for many decades. I am especially grateful to my dear friend Michael Weiss, who generously spent an afternoon interviewing Paco in Barcelona about his early adventures with François and made an exceptional translation of their conversation.

Lastly, I would like to thank those who contributed to the success of this project. Thanks to Dean Charles O'Connor and the Hixson-Lied College of Fine and Performing Arts for their continued support, notably for my faculty leave to work on the manuscript and for my travel costs. I am especially indebted to Dr. Sergio Ruiz, director of the Glenn Korff School of Music, for his enthusiastic and generous grant support, without which it would have been virtually impossible to bring this project to completion. Many thanks to Mike Levine for his developmental editing, which brought the biography into focus, and for suggesting Mary Klein as the person best suited to help with final refinements to the manuscript. And to Mary Klein, the ne plus ultra of copyediting and publishing expertise, a very special thank-you for her experienced hand, eye for detail, and joyous demeanor.

Hans Sturm
Lincoln, Nebraska, 2021

Avec Quatre Cordes

(With Four Strings)

François Rabbath

In Beirut, Lebanon, I started working at the age of thirteen as a musician playing the four-string double bass to help support my family.

At sixteen I stopped playing on my four strings for two years to set up a factory of women's underwear by working twelve hours a day to help my sister Loulou and my brother-in-law René Cabbabé, along with their four young children.

From eighteen to twenty-three years old I returned to my four strings. In this period, I helped to pay the full board of my two brothers Jean and Henri for a year, so that one could continue to study piano and the other search for work. (I remember my father telling me, "My son, your brother is never going to reimburse you for this money." And my response, "Daddy, someone has to help them.")

With my four strings: I managed to enter the National Conservatory of Paris.

With my four strings: For two years, I helped my brother Jean pay for his living expenses in France and his lessons with his piano teacher Magda Tagliaféro. When I was absent on my tours, I gave him signed blank checks for his needs.

With my four strings: I helped an Armenian violinist who landed in Lebanon. He did not have enough to live on, nowhere to stay. I let him stay in my nine-square-meter apartment and fed him for several months until I was able to find him a job.

With my four strings: I helped my first wife, who had left me, until she found another husband.

With my four strings: I wrote a six-volume method to help other bass players to progress.

With my four strings: I have accompanied singing celebrities.

With my four strings: I joined the Paris Opera at the age of fifty.

With my four strings: I had a career as a soloist. My bass made me famous all over the world.

With my four strings: I helped my three children to settle down.

Finally, it's amazing what we can do with four strings.

Finally, I am very happy to have had the chance to find my bass that supports my four strings and my bow that makes them vibrate.

prelude

I magine you have arrived at a concert venue. Any venue will do: an ornate theater in Venice, a modern performing arts center in Tokyo, a rustic church in rural Kansas, a garden in Copenhagen. Perhaps you were invited by a friend—an amazing double bassist was to give a recital. Not to be missed!

A bass recital? Really?

That large, cumbersome instrument?

The instrument that the baroque flutist Joachim Quantz once described as sounding like the furniture was being rearranged in the upstairs apartment?

But your friend was insistent, so here you are.

The lights are low onstage, but you can make out that the grand piano is fully open. (You wonder, How will the bassist ever be heard?) François's famous Quenoil bass, with its distinctive gently sloping shoulders, leans on a conductor's podium, placed just in front of the curve of the piano.

As the lights come up, the audience begins to applaud, and an elderly gentleman approaches the podium at a measured pace. He is dressed in an untucked dress shirt with flowing sleeves, and you notice the gold chains around his neck as he acknowledges the applause with a warm smile and waves. His sparse silvery-gray hair, unshaven chin, and warm smile remind you vaguely of somebody's great-uncle. He leans over and picks up the bass in a single graceful motion, and after a few deliberate bow strokes to check his tuning, he looks up to the audience and says in his strong accent, "*Poucha-dass*. I always begin with *Poucha-dass*. A raga."

And so it begins. Slowly unfolding.

The music sounds vaguely familiar, this bass raga. With the bow swiftly alternating between strings, you sense the presence of the sitar's drone, but much deeper and more profound. Small glissandi and subtle accents give the music flavor and rhythmic character. The bow moves toward the bridge and back toward the fingerboard, changing the timbre of the sound from clear to otherworldly and back again. He looks up to the ceiling, smiles again, and looks to his bow. He is enjoying the sounds. You become transported by the ever-evolving music as the piece grows in intensity. In a sudden blaze of double-stops, the percussive tabla interrupts and then melts back into the sitar. And then interrupts again. The piece grows ever faster. Higher. More intense. The bow is a blur, and the whole room seems to be ringing with the drone. And then, after a single harmonic flourish, he lifts his bow off the bass in a long, slow arc as the harmonics ring and then fade into an explosion of applause.

The music was transcendent—beautiful and intense. Yes, it was the sound of a bass, but what you heard was sitar and tabla. It was the ultimate demonstration of a tremendous virtuosity perfectly serving the music, a mélange of Middle Eastern scales, jazz-inspired improvisation, and classical techniques, played effortlessly. And always with a smile.

1

The Early Years

Each one is unique.

fter World War I, a League of Nations mandate gave France control over the Syrian territory. Although Syria was declared independent of France in 1930, the French parliament was unwilling to relinquish control. It was not until 1944 that the proclamation of independence was finalized and French troops began to leave. Despite complex problems caused by the occupation, there were humanitarian benefits. The French had funded education, infrastructure, and agriculture projects. Aleppo had been competing with Damascus to become the cultural and intellectual capital of the newly formed country, albeit in different states, and the French, seeking to exploit this competition, offered Aleppo significant assistance.[1]

Aleppo is one of the oldest continuously inhabited cities in the world, and for centuries it was one of the largest in the Middle East, rivaled only by Constantinople (now Istanbul) and Cairo. Located between the Mediterranean Sea and the populous region around the Tigris and Euphrates Rivers known as Mesopotamia, Aleppo was an important stop along the Silk Road and thrived on international trade.[2] But the completion of the Suez Canal in the late nineteenth century diverted much of the trade away from the land route through Aleppo. By the early 1940s Turkey had annexed the areas to the north and west of Aleppo, which further isolated the city from the rich cultural influences brought by international trade.[3]

The Citadel of Aleppo, a medieval fortress, rises up from the center of the city. Sun-baked stone homes, nestled tightly together, form continuous walls that wind their way to the horizon, their second-story balconies partially shading the sidewalks. The wide, dusty streets surrounding the fortress saw few cars in the early 1930s, and were traveled primarily by camels and horse-drawn carriages. The covered souk marketplaces are a maze of tall, arching stone tunnels with cobblestone walkways, the ceiling interrupted every few feet by rectangular holes to allow shafts of light to penetrate the interior passages, creating long, sharp shadows. Guided by carved stone walls, the Queiq River flows through the city center and brings a source of water for palm trees and green spaces.

François Rabbath's father, Georges Séyes, was the youngest of seven children. Georges's father had died very young, at the age of thirty-three, forcing his mother, Farida, to work as a laundress at home to support the family. Electricity was a luxury the family could not afford, so in the evenings Georges studied by candlelight. Eventually, the family's financial troubles forced him to leave school at age eleven to take a job. Being his family's primary means of support, Georges could not afford to perform the required military service when he reached eighteen. In order to avoid conscription, and since he looked much older than he was, he paid a fee to have his name and birth date changed on his birth record to make it appear that he was ten years older, thereby avoiding the military. Georges Séyes took the name of his maternal grandmother and became Georges Rabbath.[4]

Georges married Bahija Ballyan, a Christian Armenian woman whose family had fled what is now Turkey during the Armenian Genocide. Bahija's father had been a successful businessman, and the couple received a generous dowry. Georges had also received a small inheritance from his father, and he approached Karim, his new brother-in-law, with a proposition to combine their assets and invest in the recently formed Beirut Stock Exchange. Karim, aware that Georges was an astute businessman, agreed.

The total sum of their investment was a twenty-liter gas can filled with gold coins. After purchasing the stocks, Georges brought the stock certificates to Karim to put them in a safe place. Karim, who did not understand much about the stock market, looked down at what Georges handed him and said, "But Georges, I've entrusted you with gold and you bring me back paper."

A few years later Georges decided the time was right to cash out of the market. He invited Karim to dinner and afterward asked him to close his eyes and then led him by the hand into the bedroom. There were ten gas cans on the bed.

"But, do I guess right?"

"Yes! And we will open our own bank and call it Bally Bank!"

And so François was born into an upper-middle-class family on March 12, 1931. He was the eighth of George and Bahija's ten children and the youngest boy. In addition to the immediate family, both grandmothers and three live-in housekeepers slept under the same roof, a normal living arrangement for a large middle-class family in Syria at the time. The large family house, Beit el-Samane (House of El Samman), had ten bedrooms, two living rooms, a dining room, an inner courtyard, a summer garden, a laundry, a large cellar, and two wells. Double carriage doors served as the main entrance to the home. Two oval air vents near the base of the doors, each the size of a large platter, provided a measure of air circulation. François would spend hours playing near the doors. He would open one of the vents, sit on the floor, and hold the vent's wrought-iron grate like a steering wheel. Peering through the vent to the street beyond, the warm wind whipping through his hair, he pretended to race a car through the city streets.

In the mid-1930s life around Beit el-Samane moved slowly and softly. Sounds from around the neighborhood would capture François's imagination—hammer blows from the nearby blacksmith or an occasional passing tram would inspire visions of swordplay or exotic travel. Horse-drawn carriages often parked single file across from the Rabbath home. He would hear occasional neighing and the percussive sound of the horses' hooves on the pavement, stomping to rid their thighs of flies. From time to time, François's curiosity would lead him out the front door to see the enormous horses up close. His brief encounters with these noble animals—the sound of their lips as they ate, the feeling of their breath on the back of his neck—would enter his dreams.

Summer evenings were particularly exciting for the Rabbath children. Air conditioning did not yet exist, so mattresses were carried up to the flat roof of the house where they would sleep under the stars in the cool evening air. Georges would read them bedtime stories by candlelight.

Business for the bank was doing well, and both families lived comfortably for several years. However, there was virtually no oversight of Middle Eastern banks during the first half of the twentieth century.[5] In essence, Bally Bank was a family operation—the bank accepted deposits and the family invested the money back into the community, keeping only limited liquidity on hand to cover day-to-day operations. Larger sums were invested in projects that in turn generated interest for their customers and profits for the bank. Karim died and his eldest son, Antoine, took over his father's position. Advised by a dishonest lawyer, Antoine decided to use the bank to amass a personal fortune and embarked on a plan to declare a fraudulent bankruptcy. Due to lax banking regulations, declaring bankruptcy allowed Antoine to sidestep his obligations to the bank's depositors and investors. Georges, unaware of Antoine's plan, first learned of the bankruptcy when panicked customers began rushing to the bank's office to withdraw their savings. Georges tried to reason with the crowd, but there was nothing he could do. He reimbursed as many people as he could with the cash on hand, which, as François bemoaned, "had the effect of throwing us out of our beds and onto the straw overnight."

As a banker, Georges had enjoyed a great deal of respect in Aleppo. He had been seen as a community leader, and his advice was frequently solicited on business matters. Once Bally Bank declared bankruptcy, all of this changed. During the following months he became bitter about the experience and in a particularly disheartened moment told François, "My son, what you have in your pocket is what you are worth."

François later confessed that this conversation had haunted him—he came to believe that his only talent was playing the double bass and that without money he was worth nothing. Years later, Georges had become an executive with the Jacob Safra Bank in Beirut, and François came to visit while on tour. He was featured on the front page of the city's most important newspaper, *L'Orient-le jour*. Both men had become successful. In the evening following his recital, François found himself alone with his father on their balcony overlooking the city, enjoying a glass of arak (an aniseed Lebanese drink). François abruptly turned out the two empty pockets of his pants and said, "Look, Dad, I do not have a penny in my pocket." Having lived a life rich in experiences, François now knew that his father's earlier comment was born out of his frustration at losing Bally Bank. Nevertheless, the comment had made a lasting impression on François and planted seeds of concern for his financial health that would preoccupy him for many years.

Aleppo had few hotels in the 1930s, so occupying French leaders, generals, and officers often lodged with private individuals. After the failure of Bally Bank and now in need of money, Georges and Bahija decided to rent out rooms in their large home to officers in the French army. They sent François and three of his brothers— Pierre, Victor, and Jean—to study in Lebanon. At the tender age of six, François was sent from Aleppo to Lebanon to attend Antoura, a French boarding school.

Antoura was in the mountains above Beirut, 350 kilometers (217 miles) south of Aleppo. This was a painful time for François. He missed his mother terribly, and although his brothers attended the same school, he saw them infrequently since they were older and lived in a different dormitory. He was distracted by his homesickness, having been plucked out of a large, loving family and placed into a school where he knew no one. François was continuously anxious and suffered from chronic headaches. During each recess period he would visit the infirmary to ask for some aspirin. The "doctor" was a tobacco-chewing priest who reminded François of a character out of a cowboy movie. He would put his hand on François's forehead and, frowning deeply, spit into a can next to his desk. The consultation complete, he would reassure François with a smile. Then, handing him a sweet lozenge accompanied by the most serious look in the world, he sent François off to go back out and play.

One day, François came as usual to ask for a lozenge, but to his surprise, after feeling his head, the priest instead asked him to undress and put him in one of the six beds of the little clinic. François saw him approaching with glass cups that he intended to put on François's chest and back—cupping therapy. Frightened, François refused. He only wanted his lozenge, but apparently this time it was more serious. The priest called for Father Sarloute, the director of Antoura, an impressively tall man with a mountainous belly draped by a dark brown cassock. François loved the director and allowed himself to be treated. He stayed for a week in the clinic, with a beautiful view of the ocean. This is where he saw waterspouts for the first time—conical swirls of water that, as if by magic, rose up out of the sea and melted into the clouds.

François's teacher often put the class in lines to take turns reciting their lessons. Being at the front of the line was nerve-racking, and when François's turn would come, he often found that he had forgotten everything. Without asking, he began to return to the back of the line. When his turn came for the second time, having heard the others, he could recite his lesson effortlessly. Noticing this, the teacher began to send students who had the same problem to the back of the line. The process of reviewing the lessons did not take much longer, and every student met with success.

When François returned to school in Aleppo, he discovered that the Syrian schools had undergone a transformation mandated by the French protectorate. The French language had become a new requirement in the revised school system. The school day was divided, and students were required to speak French in the morning and Arabic in the afternoon. At home, François found himself speaking one word in French and another in Arabic, mixing the languages. While both languages apply gender to nouns, Arabic assigns gender more frequently, and consequently does not allow for the confusion between genders in a sentence that might result in a witty double entendre. François grew very fond of French wordplay, and years later, he would admire the art as practiced by the brilliant comedians in Parisian theaters.

By age eleven François was tall for his age, almost as tall as his teachers. The public school teachers would hit children who did not know their lessons—often across the fingertips of one hand with a ruler. The teachers would repeat, "We hit you because we love you and we want you to learn." One day, frustrated by François's lack of understanding, one of his teachers asked him to show his fingertips to be hit again. As the ruler came down, François opened his hand, caught the ruler, and in a single motion, threw it violently across the room, hitting the window. He said in a firm voice, "Never hit me again." The teacher sent him to the main office, but instead François ran home.

For the next several months, François stole small sums of change that his grandmother had left around the house. In the morning he would take his book bag and head out the door with the other children toward school, but then double back into town to the theater. There were three daily showings at the cinema: at 10 a.m., 2 p.m., and 6 p.m. Each weekday he would watch the first two showings and then return home, becoming somewhat of an expert on films released in 1942.

After six months, the director of the school came to the Rabbath home to inquire why François had not been attending. François said that he was tired of being hit and did not want to return. His father asked him what he planned to do instead. François responded, "Anything!" His father turned to the director and said that he supported his son's decision and would withdraw him from the school. François was elated.

He began working in a fabric store. His job entailed climbing the tall ladders to retrieve bolts of cloth from the high shelves surrounding the sales floor. François was a quick learner, and the owner allowed him to begin measuring and cutting fabric to size. The whole experience was exciting, especially since the store was in the middle of the souk, the large mysterious marketplace filled with dark, winding passageways, exotic smells, and the patter of vendors hawking all manner of unusual goods. The store owner enjoyed François's energy and enthusiasm, and François loved the work—at first. He was happy to be doing something productive and to be appreciated, so very different from school. But after a short while, he began to understand that there wasn't much more to the job, and after two months he told his father that he wanted to quit and find something else.

François's brother Henri had also left school and was working as an apprentice mechanic. Each day he would come home covered in grease and talk excitedly about the cars and trucks he had seen. François looked up to his brother and loved the idea of working on cars. Cars had been a rarity in Aleppo when he was younger and were still considered a luxury for most Syrians. The idea of being able to get close to these mechanical wonders was intoxicating, and François applied for an apprenticeship. He found he had an aptitude for mechanical problems and one day even removed a truck's engine from the chassis by himself—wrapping the large chain around the motor and using the mechanical winch to raise it out of the engine compartment. He found a great deal of satisfaction in this work and stayed at the garage for six months. It was Bahija who made the decision that he had to find other work. Having one son with oil- and grease-stained clothes to clean was enough. Two was at least one too many. François once again needed to find another line of work.

2

Introduction to the Bass

> **What you cannot do today,**
> **you will do tomorrow.**

*I*t was Elie who suggested that the brothers form a band. Elie was the oldest boy and played the violin. Henri played the clarinet and saxophone, Pierre played the piano, and Victor the drums. None of them had much training, and the quality of their instruments was what was available and affordable in Syria at the time. Victor's drum set, for instance, consisted of a single marching snare drum that he played using a pair of heavy drum sticks purchased from an army surplus store. He had seen jazz bands in the newsreels at the movies and noticed that the drummers also played with brushes, so he cut a piece of thatch from the roof of a nearby shed and fashioned the straw into a pair of brushes.

During better times Georges had built a modest country retreat in the mountains above Aleppo. Fortunately he had put the property in Bahija's name, so it was safe from the creditors after Bally Bank had failed. Every summer the family would spend several weeks in the mountains while school was not in session, enjoying a refreshing break from Aleppo's heat and dust during the scorching summer months. Occasionally, the youngest siblings—Vivienne, Betty, Jean, and François—would travel to the country with their father, while the four older boys remained in Aleppo with their mother. By this time the two eldest sisters were married and had moved with their husbands to Beirut.

Upon returning home from the mountains one summer, the younger siblings were met with a wild cacophony! While Georges and the younger siblings had been away, the older brothers had learned four jazz tunes by ear. Elie, standing tall, gracefully swayed back and forth as he played the familiar melodies on his violin. Henri ornamented the tunes on the clarinet, punctuated by an occasional squeak. Loudest of all, Victor pounded away on his drums, grinning from ear to ear. Pierre somehow managed to keep the group together on the piano. Bahija adored the music—after three months, she knew it well—and sang along. Georges was ecstatic that his boys were making music and asked what they planned to do with their new ensemble. Elie announced proudly that they had already booked an engagement in a nearby café: "We're going to play and earn money!" It was the auspicious beginning of the Rabbath Orchestra. After dinner, the café was transformed into a small nightclub, and people would drink and dance. Although the boys knew only four tunes, the café owner was happy with the band simply repeating what they knew over and over again. People enjoyed the live music and stayed longer into the evening.

Ever ambitious, Elie arranged an engagement in Damascus at a fashionable cabaret. The contract required an ensemble of eight musicians, though, so he planned to supplement the Rabbath brothers with four additional Armenian musicians from Aleppo. He asked Bahija to make stage costumes for them. For the tangos he wanted blue shirts with large, puffy sleeves and red velvet waistcoats set with sequins. Jazz suits were also planned, patterned after the extra-long jackets of the Count Basie Orchestra that the brothers had seen at the cinema. Bahija, assisted by François's aunts, sewed continuously for two weeks—every sequin on all eight vests was sewn on by hand.

When the Rabbath Orchestra arrived in Damascus, the owner of the cabaret invited them to attend the final performance of the group who was leaving, a quartet of accomplished Jewish musicians from Poland. They were seasoned professionals who played both light classical and variety music. Little by little, panic seized the brothers as they listened. At the end of the evening, the first violinist came to see Elie and said to him quietly, "The place is yours. We will come tomorrow to listen to you." Elie saw that he needed to quickly find a way to disguise the weaknesses of the amateur Rabbath Orchestra in order to save their jobs.

The next morning, Elie went to visit the Al-Hamidiyah Souk. Located within the ancient walled district of Damascus and covered by an arched metal roof, the souk occupied several city blocks. In one of the shops, he found doumbeks—deceptively loud, the small goblet-shaped oriental hand drums are traditionally placed under one arm and played with the fingers. He bought four and distributed a drum to each of the musicians except his brothers. He needed Victor to drive the rhythm from the drum set and Pierre to provide harmony on the piano. Henri was going to be the star. He was to play the famous clarinet introduction to *Rhapsody in Blue* by George Gershwin. (The introduction was the only part of the piece Henri knew.)

That evening the cabaret was packed. The public was attracted by the announcement of a new Syrian ensemble, the Rabbath Orchestra, and eagerly awaited their performance. The Polish quartet, sitting at a rear table, were just as eagerly anticipating an impending disaster. The group's hopes had been raised by their leader, who had already solicited the owner for an extension. Why not demand a raise after this new amateur ensemble failed?

The morale of the Rabbath Orchestra was low. Elie tried his best to encourage them, almost having to push the men onto the stage. Pierre had a twitch when he became nervous, and his head was now moving visibly from side to side.

Once the orchestra was in place, welcomed by a warm round of applause, the eyes of everyone fell on Elie, the leader. In deathly silence, violin in his left hand, he lifted his bow as a baton and cued Henri. Raising the bell of his clarinet high into the air, Henri began—a long, solo clarinet trill, followed by a swooping ascending glissando, into the soaring Gershwin melody. At that precise moment, Elie lowered his bow, and the four musicians armed with doumbeks began to play furiously.

The Arab-American-African groove was deafening. Henri's shrill clarinet floated above the melee, improvising freely on a single chord. The audience, accustomed to the staid, refined tones of a string quartet, got up and began to dance. People were excited, exclaiming, "We finally have a good orchestra!"

At the end of the evening, the leader of the quartet came to Elie and told him, "You know, you're very clever." With that, he turned and left. Elie, smiling broadly, followed him to the door.

One evening, three months later, François's older brothers returned from Damascus while he was sleeping. Early the next morning François found Elie in the inner courtyard having breakfast. He was elated to see his older brother and ran to kiss Elie to welcome him home. In a casual manner, Elie asked François for a favor: "Please run up to my room and fetch me a handkerchief."

François dashed upstairs and to his astonishment discovered a huge violin leaning in the corner, ten times the size of Elie's!

Upon seeing the bass, François became paralyzed, frozen to the spot by the instrument's size and majesty, completely forgetting why he had come upstairs. He was forbidden to touch his brother's musical instruments, but the allure of the enormous violin was irresistible. He moved forward apprehensively and pulled a string. The sound was deeply profound, rattling the window—almost shaking the entire room.

François raced back down the stairs to Elie.

Barely able to contain himself, he blurted, "Who is that fat violin for?"

"First, it's not a violin," Elie replied. "It's called a double bass."

"Who does she belong to?"

"Who wants it?"

"So, I can take her?"

"Well, my god, yes! As long as you play it, I want to give her to you, and you will join the orchestra immediately."

With overwhelming eagerness, and afraid that Elie might change his mind, François ran back upstairs and gently took the precious bass up the narrow staircase to his room on the highest floor.

It is not difficult to see why François became so passionate about the double bass from the beginning. The instrument was a gift from his beloved older brother and represented family, acceptance, and an insurance policy to keep from being separated from his brothers ever again. The gift of the bass was exceptionally meaningful.

Every year, Bahija sent her six growing sons to the neighborhood tailor to purchase a new suit for special occasions. For all François knew, the tailor's window display might have been the same for years, but on one particular day he took notice of an old, ornate wooden music stand. Curious, he took a closer look as his brothers were being measured and was astonished to see that the music on the stand was Édouard Nanny's *Méthode complète pour la contrebasse*, a book written by the professor of double bass at the Paris Conservatory. François had been searching everywhere to learn how to play the double bass correctly—and right here in front of him was a bass method from Paris!

He now faced a painful dilemma. If he asked the tailor to sell it to him, the tailor might ask for a lot of money or just say no. In that moment, François decided he could not take that risk, so he stole the book. He knew he was committing a crime for the first time in his life, but he believed he had no other choice. With the tailor momentarily in the back room, François quietly slid the method book under his sweater. When the time came to have his measurements taken, François reached out one arm at a time, tightly pressing the prized book to his chest with the other. His heart beating wildly, he bolted for home after the measurements were taken. Shaking, filled with equal measures of fear and excitement, the conflicting feelings of joy and remorse whirled through his mind.

That night François put his bass next to his bed and hid the method book under his pillow, holding it firmly. He clung to these two treasures like a shipwrecked man.

As he was drifting off to sleep, François overheard Elie tell Pierre, "You'll see, he will be the only great musician in the family."

Now that he had the method and the bass, François began studying in earnest. He started by meticulously following the sketches illustrated in the book. The drawings represented how to hold the bass, how to hold the bow, and the different positions of the left hand. But without a teacher's guidance, sketches and photographs can be misinterpreted. François later learned that his bow hold was incorrect, causing the large muscle of his thumb to cramp. Another impediment that François faced was that he did not read music. The method was written in such a way that it was necessary for him to learn where to place his fingers on the double bass from notes written on a musical staff. Although he did not know the names of the notes, he was able to discern that Nanny had assigned a number to each finger. Seeing the numbers written above each note, François observed that each note on the staff corresponded to a precise place on the fingerboard, and that open strings were indicated by a zero. He slowly began to determine where to place each finger on the bass. Each time a note appeared at the same place on the staff, he put the prescribed finger on the string that corresponded to that place on the fingerboard. In this methodical fashion, François started reading music even before he knew the names of the notes.

In July 1945 the Rabbath Orchestra began its first long-term professional engagement, in a Beirut nightclub called the Coupole. The club offered a complete evening's entertainment: light dinner music with a trio, a large jazz band for dancing, and a late-night variety show that featured singers, dancing girls, and jugglers. Stéphane Benjamin managed the dinner theater and Harry Fleming served as the music director of the Coupole. A tall elegant Black man, gracious in manner and speech, Fleming was also an excellent tap dancer. He would dance up and down the stairs to the host podium, entertaining guests as they approached. It was Fleming who had hired Elie to form an orchestra for the six-month engagement. Elie was to organize all the ensembles, and he hired François to play the bass. François had little idea of what he was doing and stood in the background, plucking the strings gently in tempo, like a mime with decent rhythm.

The first day of the engagement was a day of celebration, and François felt a rush of joy at being in the midst of a jazz orchestra, surrounded by his brothers and such rich harmonies. Harmonies were virtually nonexistent in Arabic music of the 1940s and were heard only in Western movies. For centuries the music of Syria had featured drones and modal melodies, ornamented by exotic quarter tones but without harmonic progressions. It was a marvelous experience for François—wearing a tuxedo in front of a well-dressed audience, performing jazz and popular music in a nightclub. He felt as if he were in the movies he had seen while skipping school.

The late-night variety shows began around midnight. The waitresses, whose job was to sell drinks to the customers, were required to perform a number with the orchestra. The management was not concerned with the quality of their performance, so long as they kept the customers engaged and drinking. In addition to their salary, the waitresses were paid a percentage of what their customers drank, so to encourage their customers to drink while staying sober themselves, the women often drank tea as a substitute for whiskey and lemonade for champagne.

One of the dancers, skinny and maniacal, always had a tambourine in her hand, waving it about her head and body. She wore a feathered hoopskirt and had created a pseudo-acrobatic dance number in which she raised her arms and kicked up her legs while dancing about, shaking her tambourine. She made a request of Elie during an afternoon rehearsal.

"Mr. Eliasss," she purred, "would you tell your brother, the drummer, to be kind enough to accentuate the movements of my arms and legs with cymbal strokes, pleeease?"

The Rabbath Orchestra were still amateurs. They were getting better, but the instruments they played were not of very high quality. Victor's drums were solid, but unresponsive, and in the words of François, "he had to bang on them like a deaf man to make them ring. Add to this a certain lack of professional experience . . ."

That evening, the dancer began her number by raising one of her arms while looking back at Victor with an impish grin. There was no time to hesitate—this was the moment! Victor tapped on the cymbal. She gave him a nod and raised her leg. Victor hit the cymbal harder. Every time she moved, Victor hit the cymbal. Then she suddenly leapt dramatically into the air, throwing open her arms and legs at the same time. Surprised by this novelty, he hit the cymbal from underneath with so much force that it came flying off its stand. Alarmed by the intensity of the sound, she turned just in time to see the flying cymbal hurtling toward her head. She immediately ducked and began to scurry away, bent over, buttocks in the air. Her wriggling feathers gave the impression of a startled ostrich who somehow managed to run with her head still in the sand. Witnessing this unexpected moment of slapstick, the audience burst into fits of laughter and applause. Harry Fleming was so impressed by the commotion and the audience's energetic response that he requested the group repeat the act every evening.

The six-month experience at the Coupole helped to shape François's approach to his instrument. When a note he played happened to correspond with the harmonies of the piano, it was a moment of great satisfaction. These coincidences encouraged him to focus on seeking the correct pitches to play with the piano. To be confronted with the circumstance of having to play in an ensemble by ear as a beginner is a unique challenge, and the combination of performing every evening and studying during the day proved to be very motivating for François.

As exciting as the engagement was, François became increasingly frustrated with his bass. The plywood instrument was as unresponsive as Victor's drums, and to make matters worse, the gut strings made only an indiscernible thump. The result was that playing this bass was really more like playing a bass drum, adding a low percussive rhythm but without a clear pitch. More than anything, François wanted to sound like the bassists he had heard in the movies. After another month of playing, he had become desperate. It almost didn't matter which note he played; every note sounded dead. He begged Elie for a new bass, but the response was always the same: "It's good enough for us." Knowing that his brother would not approve of purchasing a new instrument because of his complaining, François decided to take drastic action.

He went into a music store and discovered a new bass with metal strings instead of gut. When François played this bass, he finally heard the real pitch of each note. He gave the store clerk a small deposit to hold the instrument and began to scheme. He knew that in order for him to obtain the new instrument, the old one would have to be damaged badly enough to need replacing. The more François stewed over his problem, the more he realized that the bass must be completely destroyed.

One day, out of sheer frustration, he took his bass up to the fifth-floor balcony and held it over the railing. With a deep breath and a short prayer, he let go. The bass fell away from him as if in slow motion, getting smaller and smaller until . . . bang! The instrument shattered into a dozen pieces, scattered across the inner courtyard. François grabbed a sheet from his bed and ran downstairs. He bundled the pieces into the sheet and took them to Elie.

"She fell down."

"From where? How?"

François pointed to the balcony. "I was practicing and . . . and leaned over too far."

Elie looked at him with one eyebrow raised, but realized there was nothing to be done.

"I hope you know where to find another one for tonight."

"Yes!" And François sprinted to the music store to purchase the bass.

Playing his new bass in the orchestra was a revelation. François's intonation was a disaster, but he could now hear each note clearly and learn more precisely where each pitch lived on the fingerboard. Exploring the connection between his ear and hand led him to develop the concept of the "pivot." He found that he could play more pitches in a single position by leaving his thumb at the same place on the neck and rotating his hand along the fingerboard. With this new technique and its focus on the relationship between his fingers on the fingerboard and the placement of his thumb on the back of the neck, he was able to play more notes accurately in a single position than the Nanny *Méthode* described. It was a discovery that allowed him to quickly excel.

François's early playing career unfolded in much the same way it does for most musicians—feast or famine. Opportunities come in waves, and after a high wave often comes a deep trough. His earliest opportunities were tied to the family band. If they had work, then he could play music. When the musical work ran out, then he had to find other employment in order to help support the family. The experience at the Coupole inspired Elie to dream of forming an orchestra with all five of his brothers and touring Europe. Unfortunately, the dream faced prohibitively high hurdles. First there was a problem with Jean. He was still attending school and studying piano privately with the brilliant Russian pianist Michel Cheskinoff. Formerly a professor at the St. Petersburg Conservatory, Cheskinoff was now teaching at the Lebanese Higher National Conservatory in Beirut. Jean was an excellent pianist and would have been terrific in the ensemble, but Cheskinoff believed that playing jazz would interfere with his refined classical phrasing. With Cheskinoff being such a highly respected and demanding teacher, it is easy to understand why Jean would never agree to be part of the orchestra. The remaining brothers—Elie, Pierre, Victor, Henri, and François—continued to perform nightly and contribute toward the family expenses. This arrangement was acceptable to Georges, and Jean was exempt from making contributions while he remained in school. But Jean's decision to drop out of school and devote himself solely to studying piano was another matter. Georges could not understand why all his sons studied during the day and worked in the evenings except Jean. In a diplomatic gesture, François intervened and agreed to pay Jean's share of the expenses in addition to his own.

Then Pierre got married. He was attracted to a woman who worked at the Coupole. Originally from Hungary, she had fled a life of poverty and, to avoid being sent back, was seeking to marry a Lebanese man. Pierre, enjoying her attentiveness, was oblivious to her ulterior motives. After they were married, she convinced Pierre to insist that Elie double his salary. Pierre, being the pianist, was indispensable to the success of the Rabbath Orchestra. But the orchestra couldn't afford to double Pierre's salary, and Jean had no interest in being Pierre's replacement. This left Elie no alternative but to dissolve the ensemble, only three years after its creation. François once again had to seek alternative work.

René Cabbabé, François's brother-in-law, had traveled from Beirut to Paris to visit his uncle, who ran an undergarment factory. His uncle convinced René that he could open a similar factory in Lebanon and gave his nephew two sewing machines to take back to Beirut: a zigzag sewing machine and a complex overlocker.[1] Excited that he could finally be his own boss, René returned home with his new machines and three bolts of cloth. He begged François's sister Laurisse to convince Elie and Henri, both idle, to join him as partners. They would call the company REHL, a name created from the first initials of the associate partners (René, Elie, Henri, and Laurisse). René suggested to Elie that they hire Victor, Jean, and François as workers. The brothers received a symbolic salary, equivalent to their family expense contributions.

The result was that François, now sixteen, stopped performing as a bassist for two years in order to work as a laborer on a sewing machine twelve hours a day. Rather than feeling depressed by the experience, he found that he had the same desire to excel in sewing a seam as he had in playing the bass—although he would have much preferred to make music. He took pleasure in trying to exceed his own high expectations, which kept him focused on his work. After a year François was able to sew five hundred pairs of women's underpants in a single day.

Georges had moved the family to Beirut to begin anew and took a position at the Jacob Safra Bank. Originally a local money-changer based in Aleppo, the Safra Bank grew in part thanks to Georges's banking acumen. The business quickly expanded and within several years had branches throughout the Middle East. In an effort to support the family's business, Georges approved loans for REHL from his new position at the Safra Bank. After two years without receiving any returns on the investment, Georges reviewed the company's books and discovered that all the profits had been squandered by René. The company had not made any money to either reinvest or pay back investors. Georges and Elie felt betrayed and believed their only recourse was to remove the immediate family members from REHL. They returned the remaining fabric and helped train replacement workers. François felt deflated by the experience. The brothers were in the same situation as two years before, after having worked twelve-hour days for twenty-four months with nothing to show for it.

Almost as quickly as the underwear business folded, a new musical opportunity presented itself. Pierre approached Elie with a request to speak to Victor and François. He wanted his blessing and assistance to form a Rabbath Trio for an upcoming six-month engagement in Cyprus. Elie was not happy with Pierre. After all, it was because of Pierre that the orchestra had been dissolved. However, the brothers had nothing left to lose, and in the end, Elie gave the project his blessing and encouraged Victor and François to go. As the trio was about to leave for Cyprus, François felt obliged to make yet further contributions to the family finances. Jean had not made any contributions while he continued to study with Cheskinoff, and now Henri did not have steady work either. Elie was ultimately able to find regular work as a musician, but Henri floated along, finding only occasional odd jobs. François agreed to continue to contribute money for himself, Jean, and Henri for a year.

On the cusp of traveling to a new country with his brothers as an employed musician for the first time, François felt a heady mix of excitement and pride—excited for the impending adventure and proud to have the means to make a significant contribution to support the family.

3

the Rabbath Trio

Your ears are your professor.

The Cyprus trip was arranged quickly. The contract stipulated that the musician who played the bass had to double on an additional instrument, so a week before their departure, François purchased a cheap accordion and learned to play a handful of tango melodies. The trio embarked on a boat from Beirut to Famagusta, where François happily regained his job as a musician, playing music in a Cyprus cabaret. He remained a conscientious student of his beloved instrument, carrying the double bass back and forth from the cabaret to the boarding house to practice daily.

Sadly, by the end of the third month, the cabaret was closed due to illegal drug dealing, and the trio was forced to take the first boat back to Beirut. It was an empty cargo ship. The boat had been designed to carry large shipping containers, and its lower deck was completely flat. The unloaded vessel was light for the open sea, especially in bad weather, and 40 kilometers (25 miles) out from the Beirut harbor a storm came up. Three decks of cabins rose up at the back of the boat, and the waves were crashing to almost the middle of the second-floor bridge. Unable to sleep, François looked out over the third-floor deck, watching anxiously as the ship pitched from side to side. Almost everyone was seasick, including the captain. Only one passenger was not sick, Sarkis Surmelian. Sarkis was an Armenian musician who played clarinet and violin in the cabaret orchestra. After their last gig, at 3 a.m., François had observed a very drunk Sarkis in the pouring rain, boasting to another violinist about the fine qualities of his instrument and scratching the violin with his fingernail to reveal the layers of varnish. The sailors caught sight of him wandering across the middle of the second-floor bridge, bottle in hand. With every tilt of the deck, he would lose his balance and then catch himself at the railing—a dizzying tightrope act with roiling water some 9 meters (30 feet) below. The sea was so violent that the sailors did not dare to go out without security ties. Two of them watched Sarkis closely. Once he came near, they grabbed him and locked him in his cabin to keep him from wandering out again. François spent the rest of the night on his bunk, sipping lemon juice to help quell his nausea. The storm subsided as the ship pulled into the Beirut harbor, and a spectacular view rewarded the passengers for facing the perils of the storm. The sea that surrounded them was completely black, but the city, with its majestic mountains rising upward, was lit up like thousands of flickering fireflies—a stunning sight to come home to.

Shortly after their return, in early 1950, the Rabbath Trio was fortunate to be signed to a six-month contract at one of the city's most prestigious hotels, the Hotel Normandy. In an effort to enhance Beirut's waterfront on Saint George Bay, the French protectorate had built the avenue des Français along the seaside.[1] The new boulevard was lined with palm trees, upscale restaurants, and hotels, becoming a popular area for the locals to promenade and a destination for visiting tourists. The Hotel Normandy's eye-catching cylindrical entrance towered over the waterfront and attracted a wealthy clientele.

In addition to performing in the Hotel Normandy's dining room, the trio was required to accompany guest artists at the Kit-Kat Club, a small adjacent nightclub owned by the hotel that opened to the sea. Beirut was not considered an artistic destination, so the trio had to accompany a variety of local and regional touring acts, from singers and dancers to acrobats and magicians. They quickly learned how to negotiate the pitfalls of working with amateur artists and scant rehearsal time, making up for any shortcomings by relying on their musicianship and an almost telepathic intuition, creating arrangements on the fly. After several months the brothers were no longer the same amateur musicians who had accompanied the tambourine-shaking dancer at the Coupole. They had grown together into a refined professional rhythm section, capable of accompanying virtually any artist.

The trio's contract was extended multiple times, and they would continue to perform at the Normandy for almost five years. Since the trio did not have a solo melodic instrument, François would transcribe cello or violin pieces for the bass to play during dinner-hour sets. Playing melodies in the upper register of the double bass was like giving a mini-recital every day and helped François develop his concept for playing in the highest registers of the instrument. The dining room performances served as background music for patrons, most of whom were more interested in their food and conversation. From time to time, however, there were those who took notice. One evening he became aware of an older gentleman watching him perform. François was maybe nineteen years old at the time, and he focused on playing to keep this man's attention.

When they took a break, the man approached François and introduced himself. He was the violin virtuoso Yehudi Menuhin and happened to be in Beirut en route to India.

"Show me your fingers."

François turned his left hand over, and there was a single line across all the fingertips.

Menuhin showed François his fingers. "See, I have the same line."

"But your line is so small."

"Yes. Of course, I am a violinist." He then added, "You will go far."

This meeting made a deep impression on François and led him to consider how a few well-placed words can have a tremendous impact. Here he was in Beirut, a young bassist in a hotel restaurant, and one of the world's foremost violin virtuosi had paid him a compliment.[2]

Not far from the Normandy, the Sixth Fleet of the US Navy was stationed for a time in Saint George Bay. One evening a large number of American sailors entered the Normandy's dining room. Unlike other tourists, the men fell silent once the music began. They were a responsive audience, and encouraged by the enthusiasm, the Rabbath Trio performed a set of energetic pieces normally reserved for the Kit-Kat Club. As François began to play in the upper register, he heard the sailors say, "Shush, shush," to the waiter for making noise at the table.

After the trio finished the set, the sailors lined up to greet them. The men explained that they, too, were musicians, members of the orchestra of the Sixth Fleet. One after another, each sailor came up to François to congratulate him on playing with the bow, like the cello—fast and in the upper register. This expression of appreciation by a large group of American musicians made a strong impact on François and his brothers. It was the first time they ever enjoyed such a warm reception from musicians—and their first time meeting Americans.

One evening, the French Armenian singer-songwriter Charles Aznavour came backstage after a performance and introduced himself, saying, "If you ever come to Paris, let me know." Aznavour's career was in its early stages when he appeared in Beirut. He was touring the Middle East with his pianist and arranger, Jean Leccia, when the two men came into the Normandy to have dinner. They initially thought that the Rabbath Trio was European and that François was Russian because of his abilities with the bow. Leccia was planning to leave Aznavour in six months because he had a previously booked tour. He told François privately that he had said to Aznavour, "If you have a chance, take them."

Having days to himself with little to do aside from practice, François began to pursue bodybuilding. He discovered a book by the French bodybuilder Marcel Rouet[3] and used it as his inspiration, training with the same focus he brought to music. He purchased a few pieces of exercise equipment that he kept in his room and would show off at the beach by lifting large water jugs with other bodybuilders. At his peak he could curl thirty reps of over 130 kilos (250 pounds) and his biceps were more than 52 centimeters (21 inches) around—even bigger than Rouet's. But he was overtraining. François did not know about healthy lifting techniques and taking appropriate time to rest. At one point, he tried a "snatch and jerk" maneuver and injured his back. It was during rehabilitation that he discovered relaxation techniques, coming into complete relaxation by focusing on each muscle of his body in turn.

Georges admired his son's impressive physique and would occasionally ask François to stand outside the Safra Bank and "guard" shipments of gold that arrived by truck. The truck actually arrived with armed guards, but Georges reasoned that François's presence would help dissuade anyone from considering a robbery and at the same time serve as an impressive advertisement for the bank. Being the youngest son, François always looked up to his father and older brothers and was delighted to have his father's approval and attention—although he acknowledges that while he always knew that his father loved him, he would have preferred to be admired for his bass playing rather than for his body.

The Rabbath home in Beirut had a chambre de bonne, or maid's room, on the fifth floor. The family was not employing any live-in help at this time, and the tiny room sat vacant, so Georges decided to use it to store his collection of old newspapers. Late one afternoon, François heard his father cry, "Catch him!" A young man had snuck into the house and was stealing newspapers from the fifth floor. François jolted awake from a nap and ran out to the second-floor landing without his shirt on to see what was the matter. The young man took one look at François's physique and was so frightened that he jumped down the center of the circular staircase from the fifth floor to the ground floor to escape. Fortunately, he wasn't injured and scampered off. François was devastated. He was so afraid for him—the boy could have died. François looked down to his father on the ground floor and shouted, "You're crazy. For your newspapers? For anything?" He couldn't sleep for three days—whenever he closed his eyes, all François saw was the young man's body suspended in the air over the stairs.

Once the engagement at the Hotel Normandy came to an end, the brothers debated where to relocate. The hotel engagement was by far the best gig in Beirut, likely one of the best in the Middle East, and the trio knew they needed to travel to continue to have success in the music business. They considered moving to either New York or Paris. Pierre and Victor wanted to move to New York, but François was adamant about moving to Paris. France had several things to recommend it. First, their experience with the French in Syria had been good. Despite the occupation, France had sent over many of their intellectual elite to help rebuild the country's institutions after World War I, and almost without exception all the French people that they had interacted with were highly educated and gracious.

Second, they already had an understanding of French, while moving to New York would require learning a third language. But most importantly, for François, he longed to go to the Paris Conservatory to meet Édouard Nanny. He was excited to study with Nanny, to share his discoveries, and to discuss his suggested "improvements" to the Nanny *Méthode*.

Pierre and Victor finally acquiesced. Their time at the Hotel Normandy had enabled the trio to save enough money to pay for their trip from Beirut to Paris and cover living expenses for a while after they arrived. François had mixed feelings. He was sad to leave his family, and the trio was very popular in Beirut. He had warm memories of making new friends and meeting famous artists. But at the same time, he was thrilled to fulfill his dream of traveling to France and having the opportunity to finally meet Édouard Nanny!

4

Paris!

You must dare to do it—you must
throw yourself on the water.

François, Pierre, and Victor arrived at the Paris Orly Airport in July 1955.[1] They wrestled their luggage and instruments onto a shuttle bus that would deposit them at Les Invalides in the 7th arrondissement. François settled into a window seat, allowing himself to be cradled by the hum of the engine. After so many years of waiting and hoping, he was finally on a bus headed straight into the heart of Paris—a new immigrant in the city of his dreams. Excited to see the country that had filled his childhood imagination with her tales, he couldn't wait to immerse himself in the sounds of the inimitable French accent and savor the legendary food. As the landscape became more urban, François sat up in eager anticipation of catching the first glimpse of the most beautiful city in the world. They began to pass by ornate buildings, broad boulevards, fountain squares, shops and restaurants—all the stories that he had heard or read seemed to materialize behind each city gate. It was dizzying. He was determined to do what was necessary to live here forever.

They had arrived early in the morning, and François noticed that the garbagemen were white. He asked the man sitting next to him on the bus, "Excuse me, sir, can you tell me what nationality these garbagemen are?"

Surprised by the question, the man glanced over at François with a smile. "Let me guess. You're Lebanese."

"How did you guess?"

"I was sure of it. You know, I lived more than three years in Lebanon."

He shared everything he knew about Lebanon, and then, realizing that François was waiting for an answer to his original question, he responded, "There are all nationalities working here. Yes, even French."

He paused on this last word, staring directly into François's eyes.

François was dumbfounded, replying, "It cannot be—a Frenchman would never accept a job like this!"

When François was growing up, Syria and Lebanon were a part of the French protectorate. France had sent scientists, engineers, and teachers to Syria. In his mind it was inconceivable that a Frenchman could be a garbageman.

A sudden squeal from the brakes brought François back to reality. They had finally arrived at Les Invalides.

François took leave of his neighbor, thanking him and wishing him luck. The trio gathered all their luggage and instruments and began to seek a taxi. Fortunately, there was a taxi stand near the bus stop. They looked down the taxi line and chose the only car that had a roof rack. This car, however, was in the middle of the line, and taxis were assigned to passengers in the order they arrived. By the time the three brothers reached the front of the line, the driver they had chosen rushed up to take the luggage from the gentleman who had spoken to François on the bus. It was a coincidence that actually saved them. Seeing the situation, the gentleman took his suitcase from the driver's hand and gave his place in line to François, smiling and patting him on the shoulder. He then got into the next taxi.

The driver, who had hoped to avoid the trio and all their luggage, was forced to take them. He climbed back into his cab and exclaimed, pointing to the double bass, "I cannot take so much."

A police officer standing nearby was following the conversation and stared at the driver with a frown.

François protested, "We chose you on purpose, because—"

"And, so what?" he replied, cutting François off.

"But, we need your roof rack."

The officer approached the taxi, smiling at the brothers. He pointed to the luggage and turned to the driver, saying, "Take this, and right now."

François observed that the officer was perhaps middle-aged, with a long scar on his left cheek that gave him a hardened air.

The driver came out of his taxi angrily, seemingly prepared to confront the officer.

But the officer was having none of it, and before the cab driver could utter a word, he added, in a steely tone, "If the minister has seen fit to give them his place, you *will* take them."

The driver insisted that they hire a second taxi to accommodate the trio in addition to the luggage, but the officer did not move from his place and looked to make sure everything was packed correctly.

Pierre and Victor got into the back seat of the taxi with difficulty, squeezing next to the luggage that was stacked to the ceiling. François noticed that the car visibly sagged under the load as he put the final bags at his feet and climbed in. It took the officer's help to get the door closed behind him.

The poor driver was furious. Speaking to himself, he muttered, "If I told this to my wife, she would never believe it."

The brothers could not understand why the load was such an issue for a taxi in Paris—it would never have been a problem in Lebanon. They gave the driver the address for the Hotel Victor Massé. It was a cheap place to stay for a couple of nights while they attempted to gain a more permanent place at the Foyer Franco-Libanais (Franco-Lebanese Home). The home was in the Latin Quarter, near the Panthéon, but they were unsure if it was open during the month of July. They asked the driver how much he would charge, being used to haggling for the price of a ride. He pointed at his counter and said with some annoyance, "Where did you say you were from?"

When the hotel manager saw all the baggage and the instruments, he asked how many nights the three were planning to stay. "Not more than two or three," François replied. Relieved, the manager gave them two rooms on the highest floor and insisted that the hotel did not rent by the month. The brothers were a little curious why the manager had said this, since they had told him that they intended to leave as soon as possible. Later it became clear. Located near the red-light district, the hotel found it more profitable to flip rooms several times in a single night than to cater to long-term boarders.

For three straight days, the brothers went to the Franco-Lebanese Home to request a place to stay. Each day they rang the doorbell and never got a response. On the third day, they saw someone ring the bell and then simply push the door open. They groaned. Even though it had been an expensive mistake, they later laughed at their ignorance, happy they now had a place to live. Once settled, the trio began to search for work.

Parisian musicians would gather nightly at cafés in place Pigalle near the Moulin Rouge to connect with music contractors. There the brothers met Jimmy English, an agent who supplied dance bands to the American army camps at Orly. The Rabbath Trio began to play Saturday nights in the camps, accompanying singers, and they were paid fifty francs each per evening. Despite the low wages, there were a few perks. They could purchase supplies from the camp stores very cheaply—for instance, a kilo of tobacco was only a few francs.

It was during this time that they met and accompanied Dalida, who was singing for the first time in France. Born in Egypt to Italian parents, Dalida would become a famous French actor and singer, but her theatrical style was not appreciated by the troops, who were fans of American jazz. For lack of anything better, the brothers arranged to live modestly while they continued to seek more lucrative gigs and hoped one day to be reunited with Aznavour.

5

Boussagol

**Don't try to be better than the neighbors—
be better than yourself, every day.**

lthough François loved Paris and all his new exhilarating experiences, he did not lose sight of his aspiration to meet Édouard Nanny. He wanted to thank Nanny for creating his most prized possession—the *Méthode* that had taught him how to play without a teacher. He was also excited to discuss his ideas. Every time he had found a fingering that he thought was impractical or illogical, he had noted alternatives in Nanny's score. Above all, François wanted to share his discovery of the "pivot" technique.

One day, without an appointment to meet with Nanny—or anyone else, for that matter—François set out for the conservatory on rue de Madrid and asked to speak to the bass professor Édouard Nanny.

The concierge answered abruptly: "Are you joking or what?"

Not understanding what the man had just said, François tried asking differently.

"Excuse me, I think you did not understand me. I wish to see Édouard Nanny."

(At that time, François addressed everyone as "tu," which was inappropriate. He did not distinguish between *tu* and *vous*, the more polite and general form of the word *you*.)

"Listen," the concierge replied, "the shortest jokes are the best." He added softly, "If we can call it a joke."

François was insistent. The concierge, seeing that he could not get rid of François easily, indicated that he was going to make a call.

As the concierge picked up the phone, he noticed a distinguished-looking gentleman heading for the conservatory's exit. He rushed out from behind the counter and spoke to the man, gesturing toward François. The older gentleman frowned and came over.

"Hello, young man. The concierge tells me that you wish to see Mr. Édouard Nanny?"

"Yes, please, I came all the way from Lebanon to meet him."

"Why are you so anxious to meet him?"

"To thank him for having guided me with his method when I was alone in Beirut, and I would also like to study with him, and most importantly, I would like to give him this gift."

François showed the gentleman his well-worn copy of the Nanny *Méthode* notated with his corrections, explaining, "There are so many gaps in these fingerings!"

The gentleman leaned over to the concierge and said very softly, "God bless that Nanny is dead."

Then, addressing François, he said, "That's very nice of you, but unfortunately Mr. Nanny has been dead for over ten years."

He saw in François's face that it was as if he had just told him about the death of a loved one.

François collapsed onto the nearby bench in tears.

The gentleman sat down next to François and, putting an arm around his shoulders, said gently, "I am going to introduce you to his former pupil, Mr. Delmas-Boussagol."

Addressing the concierge, the gentleman added, "You will please give this young man his information."

Standing, he then wished François good luck and shook his hand with a smile.

The concierge returned with a piece of paper on which the contact information was written in red pencil. François took it mechanically and left the conservatory. He took a deep breath, closed his eyes, and said aloud, "May God have his soul!"

This was the end for François. He was no longer interested in the conservatory, because for François, the conservatory *was* Édouard Nanny. Pierre and Victor, however, urged François to call the bass teacher and enter the competition for a place in the incoming class.

"We came to France especially for you," they argued, "when we could have gone to the United States. So, phone!"

François called and, to his surprise, discovered that Professor Boussagol was already aware of him, having been told about his experience in the conservatory office. He sympathized with François and told him that Nanny had been his teacher and that he would like to meet and talk. Touched by Boussagol's kind words and gentle manner, François considered the invitation to be an inheritance left to him by Nanny. He hurried to see Boussagol at the appointed time, arriving at his house with his bow and a kilo of American Half and Half tobacco.

Boussagol was a portly, baby-faced, and bearded gentleman, about sixty years old, a pipe permanently affixed between his lips. Seeing the pipe put François's mind at ease about negotiating the price of lessons with tobacco. Boussagol took the round red package from François, opened the tin, and after inhaling the rich scent of the tobacco, placed it on his grand piano with a small smile of satisfaction. He asked François to please take one of his basses and play something for him.

Apparently François's demonstration was not to Boussagol's liking. First of all, François owned a German-style bow, but he played it overhand, with a French hold. He had seen only the bow hold pictured in Nanny's *Méthode* and was not aware that there was more than one type of bow. Not knowing the standard repertoire of the bass, François played his own transcription of Paganini's *Perpetual Motion*. Boussagol's initial reaction was to tell him that his sound was scratchy. Stung by the abruptness of this remark, François handed the bass to Boussagol and turned to leave. Perhaps it was because of the tobacco—or just curiosity—but Boussagol reached out his arm and, holding François back, asked him to please play something else. François knew Nanny's *Méthode* almost by heart and began to play one of his études.

Boussagol leaned back into his leather armchair and listened intently, smoking his pipe with closed eyes. François's attention was drawn to a drop of spittle slowly sliding down the length of pipe and then falling onto the oriental rug. As he continued to play, he saw Boussagol's face blossom with pleasure as the professor heard something familiar well played.

When François had finished, Boussagol opened his eyes and said, "I'm willing to prepare you for the next year's competition."

François asked why he had to wait until the following year.

"But it is too late, we are only one week away from the competition," Boussagol replied.

"Listen, please give me the music, and I'll come and play it for you in three days. If you find I'm not ready, I will not show up to the competition."

Seeing that François was serious, Boussagol shook his head and then began rustling through a nearby stack of music.

"You must play the first movement of the Bottesini concerto and there will be a second audition later that will require the Birkenstock sonata—á bientôt!"

Riding the metro on his way home, François read the concerto in its entirety. He was so engrossed in the piece that he missed his station and had to change trains to head back in the opposite direction. He took the opportunity to read the sonata.

François practiced diligently and studied the scores until late at night. After three days he returned to Boussagol as agreed, with another tin of tobacco.

François had barely started the first phrase when Boussagol stopped him: "You are not using the proper fingerings."

François then turned his back to Boussagol and asked him to listen without seeing his hands.

Upon finishing, François turned back and said, "Three more days, and I'll be ready."

Incredulous, Boussagol asked, "You have never played those pieces before?"

"But it's you who gave them to me!"

"In this case I will introduce you this year. How old are you?"

"Twenty-five."

"Because you are older, we must write a letter immediately to the director to ask for an exception for your age."

Boussagol penned a letter, which François signed in a hesitant hand, not being used to writing in Latin characters. François deposited the letter in the conservatory's office and was permitted to register the following day.[1]

Since he had no money to take a taxi, François asked his friend Francis, a medical student, to bring him to the conservatory on his Vespa. François clung to Francis's back with one arm, his bow tucked tightly under the other, as they wove through the maze of Parisian traffic.

Boussagol was waiting in the antechamber with the other candidates, encouraging some, giving advice to others.

He looked up and saw François: "But where is your bass?"

"I did not bring it."

"Why did you come without your instrument?" he replied, clearly disturbed.

François explained his transportation problems.

"But what are you going to play with?"

"May I borrow a double bass?"

Boussagol gave François a stern look and shook his head out of exasperation. With a sigh, he then asked if another prospective student would do François the favor of loaning him their bass. Several people spontaneously volunteered their basses, and François chose one that was shaped closest to his own. The student whose bass he was borrowing would play his audition first. Students were not allowed to return to the waiting room, so the student left his bass for François on the side of the stage. François assured him that he would return it to him directly after the audition.

Never having auditioned before, François did not know what to expect. A handful of jury members were seated in the concert hall. Boussagol was on the stage helping the prospective students get settled and then went down into the hall to join the other jurors. François was perfectly calm—he had already spent half of his life on the stage—but he was surprised by the presence of a pianist. She was required to accompany all the auditions. She played the tuning note before François had finished setting the endpin on the unfamiliar bass to the correct height, giving him the impression that she was in a hurry—not surprising, since she had to play the same piece for fifteen nervous students. However, the piano was not in tune. François tried to tune the bass to itself using harmonics, but was having problems. He turned to the pianist and said, "But your piano is out of tune, please, I cannot match the pitch." (Once again, he used the word *tu*, the inappropriately familiar version of the word *you*, which also made it appear as if the piano were her personal instrument.) A few jury members chuckled quietly at the manner of François's speech. The pianist looked up at the jury as if to ask what she should do. The gentleman François had met at the conservatory was seated in the middle of the jury. François would learn later that he was the director, Raymond Loucheur. He asked the pianist to play a full chord so that François could tune carefully.

After François appeared satisfied, she began the introduction to the Bottesini. The tempo, however, did not suit him—he thought that once he entered with the theme she would follow his tempo, but she continued playing as though he did not exist.

François stopped playing, turned toward her, and asked, "Where are you going? Please, you must follow me."

Agitated, she threw a look of consternation at the director, who motioned for her to continue.

As he approached the cadenza, François overheard Boussagol say to the director, "And he plays like that, without ever having had a teacher."

Upon hearing these words, François felt his heart race, and he attacked the cadenza "with such force and brilliance that I surprised myself."

For the second round of auditions, in addition to the Birkenstock sonata, there was a requirement to sight-read a new piece composed for the occasion. To the jury's general astonishment, François played the new work easily and musically, receiving several compliments on his performance. Unlike the other candidates, François had years of professional experience sight-reading for singers. He later learned that Boussagol had taken the precaution of telling the jury that he was a weak reader, not knowing if he could sight-read, despite his success with the Bottesini and Birkenstock on such short notice. So, François was officially admitted as a student to the Conservatoire National Supérieur de Musique and celebrated his success at the Café Capoulade in place Saint-Michel, with his brothers and their friends. François's special guest was Francis, who had so generously chauffeured him on his Vespa and patiently waited to bring him home.

François found that his only pleasure in bass class was the freedom to smoke. Boussagol enjoyed his pipe, and François his cigarettes, while listening to students play. Some were better than others. One of the students played like a dilettante. The fingers of his left hand fell more or less where they were supposed to land, but without any accuracy. His bow was likewise imprecise, resulting in a muddle of inconsistent tones that followed the general shape of the music.

The performance made François laugh out loud, but at the same time, he realized that the student must have had some talent to succeed in managing such acrobatics despite his lack of refinement.

Not long after François won acceptance into the conservatory, the trio reconnected with Charles Aznavour. Charles was looking for a full-time trio and wanted to hire them on a monthly retainer. François considered his options. In his mind, the choice was easy— either he spent his time at the conservatory in order to have a diploma and starve, or he left school now and began to make a living accompanying Aznavour.

Boussagol's initial reaction when he learned of François's decision was frustration: "But after all the trouble you've given yourself, you're not going to give up now, after just three lessons? I'm predicting a great career for you, in one of the best orchestras, coming directly out of the conservatory!"

But François had an obligation to his brothers. After explaining his circumstances to Boussagol, he began the process of dropping his academic courses.

Despite the formal rigidity of the conservatory, François believed that Boussagol sought to improve the level of the bass studio, that he somehow understood that François's unconventional professional life could serve as a source of inspiration to other students and a source of new pedagogical ideas. If François had stayed at the conservatory, he likely would have pursued a more traditional classical career and would not have continued to develop his method. Leaving the conservatory represented the end of a chapter in François's life— the conclusion of his search for Nanny.

A few years later, François learned the sad news of Boussagol's death. "This man who was adorable, willed to me, in memory of our meeting, a bow commissioned and made especially for him. It is signed Dupuis. It is a very light bow to play solos, almost a cello bow. However, I barely knew him. The total of our relationship was maybe five hours. I did not realize the impact our meeting had on him.

"I remember what I told him at our first meeting, in response to his question 'But what are you trying to do with this instrument?'

"Without hesitation I answered him, 'Make it as important and noble as a violin.'

"I now know deep down that it was also his dream."

6

Fast Cars & Aznavour...

Don't be smart, be slow.

The Rabbath Trio began touring with Charles Aznavour in 1956. Their monthly salaries were not large, but thanks to their contract, the brothers were able to secure the coveted permis de travail, or official French work permit, which was very difficult for immigrants to obtain and enabled them to work legally. François was delighted. To have a stable livelihood, to have a work permit, to be working with his brothers—he was on top of the world, making a life for himself in Paris.

As Charles became more well known, he began to tour with the trio outside of France more frequently. Itineraries, venues, and lodging were arranged by a manager through various booking agencies, but the bureaucracy involved with touring to countries outside France was an administrative nightmare for the musicians. Exit visas were required to be submitted at police headquarters prior to departing France, and entry visas had to be prepared for each country. Traveling to several countries in a single tour meant countless hours of paperwork and trips to a variety of offices for the appropriate approvals. After repeated visits, receptionists got to know the group, so all three Rabbath brothers no longer had to appear in person. François, being the youngest (and the most patient), was assigned the task of making sure the documents were completed and submitted to the proper authorities.

In spite of Charles's increasing popularity, engagements were still erratic. Playing primarily one-nighters, the ensemble frequently had to drive hundreds of kilometers between dates. Their lives were relatively simple—traveling and performing—but François found that life on the road could become grueling. Since neither Victor nor Pierre had learned to drive, François found himself perpetually behind the wheel, chauffeuring his brothers, the instruments, and luggage in his tiny four-seat Renault sedan. Octagonal in shape, Victor's drums fit into one another like a set of Russian dolls and went into the luggage space under the front hood. François's bass was tied onto the car's roof rack in a lightly padded cloth case, and their suitcases were stacked to the ceiling on one of the back seats, leaving the three remaining seats for the brothers. Loaded down like this, François's small car could manage only about 70 kph (44 mph) on a straightaway. Meanwhile Charles drove himself and occasionally his manager, Jean-Louis Marquet, in a sports car. At one time or another he owned an Alfa Romeo, a Thunderbird, a Jaguar, and later, a chauffeured Rolls Royce.

Touring by car across Europe in the 1950s with Charles presented its own set of unique challenges. While François's Renault could maintain only a modest speed, Charles and his manager would sprint ahead. They purposely followed the same route in case something unforeseen happened. The traveling protocol proved useful during a tour of the Brittany region in northwestern France. On the advice of his manager, Charles had recently purchased a bright red Thunderbird convertible and was infatuated with its power and speed. They were traveling on a quiet two-lane country highway late at night, and Charles had pulled quite a bit ahead of François and his brothers. Jean-Louis indicated, a little too late, that Charles needed to take a turn. Instead of bringing the car to a complete stop and backing up to the intersection, Charles swung the steering wheel to the right, and the car careened off the road and into a tree. Fortunately, the two men were thrown clear of the car onto the grass—the Thunderbird did not have seatbelts. The car, however, did not fare so well. The violent impact had crushed its front end. An hour or so later, François passed by a gas station and saw Charles near the pumps, waving. At first he thought that they had decided to stop to get gas, but as he drove past, he saw in the rear-view mirror that Charles was now frantically waving both of his arms. François slowed and turned back to the station to see if there was a problem, and then he saw the remains of the car. The front of the Thunderbird was completely mangled—he was amazed that no one had been seriously injured. Having no choice at such a late hour, the two men squeezed into the back of François's Renault with Victor and the luggage.

As they started off, Charles pleaded, "Please go slowly."

François's response was simply, "I have no choice."

Charles's next car was a silver Jaguar. It was a showpiece—sleek, fast, and powerful. They had been engaged to perform at a gala in a chic ski resort in Switzerland, and true to form, as they left Paris, Charles passed the trio with a smile and a wave. The brothers continued to ascend through smaller villages in the mountains when they noticed that there were a few scattered groups of people chatting at the side of the road and pointing. A little farther on, François saw Charles standing at the side of the road in front of his new Jaguar. He was clearly furious and kicked at the tires. François pulled over and asked him what the problem was. He told François to get in and rev the engine. The sports car immediately started backfiring. Onlookers had begun to gather nearby, some joking, others giving advice. One of them peered closely at Charles and, hoping for confirmation, asked, "You are not, by chance, Charles Aznavour?"

Charles was exasperated and handed the keys to François: "Do what you want, I give up."

Charles took the driver's seat in the Renault, leaving François alone on the side of the road with the brand-new Jaguar and his toolbox.

François opened the hood and noticed that there were two carburetors. He had learned enough from his brief experience as an apprentice auto mechanic to know that a double carburetor system requires the two to be in alignment to achieve the same flow rate. He found that it was easy enough to unscrew one of the two rods that connected the carburetors, realign them, and then screw everything back together. The trick worked and the Jaguar roared to life. In less than an hour, François had overtaken Charles and his brothers and, with a smile and a wave, flew ahead. François saw Charles's reaction in his rearview mirror. "I had the impression that if he could, he would have killed me on the spot."

François arrived at the resort and, to avoid a misunderstanding, checked in as Charles Aznavour. He had the bellboy take the luggage up to the room and then went to the bar to wait. Sometime later, Charles arrived. He was tense after having driven the final 350 kilometers (215 miles) of the trip in the Renault, a car that could barely do 50 kph (31 mph) up Switzerland's mountainous inclines. Finding François sitting at the bar, sipping a beer, Charles sat down next to him and asked the barman for the same thing. Pointing to François's glass, he said, "Put everything on the account of Mr. Aznavour's room."

He then looked at François and, taking the room key, shook his head.

"Bastard," he added in a low voice.

François knew he was not really angry. Charles got the joke—a smile and a wave—and he had just had his brand-new Jaguar repaired for the price of a beer.

Charles would return to Brussels every year and spend a week performing in the Old Belgium Cabaret, a lively venue with excellent traditional Belgian food. This is where François first discovered steak tartare, a dish they called "the cannibal." He also found the eccentric Belgian sense of humor amusing, and on each trip made a point of visiting the Manneken Pis, a seventeenth-century fountain featuring a small bronze boy urinating.

One evening when they were performing at the Old Belgium, the microphone stopped working. It was a full house, and Charles did not have a particularly powerful voice—he relied on a microphone as if it were his instrument. The lid on the grand piano was fully opened on the tall stick, and the combined volume of the piano, bass, and drums meant that Charles didn't have a chance of being heard. François was nearest the piano lid and proceeded to lean back into the piano while he continued to play. Deftly maneuvering his shoulder while bending down, he gently lowered the lid. The effect was perfect, as if someone had just turned down the stereo. Charles finished the set without the sound system and, for the first time, heard his voice acoustically with the trio.

As he became more popular, Charles typically performed in venues known for presenting high-quality live music. But hastily arranged dates in second-tier rooms—often the result of a booking agent thinking only of their percentage—had the potential to be disastrous. Many smaller cabarets catered to regulars who would come out to drink heavily, flirt with the waitresses, and sing along with the evening's entertainment. Such an audience was not likely to respond with enthusiasm to a diminutive Frenchman renowned for singing romantic love songs.

The group was booked for a weeklong engagement in Madrid at just such a venue, and Charles became anxious, wondering how he was ever going to manage such an unruly crowd. He spit up in the sink after hearing the emcee announce his name over the drunken racket. Visibly shaking, he led the group onto the small stage through a low door on the back wall. The stage was so cramped that François had to position himself in such a way that he and the bass were blocking access to the backstage door. Completely unnerved by the noise of the rowdy patrons, Charles asked François to move so he could leave the stage after the first song. François, unable to move easily, shook his head no. He gestured to Pierre to immediately begin the energetic introduction to the next tune, encouraging Charles to sing. Fortunately, the waitresses hired by the cabaret were there to calm unruly customers as well as to entice patrons to drink. As it was always the same customers who frequented such a place, the scene was almost ritualistic: good behavior was rewarded with a sweet, suggestive smile and extra-attentive service.

Charles noticed that after a few songs, the crowd began to quiet down, and they completed the first set in relative calm. From evening to evening the audiences grew more attentive, and as word spread, more-serious music lovers came out to hear them. By the end of the week, Charles exclaimed, "I succeed to have them!" So, in Madrid, silence finally reigned, imposed not by the charm of the women, but by the talent of the Frenchman's voice. To celebrate his triumph, Charles brought the trio to see a bullfight. Unfortunately, the toreador was inexperienced and the result was a bloody butchery—the four men left the arena feeling queasy.

Touring with Aznavour gave François the opportunity to meet a variety of artistic celebrities. Because François was from the Middle East, most European stars were unknown to him. As a result, some of the encounters were both humorous and moving, and at times led to future opportunities.

On one occasion, Charles invited François to drive him to a meeting with an old friend ("there may be drinking involved"). They pulled through the ornate iron gates at 5–7 rue des Grands Augustins, the former Hôtel d'Hercule, and parked on the circular driveway in front of the grand mansion.[1] The door was opened by a rather short man who was balding and wearing a blue work apron. François thought he was the gardener. As they entered the home, François was stunned by what he saw. The entire place looked as if it had been struck by an art explosion. Every visible surface was strewn with art, from the ceiling to the floor, on every wall, and on almost every table and chair. His mind raced, trying to make sense of the images he saw: one beautiful, another strange, this one otherworldly, and that one grotesque. It was a madhouse of art. Seeing the expression of wonder on François's face, the "gardener"—Pablo Picasso—took François by the arm and led him around the room, asking what he thought of each piece. François, not knowing Picasso and never having seen abstract art, gave his unvarnished opinion of the artwork, as through the eyes of a naïve child. Abruptly, Picasso spun around on his heels and strode off down the hallway, gesturing for the men to follow. Charles leaned toward François and hissed, "Don't say another thing! That is the artist Pablo Picasso!"

They settled in a room at the back of the house, where Picasso held court. Picasso and Charles drank wine, while François sipped tea. Although Picasso was known for being temperamental, François actually found him to be a very gregarious man, speaking animatedly with his hands. As he spoke, Picasso would look from Charles to François, occasionally trying to elicit a response. Each time he turned toward François, François could see Charles out of the corner of his eye, discreetly drawing a finger across his lips. So François remained quiet, simply nodding his head in agreement with what he thought to be the general consensus. When asked directly for his thoughts, he responded by saying he had no opinion.

Finally, after about an hour, the men rose to depart. As they were heading out the door, Picasso asked them to wait. He returned with a small, strange piece of pottery.

Addressing François, he said, "When I ask people what they think of my art, they always tell me what they think I want to hear. But you have been honest, and I would like to give you this as a memento of our meeting."

François looked at the pottery for a moment and said gently, "Monsieur, I live in a very tiny place at the roof of my building and really only have room for things that have a personal meaning for me. Perhaps this would have meaning for someone else."

Picasso looked down at the piece in his hands as if for the first time and then bluntly retorted, "You're right. It's shit." And he threw the pottery to the tile floor, smashing it into pieces.

When they got into the car, Charles exploded, "You idiot—that was Picasso! He is a genius! That piece would have been worth a fortune one day!"

Even though their meeting appeared to end on a disastrous note, and they would not speak again for years, both Picasso and François had left a memorable impression on the other.

Having been a bodybuilder on the beaches of Beirut, François cut an imposing figure. Backstage he was occasionally called upon to act as a bouncer, gently removing audience members who came back uninvited. Such was the case in 1956. It was Charles's first appearance at the prestigious Alhambra–Maurice Chevalier theater, in central Paris.[2] A small woman bustled into the crowded greenroom filled with well-wishers. Her wild curly hair and oversize fur coat made quite an impression as she pushed her way into the room trying to get Aznavour's attention. François turned from his conversation with Charles and began to guide the woman, gently but firmly, toward the door, thinking she was a hotel concierge.

Charles laughed and cried out, "Wait, wait. She is a good friend."

At first François couldn't imagine that this woman and Charles were friends, but he let her go and was a little surprised to see that she found his response amusing. He had no idea that Charles had known Edith Piaf since the earliest days of his career and had even been her manager for a time. After the two spoke for a few moments, Charles called François over.

"She wants you to perform with her."

"Perform? With her?" François was confused. She was such a small woman—what did she perform?

"I gave her my permission. You may do this if you wish."

"Well," François responded hesitantly, "I'd like to hear her before I accept."

Piaf enjoyed the confusion on François's face. She smiled, clucked her tongue, and asked her manager, "You have tickets for L'Olympia?"

She handed a ticket to François.

"I am performing at L'Olympia next week. Come and see for yourself if you would like to join me. I have a special concert in mind for you."

The day of Piaf's concert had been busy for François, who had been in the recording studio for hours. Although he was tired, he was curious about this intriguing woman and rushed over to the Olympia theater. The concert was beginning a little late, and he took a closer look at his ticket as he entered. The ticket was for the first row, front and center. As he came down the aisle, he couldn't believe how packed the theater was. Who *was* this woman?

Piaf shuffled out across the stage, looking every bit as he had remembered her, a small, not entirely attractive woman. Then she began to sing. In his eyes, she grew and grew and grew, until her presence filled the entire stage through her voice, her personality, her artistry. The crowd rose as one in an enthusiastic standing ovation, and as she bent over to take her bow, she looked directly at François and mouthed, "Well?" Overcome with emotion, he dropped his head and nodded *Yes!*

Over several years Piaf hired François to play numerous concerts and live television and radio appearances.

––––––

In 1960, the celebrated French movie director François Truffaut decided to make a film in the style of New Wave crime drama. Truffaut wrote the script for *Tirez sur le pianiste* (Shoot the Pianist), based on David Goodis's 1956 novel *Down There*, with Charles Aznavour in mind as the central character—an unsuccessful classical pianist who winds up playing in a dive bar and gets involved with gangsters. Both François and Victor performed and acted in the film. In the film's opening scene, François is playing piano, accompanying "The Singer," played by French singer-songwriter Boby Lapointe. In the film's voice-over narration, Truffaut remarks, "Victor, the drummer, is always smiling, and François Rabbath, the bassist, with black hair on his hands." As a result of their work together on the film, François later collaborated with Boby on the novelty pop tune "Diba Diba," which became a hit in France. Known for his lighthearted, fun-loving personality, Boby wrote the lyrics (the opening line: "Don't tell me that this Diba-diba is not funny") and invited François to compose the music.

When not on tour, François often worked in the Parisian recording studios. Even with his stellar reputation and work ethic, he was still occasionally made to feel unwelcome. During one such session, François had been contacted by the union to record in the Europe 1 radio studios. The singer was Jean Arnulf, a successful French artist with whom François had toured. Arnulf had requested that the contractor call François specifically because he already knew the music. On that day, however, the union had decided that foreigners would not be allowed play on union sessions. The apparent reason for the ban was because an ensemble from South America had recently recorded without hiring any French union musicians. François was both a member of the union and had a work permit.

He had arrived at the studio and was unpacking his bass when he was confronted by the union steward, a man named Brasco, who announced, "We cannot play with you today because you are a foreigner."

François was taken aback. "But Brasco, I've played with you for two years, what's happened? How am I foreign?"

The contractor who had hired François interrupted their conversation and explained that he had already set up the sound stage. As François prepared to leave, Arnulf, seeing what was happening, said, "No! That's it! Stop the session. We're leaving."

The next day, the contractor phoned François back to apologize: "I am sorry, they were confused. It is the South Americans they are against, but not you, you may play."

This experience left François feeling bitter. He had come to Paris with the idea to join a family of musicians. When he performed at the Hotel Normandy, he met musicians from the United States and Europe—they were always friendly and exchanged ideas. Over the years when he traveled internationally to South America and beyond with Aznavour, he was treated with great respect. Yet in France, his adopted country, he was made to feel unwelcome, considered a foreigner. "They treated me like a foreigner, a stranger," he recalls sadly. "I don't belong to any country. I have passports from Syria, and after, from Lebanon, and now France. But bass is my nationality."[3]

While rejection inevitably comes to even the most talented and dedicated for reasons outside of their control, François's artistry enabled him to participate in simple moments of sublime musical magic. Since 1934, the "Republic of Montmartre," a neighborhood that sits high on a hill in the north-central 18th arrondissement in Paris, has hosted the Montmartre Festival of Wine. The popular five-day event is a free televised festival with continuous live music that attracts many of the biggest French celebrities. In the fall of 1962 François had been asked to put together a trio to perform intermission music between major artists, each of whom was to play a short set of three songs. François was relaxing backstage between sets when he heard the familiar and distinctive voice of Jacques Brel, a much-beloved singer-songwriter whose theatrical songs enjoyed wide popular appeal. Brel was accompanying himself on guitar, singing one of his most famous tunes, "Le plat pays," a haunting song that describes the lovely and lonely Belgian countryside where he grew up: "With a sky so low that the canal gets lost / With a sky so low that it brings people humility." He sang so beautifully that François was moved to quietly come onstage and pick up his bass. Hesitating at first, Brel continued as François took up his bow and played in counterpoint. When they finished, Brel turned to François with tears in his eyes and took François's hand. He then stood to leave and didn't play another song. François would later accompany Brel on numerous concerts.

Mauricette Guigni was a bank teller when she and François met. François was in his late twenties, actively touring with Aznavour. Beautiful, slender, and petite, with sharply refined features and long blond hair, Mauricette was just twenty and unlike any other woman

François had known. He was smitten at first sight and would wait in line at the bank, allowing others to go ahead of him, so he could have a chance to speak to her. For her part, Mauricette had never met anyone like François—a Middle Eastern man with an impressive physique, a quick wit, and a winning smile. They began to meet for coffee and spoke at length about their lives. She loved to hear his stories of what it was like growing up in the Middle East and touring with Aznavour, by now a rising star. An occasional coffee led to dinners, and the two quickly became a couple. Mauricette was still living with her parents. Her mother was from Normandy, in northern France, and her father was a builder, an Italian immigrant who built stone fireplaces and chimneys. When he drank, he often became surly and didn't like the idea of his daughter seeing an older man, a musician from the Middle East. François soon noticed bruises on her arm from where her father had grabbed her.

Mauricette was working at the Bank Société Générale in Saint-Germain. Her parents, knowing that the two were seeing each other, found a new position for her at BNP Paribas Bank on boulevard des Italiens near the Opéra Garnier, farther from where they thought François lived. But trying to keep young lovers apart is an exercise in futility. Mauricette took a sick day and spent it with François—he had just returned to Paris after an extended tour with Aznavour, and she was eager to be with him. They spent a romantic day together, and after dinner, François encouraged her to call home and let her mother know that she was fine and not to worry. But her mother was upset and told her to come home immediately, that they would be waiting up for her. This concerned François because it was late and her father had undoubtedly been drinking. Impulsively, François asked Mauricette to marry him.

Among the forms that are required to be officially married in France, you must demonstrate proof of residency for a minimum of thirty days. Both had lived in Paris for years, but since Mauricette still lived with her parents and was not yet twenty-one, they were concerned that she might be considered a dependent. The two felt they needed to establish residency for a month as a couple. They chose to travel to Versailles, not far outside Paris, and rented a room. It was close enough for them to commute into Paris when needed, but far enough away that it would be unlikely that her parents would find them. As it happened, they moved to Versailles almost exactly one month before Mauricette turned twenty-one, and they were married a few days after her birthday, on May 16, 1960. Her parents were understandably concerned for her welfare and furious with François. They contacted the police, who tracked the couple down after they had returned to Paris, and François was summoned to report to the Fifth Bureau, the criminal division. Anticipating that something like this might happen, François grabbed their marriage license and went with his new wife to the police station. Mauricette was asked to remain in the hallway as an officer guided François into an interrogation room.

The officer demanded, "You kidnapped her?"

"I don't understand. We're married," François responded as he produced the license.

Mauricette's parents had claimed that François was involved in an outrageous plot—kidnapping and selling women. François showed the police the marriage license as proof, and the couple was released with an apology.

Two years later Mauricette became pregnant and they welcomed a son, Olivier. He was not planned, but François always wanted to have a family and they both had jobs. When he was home, François spent every moment with Olivier, but their time together was infrequent due to Aznavour's touring schedule. François's repeated and sometimes lengthy absences, combined with Mauricette's responsibilities at work and raising Olivier, left Mauricette exhausted, and she didn't want to work anymore. François agreed. He was making enough money to support the family's expenses, but without the second income he would have to accept all the additional freelance work he could find, taking more time away from his young family.

———

François was thrilled when Charles announced they would be embarking on an extended tour of the Mediterranean, including appearances in Greece, Egypt, Iran—and home to Lebanon! The return of the Rabbath Trio to Beirut was cause for celebration. The brothers received a hero's welcome: the famous Rabbath Trio, formerly of the Hotel Normandy, was performing with Charles Aznavour, everyone's favorite international star of Armenian descent. The group was featured prominently in the *L'Orient-le jour* newspaper, and the concert sold out within hours of its announcement. François felt the same mixture of excitement and pride as he had performing with his brothers in Cyprus years before, only now he was sharing the moment with an audience of family and friends. The audience's response was overwhelming. Charles and the trio were held to several encores, and François left the concert hall in a state of euphoria.

To complete his homecoming celebration, François had taken the opportunity of the Beirut concert to introduce his wife and six-month-old Olivier to his parents. Although François no longer considered himself a practicing Christian, he knew Georges and Bahija would love to see their new grandson baptized, and Charles had agreed to be named Olivier's godfather. Holy water, which Bahija had taken the precaution of warming, was in a large bowl in the middle of the living room table, awaiting Olivier's baptism. Charles began the procession, followed by the family, and lastly, the Armenian priest. It was a sweet, memorable moment—the highlight of the tour.

While in Iran, Charles had been invited to perform in the courtyard of the shah's palace in Tehran. Their host was Mohammad Reza Shah Pahlavi, whom they called Shahanshah, or "King of Kings." The shah, wanting to congratulate the musicians after the performance, stood up to meet them. The moment he rose, the entire court stood up. People who were standing closest to the musicians backed up as they bowed toward the ground. François's reaction was one of curiosity: "The shah seems to be treated like a living god. But he shook hands with us and seemed to be a simple man. Why did people need to act as slaves before him?"[4]

In Egypt they found themselves floating on the Nile aboard *El Horreya*, the royal yacht. Each musician was given a private cabin for the duration of their engagement. Charles stayed in the King's Cabin, a luxurious room with solid-gold bath fixtures. François was given the Vizier's Cabin. With front-facing panoramic windows, the room enjoyed an unobstructed view of the scenery. On shore, François was delighted to be surrounded again by the percussive chatter of Arabic and the spicy, pungent aromas wafting along the narrow corridors, and he spent hours walking through the ancient souks. As much as he relished these moments, he was dismayed by the stark disparity between the luxury of the upper classes for whom he regularly performed and the poverty of the beggars and children who roamed the streets. He noticed one of their guides had filled his pockets with coins and was handing them out freely to anyone with an extended hand as they walked by. He was practicing zakat, the Muslim tradition of giving away a percentage of one's wealth each year to those less fortunate. The young man explained that while some chose to give to organized charities annually, he preferred the act of giving daily to those in need around him. His words gave François some hope for the future in the face of the vast gulf he observed between the powerful and the powerless in these countries.

———

It was in Algiers that Charles made the decision to hire Jacques Loussier as his pianist. Jacques had just completed his military service and would replace Pierre, who was leaving Aznavour to accompany the singer and actor Gisèle Robert (she would eventually become Pierre's second wife). One of Jacques's first engagements with Charles and the Rabbath brothers was in Rio de Janeiro. The ensemble stayed for a month at the four-star Copacabana Palace Hotel, across from the famous Copacabana Beach. João Gilberto, often called the father of bossa nova, came to hear Charles. After the performance he invited François to his home, where they played for hours. François was enchanted by Gilberto's music. His baritone voice was so relaxed and soothing, almost conversational, and his phrasing was marvelously elastic and free. He would hunch over his guitar and play so quietly that François found he had to play the bass very gently, caressing the strings with the tips of his fingers. And then there were the harmonies—François had never encountered harmonic progressions like those in Gilberto's Brazilian tunes.

Gilberto asked, "You are hungry?"

"A little, but I must go back to Copacabana because Aznavour—I have to play . . ."

"No, no, one more, please."

François kept coming back to visit Gilberto, returning as many as ten times during the month.

Rio is also where Jacques Loussier's famous concept "Play Bach" was born, leading to the series of popular recordings by the same name. During daily breaks, Jacques and François collaborated on the idea of playing the works of Bach in a jazz style. The trio, with Victor, was going to be called Loussier and Rabbath, and the first public performance of "Play Bach" took place at the hotel. Charles allowed his new trio to perform a few pieces as an opening to his concert, and the audience response was warm and generous. After the performance, Jacques, François, and Victor drank a champagne toast to their new venture and planned to make a demo recording for Decca Records when they returned to Paris. They made the demo, and Decca signed a contract with Loussier. However, according to Jacques, for reasons of publicity, Decca preferred to have better-known musicians—Pierre Michelot (bass) and Christian Garros (drums)—replace the Rabbath brothers in the trio. And so, "Play Bach" with Loussier and Rabbath became the album *Play Bach* with the Loussier Trio.[5]

By 1962 François had been touring with Charles Aznavour for six years. Well known throughout Europe, Aznavour was now considered the "European Frank Sinatra" and was quickly becoming known worldwide—he would be named "Entertainer of the Century" in an online poll by CNN and *Time* magazine in 1999. With Charles, François had toured the globe, met many major stars of the day, and even acted in a movie by a highly regarded director. When he was not on the road, his freelance career was blooming. He was working regularly in the recording studios of Paris, performing on commercial jingles and movie soundtracks. Due to his affiliation with Charles, he began to get calls to accompany, produce, and arrange for other singers. François's professional world was expanding, and after his rift with Jacques, he began to think seriously about leaving Charles. A concert date in Monte Carlo would provide the motivation.

7

The Sound of a Bass

Trust yourself. Believe on you.

In late 1962, legendary record producer Quincy Jones came backstage to congratulate Charles and the trio after a performance in Monaco. Jones had been living in Europe for several years and had become the first Black music director of Mercury Records, a major international recording label.[1] He was looking for artists to sign and, impressed by François's melodic virtuosity, asked him if he had ever recorded a demo. When François said that he hadn't, Jones responded, "Well, if you make one, be sure to send it to me so I can hear it."[2] This brief interaction with Quincy Jones was a pivotal moment for François—just as inspiring as his conversation with Yehudi Menuhin many years earlier. It was a validation of his work and passion from a highly regarded artist. He decided to take the plunge and gave Charles his notice.

During a break between sessions at the Philips recording studio, François took the opportunity to ask about reserving studio time to make a demo. He approached the director of Philips Studios, who inquired about the nature of the project. Knowing François's playing and learning that Quincy Jones was interested in hearing the demo, the director ran upstairs to the main offices and came back down with a contract. Philips offered to sign François to a contract for two records—immediately—and if he signed, he wouldn't be charged for studio time. The director added, "We don't need Quincy Jones." François signed.

François submitted a demo of three pieces only days later. Two songs were composed by his brother Pierre and Roland Vincent, a friend, and *Désert* was a piece he wrote at the last minute for bass and percussion. The listening committee at Philips reviewed the demo and, more interested in featuring François's bass playing than lyrical songs, chose *Désert*. They requested that François write eleven more for the recording. Certainly Philips wanted pieces that showcased his virtuosity—and who better to write for his unique abilities than François himself. It is also not unreasonable to assume that Philips, unsure about the potential popularity of a bass and percussion recording, would not want to add any additional costs to the project by having to pay composition royalties to an outside publisher.

Never having composed before, François was now required to write an entire album's worth of music. He wrote and submitted a set of six simple piano pieces in order to be admitted to the Society of Authors, Composers, and Publishers of Music (SACEM), an organization that collects royalties on behalf of creative artists. *The Sound of a Bass* was recorded in two sessions: three pieces were recorded on a single date in April 1963 and the remaining nine pieces over four dates in late September. The recording was released in 1963 in both mono and stereo versions in France and Canada; in 1964 it was released in the United States as *Bass Ball*.

The Sound of a Bass, despite its swift preparation, perfectly reflects François's musical experiences and tastes. Influences from the Middle East, the Great American Songbook, movie soundtracks, and virtuosic classical bass technique come together in a uniquely distinctive musical vision, showcasing François's astonishing virtuosity. François was joined by drummer Armand Molinetti, an accomplished European jazz drummer who had recorded with such jazz luminaries as Roy Eldridge, Don Byas, Sidney Bechet, and Clark Terry. Despite the spartan instrumentation—the recording was the first LP release to feature only bass and drums—the variety and scope of the music was vast: the loping $\frac{6}{8}$ groove of *Désert*, the intricate and fleet call-and-response of *Impalas*, the strutting, bluesy *Hésitations*, and the haunting cries of high artificial harmonics in *Prélude à l'archet*.

Philips had long been a leader in recording technologies, helping to develop stereo technology and overdubbing techniques, which used two-track tape machines to create multiple layers. François employed these new innovations, developed and introduced to major labels only a few years earlier, to great effect. He created a bass ensemble for his snappy and imaginative *Western à la Breughel*, combining influences from Western country music as if they had somehow been painted by the Dutch artist Pieter Breughel. And then there was the eerily swinging *Basses en fugue*, a choir of swooping harmonics floating over an accompaniment of walking bass and jazz drums.[3]

François conceived the idea of hosting a special celebration to publicize the release of his new recording. He envisioned a formal cocktail party celebrating what he called "a significant cultural event," the first-ever recording of only bass and drums.[4] He rented the Pavillon Champs-Élysées, an elegant ballroom near the Arc de Triomphe. The surrounding neighborhood is home to many embassies, and François invited their cultural attachés. Much to his surprise, almost all accepted and responded that they would also like to bring their respective ambassadors. Georges Meyerstein-Maigret, president of Philips France, loved the idea and agreed to attend and to receive each guest. But François learned from one of the cultural attachés that if Meyerstein-Maigret were to receive each ambassador, the event would then be considered business related, not cultural, and the embassies would have to decline the invitation. So, on April 27, 1964, François and Mauricette remained at the entrance of the ballroom and received each guest. In addition to inviting ambassadors and cultural attachés from Europe, the Middle East, and the Far East, François had reached out to many of his friends in the Paris arts community, including artists, actors, comedians, and musicians, many of whom were household names in France. He gave a list of the attending ambassadors to Philips two weeks in advance, and they created a special personalized printing of each LP. These albums had an embossed velour cover, and the inner label affixed to the center of the record featured a color image of the flag from each respective nation with a personalized inscription thanking the ambassador for attending.

Knowing that the evening was about music and culture and not about the political issues of the day, the ambassadors were relaxed and very cordial with one another. Checking his list, François noticed that the Japanese ambassador was the only one who had not yet arrived when the time came for him to perform. He performed two pieces and looked up to see an Asian man at the door waiting to be received. François set down his bass and made his way through the crowd of well-wishers to greet the ambassador. The man graciously accepted François's welcome and took his arm with a surprisingly firm grip as he led him to the bar to toast the event. François asked the ambassador how he came to have such strength, and he replied with a single word: "Endurance." This comment stayed with François, and as he began to further explore his pedagogical concepts, he came to understand that endurance through scales and arpeggios would allow him to become free and no longer feel the bass strings under his fingers.

The Sound of a Bass exceeded all expectations.[5] Capping multiple critical accolades, the recording received two prestigious 1964 Grand Prix du Disque awards presented by the Cercle des Avant-premiéres du Disque—for interpretation and composition. Given the recording's apparent popularity, royalty statements from Philips list incomprehensibly low sales numbers. François maintains that his producer, Claude Dejacques, told him that tens of thousands were sold. Nevertheless, the recording was to have a long life beyond its initial release. The original single, *Désert*, was picked up as the theme music for the Europe 1 radio broadcasts of Auguste Le Breton's popular detective series, *Rififi*, and *Basses en fugue* became the theme for *Les tréteaux de la nuit* (Night Trestles), a radio theater series on Maison de la Radio for more than twenty-five years. These high-profile placements led to opportunities for years. As strange as it may seem, *The Sound of a Bass*, a recording of bass and drums, had entered the popular audio landscape of the 1960s in Paris and propelled François's career as a soloist. The recording was reprinted in 1968 for release in France and reissued again as a CD in 2006.

Following the release of *The Sound of a Bass*, Philips presented François in a series of concerts at the Théâtre des Capucines, both as a soloist and as an accompanist to several vocalists. This in turn led to an engagement with the French singer Monique Andrée Serf, known professionally by her stage name, Barbara. She had attended one of the Philips concerts and approached François to ask him if he would be willing to accompany her. She sang the songs of Georges

Brassens, a popular singer-songwriter and poet, accompanying herself on guitar. Brassens performed with a bassist, and Barbara wanted to emulate his sound. François, not interested in copying an established artist and also aware that she was playing smaller venues and not yet very popular, declined. But he told her that if she began writing and performing her own material, he would reconsider.

Inspired by his encouragement, Barbara began writing her own material, and the two eventually performed in Paris in late 1963 and then again in Brussels at Théâtre 140 in early 1964 at an international cabaret festival, where François also performed several of his unaccompanied solos. She asked him to write arrangements for her first major recording for Philips in 1964, entitled *Barbara chante Barbara*, also produced by Claude Dejacques.[6] Although not credited, François had a major hand in the creation of Barbara's greatest hit from the recording, "Nantes." She came to his apartment to work on an unfinished piece set in Nantes, an industrial city in the northwest of France. The lyrics were complete, but the music was only in a formative state. François created a simple score that perfectly enhanced the powerful lyrics: a dying man calls the singer to return to see him in Nantes one last time. Hidden from view is the backstory— Barbara had written "Nantes" as a song of forgiveness to her father for the years he had abused her. The voice of François's poignant bowed bass enters in the final moments. The first time Barbara sang "Nantes" in public, several of her family members were in the hall, and she was in a delicate emotional state. François had to repeat the introduction multiple times before she was able to gather the courage to sing the song. *Barbara chante Barbara* became an unqualified success, critically and financially. The project won the coveted Grand Prix International du Disque, bringing further attention to François's artistry and arranging skills.

François's contract with Philips required him to release a second recording. He was not happy about the arrangement, though, because of his publishing and royalty dispute over *The Sound of a Bass*. First, he believed that his royalty payments were incorrect, and second, Philips wanted François to sign over the publishing rights to his original compositions in exchange for releasing the LP in the United States. François refused to sign over the rights to his pieces, so Philips issued a limited US release. Realizing he still had to fulfill his contractual obligation in order to pursue other projects, but no longer tethered to the approval of the Philips listening committee, François was free to complete a new recording without delay and returned to the studio in early 1965. The result, entitled *No. 2*, featured seven original pieces for solo bass or bass and drums, and one overdubbed bass piece entitled *Basse en fugue No. 2 (Les gorgones)*. One of the solo bass works, the virtuosic *Rhapsodie pour contrebasse*, is a tour de force lasting over eight minutes. More esoteric and less commercial than his first recording (if one can call a bass-and-drum recording commercial), *No. 2* proved to be less popular than *The Sound of a Bass*, but it fulfilled the terms of his contract with Philips. From this point forward, François would choose to release his own recordings only in situations where he felt comfortable and confident that he would not be taken advantage of.

Although disappointed by his experience with Philips, François found that his recordings began to lead to new opportunities. His solo recording *The Sound of a Bass*, his previous work with the now internationally famous Charles Aznavour, and his creative arrangements for *Barbara chante Barbara* led to a stream of producers seeking François's imaginative skills. During the four-year period from 1964 to 1968, François was invited to compose music for numerous films, plays, and radio shows. In addition, thanks in large part to the enormous hit Barbara had with François's arrangement of "Nantes," he was asked to serve as the music director and arranger for dozens of singers for concert and recording projects, including several on major labels such as CBS, Philips, and Polydor.[7]

Although François is not certain of the date, it was likely after he appeared on *Bienvenue chez Guy Béart* in November 1965.[8] He had performed a set of his compositions on the television show and came home fulfilled. "To give a successful live solo concert on television for the bass is very rare, and I was feeling happy and satisfied." He went out at 10 p.m. to eat, and when he returned, he discovered that his apartment had been broken into and his bass was gone. His heart raced—what could have happened? Had somebody followed him home after the concert? His head started spinning and he felt sick. Despite the lateness of the hour, he began to ring everyone in the apartment building and ask, "Did you see my bass? Did you see anyone?" But it was too late—the bass was gone.

For a professional musician, to lose an instrument is their worst nightmare. Artists can search for years to find an instrument that speaks to them, and they often spend years more refining and tailoring their technique to excel in playing that specific instrument. After all, it is their voice. Fortunately, François had a very generous colleague in Willy Lockwood. Willy was a British bassist who had emigrated to Paris and, like François, frequently played bass in the recording studios. He had once told François that he had a bass that he didn't play anymore. François called Willy and explained that his bass had been stolen.

Willy confirmed François's recollection. "Yes, I have a bass. I hate her, and if you want to have her, I will sell her to you cheap. She's in my garage."

He went on: "Every time I compete for a job with that bass, I lose. I didn't pass either my first conservatory audition or opera audition with her. She frustrates me, so I am happy to sell her to you if you like. The garage is unlocked, help yourself."

François arrived at Willy's house and found the bass in a bulky rattan case in the garage. He removed the bass and gently placed it in the back of his car—the case was too large to fit. Once home, he found that when he placed the bow on a string and played normally, three strings sounded at the same time. Looking closely at the fingerboard, he saw that it was almost flat. On a typical bass the fingerboard is curved so that a bassist can put significant weight onto the bow on one string and not engage the adjacent strings. Although the sound of the bass was bright and loud, François desperately needed an instrument and decided to purchase the bass the next day at whatever price Willy asked.

Over the following days, François began to study the bass more closely and considered the instrument's proportions. The shoulders were gently sloping, so that reaching high notes in the upper registers was quite easy. François began to understand that he had been pressing the bow vertically on the string to achieve a big sound. On this instrument, however, his technique resulted in the bass producing a tightly pinched, nasal tone. As he experimented with using less vertical bow weight and more horizontal bow speed, the bass sang with more clarity. He began to adopt this bowing technique and, in the process, began to think that whoever made the instrument must be a genius. He decided that rather than modify the bass to accommodate his current way of playing—replacing the fingerboard, for instance—he would work to adjust his approach to achieve the sound he desired. The loss of his original bass was painful, but in retrospect François appreciated the theft, since it resulted in the acquisition of the Quenoil bass from Willy, a bass that helped him further refine his technique and pedagogical concepts. The bass was teaching him how it needed to be played.

———

François frequently made live appearances on radio and television during this period, giving solo performances of his own compositions. He appeared multiple times on Guy Béart's popular television program *Bienvenue chez Guy Béart,* played *Sete-quate* and *Kobolds* on *Le nouveau dimanche,* and performed *Poucha-dass* on *Samedi pour vous* on France 1 and *Impalas* and *Kobolds* with the Jean Guelis Ballet Company on France 2. Notably, he also appeared on television as a guest with several popular stars. He performed with Simon and Garfunkel on *Bienvenue chez Guy Béart* in 1967, a few months after the duo's release of *Sounds of Silence* in Europe, and with the Rolling Stones on *Samedi et compagnie* shortly after the band's 1968 *Beggars Banquet* release.

Although François was not performing quite as frequently in theaters, in 1968 two high-profile events brought him back to the stage as a soloist. In March he shared a double bill with the British rock band the Moody Blues, who were touring in support of *Days of Future Passed,* featuring their hit "Nights in White Satin." Later that same year he received a call from Jean Serge, a popular radio personality with a show on the Europe 1 radio network. Serge proposed a fifteen-day tour of the Parisian suburbs opening for Jacques Dutronc, a French rock star. He wanted to create "a cocktail mixing the cultural with the popular." François did not see himself acting as a cultural diplomat with his bass, forcing Dutronc's rowdy rock crowd to listen to his music. But Serge was persuasive. He was a fan of François's music and programmed it frequently. Serge once gave a live, on-air interview with Jacques Brel and played him a selection from *The Sound of a Bass* and asked his opinion.

Surprised by what he heard, Brel gave an animated response: "I will not leave the radio station today without a copy of that record!"

Serge responded, "You know that Rabbath performs internationally."

Brel replied, "I believe the old proverb that says, 'No one is a prophet in his own country.'"

Serge explained to François that the program would include performances by the Maurice Béjart Ballet, a highly regarded modern dance company. The plan was that the concerts were to begin with the Béjart Ballet for ten minutes, followed by François accompanied by two drummers for thirty minutes, Béjart for another ten minutes, and then the star, Dutronc, as the finale. François was still hesitant. With Dutronc presented last, the audience would need to sit through the cultural portion of the cocktail first, as if all the "banlieusards" (Parisian suburbanites) were uncultivated. However, the presence of a ballet company was enough to convince François to agree.

François had never actually seen the Béjart Ballet. He knew the dance company only by reputation. Expecting a small ballet troupe, he was surprised to see that there was only a single dancer onstage. Her first performance was to exchange two rows of chairs lined up on either side of the stage. Accompanied by dissonant electronic music, she pushed the chairs from one side to the other, slowly dragging her feet as she did so, as if she were wading across a muddy field. Hidden behind the curtains, François watched, not quite believing what he was seeing. After five minutes he grew impatient, wanting to run out onto the stage and help her move the chairs. It was not difficult to anticipate the reaction of the room, filled with Dutronc fans who always came dressed in black leather and brought all kinds of noisemakers—horns, bells, and whistles. (During his concerts Dutronc would come onstage with two signs: one said Applause and the other Stop. His audience would gleefully ignore both.) The dancer finished to a chorus of boos. She returned backstage dismayed, murmuring, "I do not understand. I do not understand."

Hearing the audience's response, François experienced a rush of adrenaline as he prepared to go on. The lights went out and the two drum sets were rolled out on platforms in total darkness. This process took a few minutes and the crowd continued yelling. As the lights came up slowly, the two drummers began a fierce percussive introduction. The combined sound of the drums and the audience was so loud that someone called the fire service from down the street. If anyone had entered the room at that moment, they might have thought a riot was going on. As François stepped onto the stage with his double bass, several members of the audience began to sing "boom, boom," imitating the pizzicato of a jazz bassist. But the sound system was loud, and François began to play with the bow. The intensity of the amplified arco sound was so sudden and unexpected, the crowd stopped yelling.

The audience remained quiet, in part because the music was so unique, but also because it was somewhat familiar. Many of the pieces François performed were frequently heard on television and radio, some used as themes for programs and others for advertisements. With all the energy in the room, François played with incredible velocity: "I played so quickly that the audience did not have time to breathe." He finished his short set in complete calm, but in about twenty minutes instead of thirty. The audience cheered wildly. After that experience François felt as if he could go anywhere and perform in any condition. The lights again dimmed to black as the stage was reset for the return of the ballet. When the spotlight came up, there was an audible sigh of relief. All hoped for Dutronc, but when they saw the dancer appear, they cried, "Not again!"

During the concert tour, the proportion of the audience who came to hear François grew. By the end of the tour, half of the room had come specifically to hear François, and he was reminded of the hard-won success Aznavour had finally found in the Madrid cabaret.

François settled into life in Paris as a first-call freelance musician. He was busy, playing as many as three recording sessions a day, often starting at ten in the morning and working until after seven in the evening. Then, if he had time, he would run home for a quick dinner, or if not, he would grab a bite to eat on his way to Gallery 55, a theater where he played every evening from ten o'clock until the early hours of the morning. The owner of Gallery 55, René Legueltel, loved François and guaranteed him a minimum salary that covered most of his basic living expenses, much like Aznavour had done. Even though he had this steady work, François was frequently anxious, waiting on phone calls from contractors for higher-paying recording sessions and concerts.

In retrospect, François found his worrisome attitude needless in light of the wonderful moments spent at Gallery 55. It was there that he met many actors and comedians who became stars and lifelong friends. Behind the scenes of this small theater on the Left Bank was a remarkable intimacy between artists. The nightly shows were fast-moving affairs, and performers followed one another onstage at a frantic pace. When it was François's turn to take a break, he was eager to run backstage to hear what he would call "the real show." The rapier wit and brilliant banter between the guest artists filled him with joy and laughter. Whenever François would see these artists in the cinema or the theater, he would fondly recall his time at Gallery 55. He played there for seven years.

In 1967 Moshe Naïm had started a new record label, Emen. Moshe was a Parisian music promoter who knew François from his concerts and first record, and he was aware that François had left Philips. Wanting to entice him to sign with Emen, Moshe came to see François frequently at Gallery 55. François, however, was not ready to be re-signed. The memories of his struggles with Philips were still fresh, and he had recently come to an understanding with the Europe 1 radio station. Lucien Morisse, husband of the now-famous singer and actor Dalida, was the new director of Europe 1 and wanted the station to establish its own record label. Morisse had helped many artists gain wider recognition, and he was well aware of François's arranging and producing work with singers. François had worked with Europe 1 on numerous occasions and trusted Morisse, who asked him to attend Midem in the South of France.

The largest annual international music conference in the world, Midem brings together thousands of artists, recording executives, agents, and managers for a week. François agreed to go, in part because while he was excited to work on projects for Morisse and Europe 1, he wanted to see if there was a major label with an interest in his solo career. It was here that he met two of the Warner brothers. They knew about the success of *The Sound of a Bass* in Europe and offered François a full-scale release of the recording in the United States. But they did not want to pay him for the rights to release the recording; instead, they offered only a minimal royalty percentage after expenses. François wanted to say yes, because Warner Brothers was such a major company, but he was having second thoughts. The trip was a revelation—he had gone to Midem to find a record company and found one of the biggest.

While at Midem, François was asked to accompany several artists. The concerts were splashy, highly produced affairs, showcasing artists for record executives. He noticed that the emcees would announce each singer by their sales numbers: "This artist sold over fifty thousand copies in the first month following his most recent release. Wow!" And the thought occurred to François that for the majority of these record executives, a musician's success was measured in sales. Disappointed by the realization, François decided to decline the Warners' offer. They had been perfect gentlemen and very professional, but he told them that he was not interested in releasing anything at this time. His experience with Philips had been reinforced at Midem, and François felt deflated. He recalls, "I felt like they wanted to sell me like a pair of shoes. Well, I am making art, man. I thought that the company was thinking about art. But no. You know, I was naïve."

Meanwhile, despite François's resistance, Moshe had kept returning to Gallery 55, pursuing François weekly for more than a year. After returning from Midem, François finally agreed. Moshe's dogged persistence had given François the impression that Moshe respected him as an artist, not a commodity. Although Emen was a small independent label with a staff of one, Moshe gave François artistic freedom, and he no longer needed to concern himself with the issues associated with a major label.

Moshe had previously signed the Spanish artist Paco Ibáñez, a powerful singer and guitarist who wrote music to lyrics taken from famous Spanish poems. Paco had already made a solo recording for Emen, and Moshe had the idea to bring Paco and François together for Paco's second release. The two musicians met for the first time in 1967 at Polydor Studios. François was recording a commercial date in the large room and, during a break, brought his bass over to a satellite studio where Paco was recording. Paco thought that "Andaluces de Jaén" would be a perfect track to add bass. He had written the music to accompany the uplifting poem "Aceituneros" by Miguel Hernández. The poem praised the noble work of the olive

growers, and Paco's song would later become a popular song of protest against Franco's dictatorship.

François asked Paco to sing it for him and listened intently. After
Paco finished, François said, "Okay. Let's do it. Let's record." They
recorded the tune live in a single take, without rehearsal. François
gracefully wove improvised melodies with the bow around Paco's
vocal. Paco was incredulous: "I've never seen anything like it before
or since. Above all, on this level of perfection. He accompanied
me, and then he left, went back to his session. And this recording
remains forever—for the ages—it was as if he'd written an arrangement, as if he'd been sitting there thinking, 'I'm going to play this
note, leave out this one, etc.' But no, no, no, it was something live,
immediate. This is pure sorcery, this is brilliance, you understand?"
After this experience, Paco would begin to call François a brujo, or
sorcerer, and, while he was regularly amazed by François's artistry,
he was never surprised.[9]

Both Moshe and Paco loved what François played and the resulting record sold well. The duo would make two records together, *Paco
Ibáñez Vol. 2* in 1967 and *Paco Ibáñez Vol. 3* in 1969. François's only
disappointment was that Moshe never paid him for his time in the
studio. Moshe would cover studio expenses, but not pay musicians'
salaries for recording. His policy was that musicians would earn
their money from publishing royalties and concerts, many of which
he produced.[10] Although François was not happy with the financial
arrangement, he understood that Moshe's intentions were pure;
Moshe's primary concern was for high-quality creative music, and
he never cared much about money. And he wasn't afraid to spend his
own money to promote his artists.

In a bold move, Moshe decided to rent the Palais des Sports in
Paris to present Paco and François for three nights in early June
1971. Built in 1959, the venue was revolutionary for its time. The
building had a capacity of five thousand and, made from aluminum
panels, was one of the lightest ever constructed. The concerts were
an expensive gamble, but Moshe was betting that between the pro-
motion surrounding Paco's latest releases and François's popularity,
the concerts would draw a crowd. Paco's most recent release to date
was a live recording made in Paris, *Paco Ibáñez a L'Olympia* (1970).
Although François had played on two of Paco's earlier LPs, he had

yet to record a solo project for the Emen label. *The Sound of a Bass* had been released eight years earlier, but it remained a popular novelty. Tracks from the recording were still appearing in commercials and as theme music to popular TV and radio shows. Moshe impressed on his artists that they needed to consider every possible idea to promote the concert series and make it an attractive event. He reasoned that even if the numbers were a little low on the first night, if the performances were spectacular, then word of mouth would more than make up for it on the following nights.

Paco often frequented La Coupole, the famous Art Deco Parisian brasserie. It was in front of this café that he first met Philippe Petit, an acrobat who performed just across the boulevard du Montparnasse at Le Select, making his living busking for tips as he rode his unicycle and juggled. They became friends, and Paco invited Petit to observe the duo's dress rehearsal at the Palais des Sports. Inspired by the cavernous size of the venue, Petit made a suggestion—as the lights in the theater dimmed, the audience would naturally look down toward the stage. What if a solo spotlight would instead shoot upward and show him walking above the stage, fifteen meters (fifty feet) in the air? Paco was excited by the idea but had reservations. It was one thing to walk a rope strung between a pair of sycamores a couple of meters above the sidewalk in front of Le Select, but this would be dangerously high and there would be no net. And then there was also the question of asking the theater management for permission. Moshe loved the idea of the spectacle, and in the end, Petit decided to avoid the theater's management altogether by breaking into the theater the night before and securing his wire to the catwalk above the stage.

Petit's breathtaking walk created a circus-like atmosphere that lightened the mood of the crowd and helped create a buzz about the concerts. By the third evening, however, the theater's management had become aware of the stunt and Petit was forbidden to make the walk, so he rode his unicycle and juggled instead. A month after the concerts Petit become famous in Paris for walking on a wire between the Notre Dame towers, and three years later he would amaze the world when he walked between the Twin Towers of the World Trade Center. For Paco, Petit was angelic, a wonder, effortless in the air, "the François Rabbath of space."

For François, the pending concerts at the Palais des Sports gave rise to personal concerns. He had played large venues in his career accompanying great singers, but always as a sideman. Now he was in a state of high stress. Would people come out to the Palais des Sports? Would they embrace the music? Would the concerts at least make enough money to cover the cost of the venue? Bassists spend virtually all of their time accompanying others, so to play the double bass as a soloist was a dream come true. But François felt a kind of panic, wanting to please all the people.[11]

The first evening at the Palais des Sports featured a "wardrobe malfunction" that would shape François's approach to performing from that day forward. Years earlier, François had become interested in watch fobs. He had a pocket watch and a collection of fobs that he would rotate from day to day. The concierge in his building remarked on his fob and asked him if he collected them. She explained that her husband was a sailor who had recently died, and her daughter needed an operation. Because she was Spanish, she did not have French national health insurance and could not afford the operation. She wondered if "monsieur might be interested in her husband's gold chain." On the necklace hung a two-sided medal of Saint Michel, the saint who looks after sailors, with a portrait of the saint on one side and the Church of St. Michel on the other. She asked François what he would be willing to pay for the chain and medallion. François was interested in the chain, but wanting the price to be fair, he asked her to take it to be appraised. She came back in tears, saying that the jeweler had weighed the gold and quoted her a low price. François said that he was sure that the price was half what the chain was worth and gave her twice the amount of the appraisal. He then attached a few of his fobs end-to-end to elongate the chain and wore it doubled around his neck.

The Palais des Sports was filled almost to capacity by the time François's name was announced by the emcee. The drummers, Marcel Blanche and André Cecarrelli, had already taken their places onstage, and realizing the stage was much larger than he had anticipated, François began jogging toward his bass to take a bow before the applause died out. In his rush, he forgot about the long chain. As he bent over to pick up the bass, the medallion swung forward and hit the back of his amplified instrument in the cavernous hall.

Hearing a massive "crack"—like an amplified gunshot—the audience gasped. But in the next moment, François angrily swung the chain around to the back of his neck. Seeing his abrupt gesture after having being startled, the crowd understood what had happened and began laughing in relief. In that instant, François had an epiphany, realizing that "the audience is here to have fun and are with me. My feeling of panic disappeared and I found I could play with excitement and without fear. This is the moment that I search for and why I continue to wear the chain."

The concert series was a major success and drew near-capacity crowds each evening. François performed solo works from *The Sound of a Bass* and *No. 2* in addition to several new works, including *Concerto in One Movement* (Concerto No. 1), *Sete-quate*, and *Ibérique péninsulaire*, dedicated to Ibáñez. He also performed Bach for the first time in public—the Sarabande and Gigue from Bach's First Suite in the same register as the cello. Moshe was so impressed by François's performance that he recorded his set on the third evening and titled the release *François Rabbath au Palais des Sports de Paris*. The recording was an artistic and critical success, and François felt he had found a new home with Moshe.

8

Picasso & Bahija

Very late one midsummer night in 1971, François's phone rang. He answered it with a yawn: "Oui?"

An unfamiliar voice on the other end asked, "Is this Rabbath?"

He hesitated. "Who is this?"

"I am Pablo Picasso."

François, thinking it was a friend out drinking, joked, "Yes, and I am the king of the Republic."

As François was about to hang up, the voice, now more agitated, responded, "Is this François Rabbath, the *honest* bass player? I am Pablo Picasso!"

François bolted upright in bed.

He had absolutely no reason to think that Picasso would have remembered him from their meeting years ago, and on his part, when he thought back on their meeting, there was perhaps a tinge of regret for not graciously accepting Picasso's offer of that strange little piece of pottery. The call only reinforced François's instincts to be true to his feelings—no one could ever anticipate how, or even if, an act of kindness, generosity, or in this case, forthright honesty would be remembered.

Picasso went on to explain that a pair of public celebrations were planned for his ninetieth birthday, and he wanted François to create a new composition for the two occasions. The first event was to be held in Vallauris, where Picasso had lived for several years and created a large mural entitled *La guerre et la paix* (War and Peace). He had painted the mural inside a small chapel in the Château de Vallauris, on two wooden panels bent to accommodate the sanctuary's curved walls. The second was to be held at the Palais des Sports in Paris, only four months after François's performance with Paco Ibáñez. Not knowing the painting, François was unsure of what to write. Picasso's response was curt: "I am Spanish. One side of the mural represents war and the other peace—use your imagination."

On October 24, 1971, the performers were flown on a chartered plane from Paris to Vallauris on the Mediterranean coast. Picasso met the plane and took François with his bass to see the mural. The sanctuary was lit by candlelight, and as he began to play, François saw Picasso staring intently at his mural. He had tears in his eyes and, as soon as François had finished, abruptly left. François called after him, "Wait! Pablo, there is an enormous crowd of people waiting to see you." But Picasso returned to his nearby home in Mougins and did not make an appearance at the celebration.[1]

The next day François again performed *La guerre et la paix*, this time at the Palais des Sports to a standing-room-only crowd of over five thousand. Immediately after François's performance, Picasso rose to his feet and shouted, "Bravo!," leading to an enthusiastic standing ovation by the overflow crowd. It was a truly intoxicating moment. (François joked, "And now perhaps I might have another piece of pottery?")

Moshe recorded François's Palais des Sports performance of *La guerre et la paix* and paired it with two previously recorded multitrack bass pieces, *Les trois basses* and *Les sirènes d'alarme*, creating a four-movement seven-inch LP for his new Les Uns par les Autres label.

Continuing to promote his artists to an international audience, Moshe arranged a two-month tour of South America for the Ibáñez-Rabbath Duo in November and December 1971. They appeared in multiple cities in Argentina, Peru, Columbia, and Chile.[2] The largest event was held in Santiago, Chile, at the Estadio Nacional to celebrate President Salvador Allende's first year in office, with some twenty thousand in attendance.[3] A high stage had been set up in the middle of the stadium to elevate the artists above the heads of the crowd. The duo was to follow President Allende, who spoke for almost three hours. Concerned for his double bass, François carried it over his head as they pushed their way through an endless maze of people to reach the platform. As he set foot on the somewhat rickety stage, François wondered if this was a conducive place to make music, but he was impressed by the massive sound system—it was loud enough to be heard for miles. François opened the concert with his seven-minute avant-garde work *La guerre et la paix*. Despite the enormity of the crowd, he played in almost total silence. He then performed a few of his earlier works and, in a courageous act, finished with unaccompanied Bach. Unprepared for the vast ocean of applause, François felt giddy with pleasure—it was exhilarating! Despite the fear that performing in the presence of tens of thousands of people engenders, it had been the experience of a lifetime.[4]

Moshe kept the duo touring into 1972. Little more than a month after they returned from South America, he sent them to perform in a dozen cities in eastern France and Switzerland to promote their respective recordings.[5] Upon returning to Paris, François found himself in high demand. Solo dates on national radio broadcasts for the Office de Radiodiffusion-Télévision Française (ORTF) were interspersed among dates with Barbara in Brussels, a return solo engagement at the Ópera de Buenos Aires, and a weeklong series of performances and lectures in Le Havre, in the Normandy region of France. François would return to the Palais des Sports with Paco Ibáñez as a part of a concert entitled 6 Heures pour l'Espagne with a host of stars, including Juliette Gréco, Arrabel, Moustaki, and Theodorakis. He also appeared on various television shows as a soloist and with numerous renowned musicians, including one of his favorites, the intrepid violin virtuoso Ivry Gitlis.

In the midst of this hive of activity, François would perform a full recital of unaccompanied Bach. The Eighth Paris Summer Festival was held on August 7, 1972, in the magnificent Gothic-style Sainte-Chapelle within the Palais de la Cité in Paris. The recital would be the first time that François would perform the complete First Suite in public, in addition to movements from the Third, Fifth, and Sixth Suites. It was the artistic highlight of his year.

By the mid-1970s François had been a regular fixture in the Parisian studios for over a decade. He had performed on countless commercial sessions as a sideman and, after the release of *The*

Sound of a Bass, had composed more than a dozen soundtracks for television and film. He was back in the recording studio in 1975, recording a soundtrack for the vampire movie *Vanda Teres*, when he was handed a message from the studio office. François knew that his mother had not been well, but learned it was bladder cancer and that Bahija did not have long to live. He went back into the studio's main room with the keyboard player and percussionist to record rhythm tracks for the final piece. Once done, he sent them home, and turning his back to the control booth, he cried with his bass as he improvised over the prerecorded tracks. He dedicated the piece to Bahija, and *Maman Bahija* became the movie's theme. François then flew to Beirut, hoping he would not be too late.

Knowing that François was on his way, and despite her pain, Bahija had asked to be helped up from her bed. She was dressed, her hair was combed, and she wanted to receive François sitting up. It had been ten years since he had last seen her, and he was eager to see her again. At the same time, he was annoyed by the part that his sisters had asked him to play. François had been told to ignore her illness and act as if nothing were wrong so that Bahija would not suspect the seriousness of her condition. Nobody had told her the truth. His sisters had been trying to make her believe that her disease was benign, even though she was clearly suffering.

François was not so sure if she was really fooled, especially when he remembered the stories of her strength of character when confronted with dangerously ill children. Jean had gone through surgery to remove large gallstones from his bladder. Bahija, at his hospital bedside, heard Jean moaning during his sleep and woke him to ask why he was in pain. Jean opened his eyes and, not seeing her, asked her to turn on the light. But the light in the room was on. Distraught, Bahija called for the nurses. She was sure he was bleeding internally. After a second emergency surgery, the doctor congratulated her for saving Jean's life, thanks to her vigilance.

Years earlier, when Victor was very young, he had developed a painful case of pleurisy brought on by pneumonia. In the middle of the night, his fever had become dangerously high, he was having difficulty breathing, and his eyes had rolled back in his head.

The attending physician addressed Bahija gently: "Madam, I am truly very sorry. I fear that there is nothing more I can do."

Holding the four-year-old in her arms, she was shocked and frightened.

After a moment, she pulled herself together and turned to the doctor and said, "So, I can do what I want?"

"But madam, since I tell you that—"

She did not let him finish.

In tears, still holding her baby in her arms, Bahija turned to François's grandmother and said, "Go get me a big tub filled with cold water and towels."

François's grandmother arrived, helped by the maid, carrying a tub filled almost to the brim with cold water. As they set it down, she whispered to Bahija, "I hope you know what you're doing." Even then, lowering a fever with a cold bath was considered dangerous.

Without answering, and with her eyes fixed on her son, Bahija took the towels and threw them into the tub. She undressed Victor, who was no longer reacting, his arms and legs hanging limply. Taking one of the towels soaked in cold water, she wrapped it around him. His reaction was almost immediate. Victor took a sudden deep, gasping breath as if he were coming up out of the water. Steam from the heat of his body rose up from the towel. Encouraged by this first reaction, Bahija asked the maid to give her another towel and then another. After ten minutes, to the astonishment of the doctor, Victor sat up on her lap.

The doctor, seeing his presence was no longer needed, stood up, saying, "Madam, it appears that you no longer need me, and further, I think I may have just witnessed a miracle."

Emotionally and physically exhausted, Bahija was apprehensive about the doctor's imminent departure. She asked for his phone number to have it nearby in case she needed his services again.

Hoarsely, Victor replied, "Don't worry, Mom, I know the way."

Everyone loved Bahija. François arrived to find her surrounded by family, neighbors, and friends. There must have been twenty people in her room, to console her, to keep her company, and to spend a few last moments with her. Through his tears, François told himself that he, too, would like to die surrounded by friends and family. He recalls, "I can say that I have never seen a person so loved and respected. Those few days spent near her taught me the meaning of the words *dignity*, *honor*, and *pride*. She was very religious, to the point that she did not want to die until she had me reinstated into the Christian faith. She could not imagine that I would go to the devil. It is true that I had lost my faith in France because of my experiences with two despicable Lebanese priests. I had become an atheist, but to help my mother, I sent for a priest and took Communion at the foot of her bed. She smiled, and I felt at that moment that she could leave peacefully."

In the face of all his recent successes and despite the disappointments and pain, François's love of his family remained his bedrock. He sought to create the same stability and culture of love for his own family—his immediate family as well as his musical family and beyond—embracing what the Greeks might well have described as agape, the love of humanity.

9

A New Life

Do in a way to not be alone.

François's personal life was in turmoil. He had to leave Bahija's side sooner than he wished and return to Paris for a court date.

He had agreed to give Mauricette a six-month trial separation and to continue to pay her bills since she still wasn't working—he reasoned that he had spent eleven years of happiness with her and wanted her to be happy, even if it meant leaving him. After six months she did not return, so they entered into divorce proceedings. He had been trying shield Olivier from the true state of their marriage. François felt that as long as the divorce from Mauricette was not yet final, there was some hope for Olivier, but as the negotiations bogged down, he began to feel that he no longer had the right to mislead him. He felt guilty that touring had kept him away from home for extended periods of time, and yet when Mauricette traveled and he found himself alone with Olivier, François realized that he enjoyed being alone with his son, even as he was impatient for Mauricette's return. So he had decided to pretend that she was on vacation, and to try to be as happy as he could manage to help them both get through this painful period. Although François wanted Olivier to avoid deep suffering and sorrow, it had become clear that it would take both parents working together to help their son through such a traumatic separation, and at this stage, an amicable resolution was unlikely.

Mauricette had told François backstage that she wanted a divorce, just before he was to play a solo recital in Studio 102 at the

ORTF's Maison de la Radio in September 1972. The live radio concert was part of a popular interactive series where musicians would play and then audience members would ask questions about the artist's music and career. The short conversation with Mauricette had been devastating, and yet François felt he did not have a choice but to play. He channeled all of his powerful, swirling emotions into the music and gave an exceptional performance. During the audience question-and-answer segment, François mentioned that he was working on a method to share his advanced techniques and help bassists learn how to play his virtuosic pieces. As it happened, Jean Leduc, the head of Alphonse Leduc—publisher of the Nanny *Méthode*—was in the hall. Jean approached him afterward and offered to publish the method once it was completed. Knowing that Leduc had published the Nanny *Méthode*, François agreed immediately.

After the concert, François was in high spirits following the exuberant response to his performance. He had experienced an emotional whiplash. The warm feelings of success and adulation he now felt were magnified in high relief against the lingering pain from his conversation with Mauricette only minutes earlier. Wanting to prolong the positive feelings, François told his agent that he would like to invite all the people who worked on the concert to join him at Le Dôme Café. The production had been well organized, and teams of people had been involved in marketing the event. François arrived a little late to Le Dôme and found a place at the long table next to Martine Richard. She had been postering for the concert and had seen him perform before. François reached over and took her hand. She lifted hers away for a moment and then put it back. He looked at her and thought she was looking at him like someone in love.

Perhaps five years later, François asked Martine, "Do you remember our first meeting at Le Dôme, when you were looking at me like you loved me?"

"No, François," she sighed, "I was looking like that because I was so tired from running around Paris for three days putting up posters for your concert."

In an unexpected twist, a year after François's divorce was finalized, Jean Leduc invited him to dinner. He said that he had something to tell him, but François already knew—Jean was seeing Mauricette.

Jean confessed, "Yes, I am very happy."

François's response was gentle. "I didn't know how to keep her. If you know how to do that, congratulations and I wish you the best."

Jean and Mauricette had a baby, but then they, too, divorced. Afterward Jean came to François and asked, "Why didn't you tell me about the problems you had?"

François replied, "I am the ex-husband and you wouldn't have believed me. And, in truth, it might have gone differently for you."

After his separation from Mauricette, François had decided to move from his tiny apartment on rue des Fossés Saint-Jacques near the Panthéon. He began asking friends and colleagues if they knew of a place. He was at Le Dôme Café with Paco Ibáñez and a few friends when a journalist at the table piped up, "I just came from a beautiful apartment. The owner has many paintings—Picasso, Dali. He must be very rich, and he's selling his apartment."

"How many square meters?"

She told François the size, 160 square meters (1,720 square feet), and the price, 80,000 francs. He couldn't believe it. It sounded too good to be true.

The journalist had the phone number and address with her.

Even though it was late, François went to the pay phone in the restaurant. It was a short call.

"You have an apartment for sale."

"Yes, but why you are calling at this—"

"I am coming tomorrow at ten."

Kosta Deltchev was, in truth, a renter. He was old, retired, and living alone, and had decided to move from the beautiful three-bedroom apartment on the sixth-floor walk-up to a smaller and much cheaper apartment on the ground floor. He had not come to this decision easily. The large apartment was rent controlled and he had lived there for over twenty years, but the building did not have an elevator and he was tired of climbing all those stairs. When Kosta told the owner that he was planning to move, the owner indicated that he was going to sell. But because Kosta was still occupying the apartment, he had the right to buy it first—and, according to the terms of his lease, at a percentage of the full asking price. François, of course, knew none of this. He had been living with Mauricette and Olivier on the highest floor of a building, in two adjacent former chambres de bonne (maids' rooms). The rooms were cramped and the ceiling came down at a sharp angle.

"Since I have lived here for so long, I have the first right to buy the apartment, at a fraction of the asking cost," Kosta explained to François. "You must pay me 80,000 francs to have the right to buy the apartment from me at that price, but it must be in cash."

It was a phenomenal deal. But François didn't have the cash. He owned his apartment, but it was mortgaged. He went to his bank to see if they would loan him the money using the equity in his apartment as collateral. From their perspective, he was paying only for the right to buy an apartment that the renter himself had not yet purchased—it was an unacceptable risk. But 80,000 francs for 160 square meters was impossible for François to resist. The asking price was perhaps a third of comparable apartments.[1]

François had one last option. He went to SACEM, the offices that disburse music royalty payments, and requested a large advance on his royalties. Hearing the amount, the SACEM representative was not receptive to the idea, but François had been very active writing scores for films and made-for-TV movies, and his account was doing well.

Skeptical, the representative then asked, "For what?"

"I have the opportunity to buy an apartment." François explained the size of the apartment and the price.

"Impossible."

"It's true."

"OK. I will approve an advance of 50,000, but our lawyer must come with you to verify everything."

François walked out of the SACEM offices with one hundred 500-franc notes in his pocket and went directly to play a concert at the intimate three-hundred-seat Théâtre Le Ranelagh, where he was performing five recitals on consecutive nights. He was thrilled—it was as if the money that they had given him wasn't real, only bits of paper. In a giddy moment, he showered Martine with all the cash, losing one bill in the process.

The meeting took place with François, the SACEM lawyer, Kosta, and Kosta's accountant at the apartment.

The lawyer asked to see the deed for the home.

Kosta: "But I am not the owner."

The SACEM lawyer shook his head and rose to leave.

François: "No, no. Sit down. What's happened?"

SACEM: "But they are only giving you a paper that says you have the right to buy an apartment that they do not even own. You can take this piece of paper to the toilet. It's nothing. It's rubbish."

François: "But I have confidence. I trust him."

SACEM: "You are crazy! But it's your money now."

Kosta agreed to accept 50,000 francs as a down payment, and François agreed to pay him the additional 30,000 over time. They both signed the contract, and François handed the cash to the accountant.

François had to wait for two weeks to finalize the sale with the owner; in the meantime, Kosta was taking his time moving out. François recalls that he was very nervous: "I was not sleeping, because I was afraid—because it's a lot of money, man. So what do you do? What can you do? Nothing."

Finally, the meeting for the sale of the apartment was arranged between the real estate agent, the owner, Kosta, and François.

Kosta began, saying, "I am going to buy this house but in François's name, because we are associates."

But they weren't associates, and the owner knew this. He was not happy with the circumstances but was primarily furious at Kosta for all the money he had lost over the years while the apartment was rent controlled. He just wanted to be done with it.

François took the pen and said, "I want to ask something before I sign. May I play music?"

The agent carefully reviewed the contract and said, "There's nothing here. You are allowed to do what you like."

"And I can practice and work?"

"Yes."

"Gentlemen, I will sign this deed of purchase—I can tell you that I have never spent so much money in my whole life."

Addressing François, the owner responded, "I'm very glad you now own this apartment and not Deltchev," as he shot Kosta a cold glance.

High ceilings, carved plaster ornaments, marble fireplaces, parquet floors, ornate glass doors opening out to an inner courtyard—the apartment was spectacular. A dream home. It was so spacious that François could only bring himself to move into the smallest bedroom adjacent to the kitchen as he began to clean the place. Several rooms were covered in old wallpaper, and François began scraping it off in the back bedroom. On one wall he uncovered quite a bit of writing in blue chalk that appeared to be measurement markings for the wallpaper. As he continued, in the center of the wall he exposed a large drawing of a treble clef and the text, "François de la Musique." He was home.

Martine eventually moved into the new apartment with François. She was all too aware of the drama between François and Mauricette and was determined to keep her distance, but emotionally draining situations still arose. The divorce negotiations with Mauricette had become contentious. During the proceedings, François had told Mauricette that if she didn't make any additional demands, he would pay her 1,000 francs every month for the rest of his life, whether or not she remarried. She didn't believe him, though, and had her lawyer ask for 35,000 francs, spread out in smaller weekly payments. When François heard this, he told his lawyer he wanted to sign the agreement. At first his lawyer thought he was joking, believing that they were in a position to negotiate for much less. But François reasoned that 1,000 every month comes to 12,000 per year. If he agreed to pay Mauricette 35,000 in total, it would be less than three years of his original offer. He signed.[2]

The divorce had been taxing, and Olivier was constantly traveling between parents, exacerbating the drama around what Martine called "the first family." For her part, Martine tried to be easygoing and welcomed Olivier, even though, understandably, he did not seem to accept her entirely. As time went on, Olivier began staying with François and Martine for longer periods, in large part because he had his own room in the new apartment. Then Martine became pregnant.

On the evening of June 20, 1980, François kissed Olivier goodnight and told him that the next day he needed to go to the hospital with Martine, who was going to have Cyril. By the time they got back from the hospital, they were surprised to find that Olivier had gone. He had taken all his belongings and left to move in with his mother. François blames Mauricette for what happened next.

Olivier sued François.

Mauricette had somehow convinced Olivier that François was a multimillionaire and that they should sue him for additional child support payments. This was very depressing for François, especially as Mauricette was now remarried to Jean Leduc. François still felt guilty about all the time he spent away from Olivier when he was growing up, and now Mauricette was using Olivier. Olivier and Mauricette went to court asking for 6,000 francs in monthly child support payments. François and his lawyer were able to show the court that this was more money than he made in an average month. The lawyers settled on 1,000 francs per month for Olivier, and for the next two years François did not hear from him. After an argument with his mother one day, Olivier called, and before saying another word, François told his son that he loved him. Olivier began to cry, and they agreed to meet the next morning. At the end of a very emotional day together, François gave Olivier an envelope with the receipts showing that he had paid Mauricette over 50,000 francs since their divorce. Olivier took the receipts home to Mauricette, and she stopped asking for more money.

François and Olivier's relationship has been strong ever since.

10

New York, Cincinnati & London

You prepare the note, form it, and throw it out—like fireflies.

With Moshe, François had thus far released *Rabbath au Palais des Sports de Paris* in 1971 and a seven-inch LP of *La guerre et la paix* in 1972. Both featured primarily live performances, the exceptions being two previously recorded multitracked bass pieces, *Les trois basses* and *Les sirènes d'alarme*, that were added to fill out the *La guerre et la paix* release.[1] François was certainly a charismatic performer—borne out by these live releases—but Moshe wanted to see if he could capture some of the magic that had made François's breakout studio recording, *The Sound of a Bass*, so popular and potentially expand the reach of his label.

Moshe began by acquiring the rights to release a collection of François's previously recorded original compositions that had not been released on LPs. The first pressing of *Multi-basse* was released in 1973 and featured music from François's soundtrack to *Vaudou* (1973), a zombie "documentary" set in Benin, Africa. The pressing sold out in less than a year, and Moshe added more recent tracks from the vampire film *Vanda Teres* (1975) to the second pressing. As with his Philips recordings earlier, François had taken advantage of the new multitrack technologies for these soundtracks and created virtual bass ensembles. Pieces such as *L'odyssée d'eau*, *Thyossane*, and *Horda* were composed for as many as five bass parts accompanied by multiple percussion tracks. The recording would be rereleased several times over the next four years through agreements with labels in Japan and the United States.[2]

In support of *Multi-basse*, Moshe saw to it that François continued to perform at major venues in France and beyond. François began the year 1974 with a live performance for Radio-Télévision Belge in Brussels. In Paris, he was featured as a soloist in three of the most prestigious venues in the city, including two nights in April at the Théâtre National de l'Est Parisien. Later that same month, he appeared for a second time as a special guest at the Palais des Sports with Paco Ibáñez and various celebrities in a reprise of 6 Heures pour l'Espagne. In July, François made his Italian debut, performing on two consecutive evenings with Paco at the Castello Sforzesco in the center of Milan. Built in the fifteenth century, the castle had been expanded several times, making it one of the largest fortresses in Europe. A stage was set up at one end of the castle's vast central courtyard and surrounded by amphitheater-style seating constructed on a raked platform. François's solo sets received rave reviews.[3]

While in Matera in southern Italy, Paco introduced François to one of his close friends, the famous Spanish painter José Ortega. Ortega had a solo exhibition in the city, and the three went to dinner at an expensive gourmet restaurant to celebrate Ortega's new exhibition and the duo's concert. At end of the meal, Ortega took one of the cloth napkins and drew François's portrait on it. He signed a second napkin, which the owner of the restaurant took from the table with a smile. They were not charged for their meals.

Moshe was delighted with the reception of *Multi-basse* and wanted to find a way to bring François to the United States. He concocted plans for an ambitious promotional concert and rented Carnegie Hall on March 13, 1975, the day after François's forty-fourth birthday. Publicity went out announcing the appearance of the "World's Greatest Bassist," and to attract a wider audience, Moshe engaged several guest artists, including jazz legend Ornette Coleman, mime Moni Yakim, and American singer Elly Stone, best known for her interpretations of Jacques Brel. In addition to collaborating with each guest, François performed *La guerre et la paix* accompanied by projections of artwork by Picasso and Ortega, premiered his Concerto No. 2, and concluded the evening with the Sarabande and Gigue from the Bach First Suite.

Of all the artists appearing with François at Carnegie Hall, the avant-garde saxophonist and composer Ornette Coleman appears to be the outlier, lacking a direct French connection. In fact, it was Ornette who originally sought out François. François first met Ornette in 1971 while living in the tiny apartment at 18 rue des Fossés Saint-Jacques. He received a phone call from Ornette, who said he was in Paris and had heard great things about the bassist. It later got back to François that Ornette had been asking musicians in Paris for a way to contact him and finally found his number in the phone book. Ornette wanted to meet François after hearing *Bass Ball.* For his part, François was aware of Ornette after hearing his groundbreaking record, *The Shape of Jazz to Come.* Carrying his violin and saxophone, Ornette climbed the six flights of stairs to François's apartment, they embraced, and without saying anything, Ornette took out his violin and began to play. François asked gently, "Please, if you want to play together, take out your saxophone." They improvised continuously for almost twelve hours, even as the neighbors began banging on the walls. When they were completely exhausted, Ornette smiled and said, "I feel you. I am coming to the source."

Every time Ornette came to Paris on tour, he would contact François and they would improvise together for hours. During a particularly memorable visit, Martine and François's second son, Sylvain, came home from daycare while they were playing.

Sylvain asked Ornette, "May I play with you?"

Ornette responded enthusiastically, "Yes!"

Sylvain was only about four years old and had a quarter-sized cello. He and Ornette began to play. François made an effort to join them, but it was clear that the two of them were having a special musical conversation. Sylvain started playing with lots of energy, standing with his cello and playing it like a bass. Eventually he gave up fingering the strings and just held the neck of the cello and sawed at the strings with the bow as fast and as hard as he could. After about twenty minutes of continuous playing, Sylvain looked up and said simply, "I want to stop, I am tired."

Knowing that François and Ornette were friends and that Ornette lived in Manhattan, Moshe felt it would be a great idea to invite him to play at François's Carnegie Hall debut. They were both somewhat surprised, however, when Ornette arrived at the hall dressed in a garish suit made out of an American flag. They were unaware that Ornette's most recent release was entitled *Skies of America.*

The piece that François had composed to feature Ornette was a lightly arranged melody followed by a free improvisation. Ornette was to begin by playing the short melody, which was answered by a series of chords, followed by another short passage, and then more chords—a repeated call-and-response pattern. As the performance began, Ornette disregarded the written melody entirely and, with a powerful sound, played enormously wide intervals spanning the entire range of the saxophone. After the concert François said, "It was not what I had written, but it was the perfect thing in that moment! When you put your soul into the music, the notes no longer matter."

Peg McCreary, an accomplished abstract artist and amateur bassist, attended François's Carnegie Hall recital. She had been volunteering for the International Society of Bassists (ISB), an organization founded by classical bass soloist Gary Karr in 1967, and was moved to write a review of the concert for the new *International Society of Bassists Newsletter.* Bass press was in its nascency, and her review was one of the first published reviews of a public performance by a bassist to appear in the ISB publication. After sharing François's biographical sketch from the concert program notes, McCreary wrote: "Whether François Rabbath is really the 'World's Greatest Contrabassist' is beside the point. What does matter is that he is a highly inventive composer and a gifted musician who makes the instrument sing. . . . Even more impressive, however, was his use of . . . extended virtuoso passages which employed the entire range of the instrument. The effect was that of hearing a complete string orchestra." She concluded, "Rabbath's personal style . . . was so obviously suffused with a love and respect for the instrument that one could not help but regard him as a serious musician."[4]

François's Carnegie Hall debut received mixed reviews from the New York press, which generally praised his performance and criticized his compositions.[5] The concert did not make the dramatic national impact that Moshe Naïm had envisioned; however, McCreary's review brought François to the attention of the bass community in the United States.

In the months following François's Carnegie debut, his career continued to accrue milestones. He performed for the first time as a soloist with an orchestra, presenting the premiere of the young composer Laurent Petitgirard's Concerto for Double Bass, Violoncello Concertante, and String Orchestra paired with a transcription of Vivaldi's Concerto for Violin in D major, op. 3, no. 9 at the Salle Gaveau in Paris in October 1975. François so loved the Vivaldi transcription that he performed it again the following year in a set of concerts he gave at the Salle Pleyel in Paris. He would continue to perform his romantic interpretation of Vivaldi's haunting second movement frequently as a part of his recital repertoire, interpreted with his uniquely elastic phrasing. The Salle Pleyel concerts also featured the premiere of François's Concerto No. 3 for double bass and piano.

In a serendipitous moment, François was introduced to the Persian three-stringed saz by the Turkish singer Toulaï. They were to share a concert to be held at Maison de la Radio in 1977, and her saz player neglected to arrive for the dress rehearsal. Upon seeing how upset Toulaï appeared, François offered to help and tried the instrument. He became intrigued by how he naturally adapted to the saz, improvising modal melodies with quarter tones interspersed with chords of his own invention. He decided to record an album with the instrument, resulting in the evocative *Sazmorphosis*. François gave an interview to the French daily newspaper *Libération* about how the process unfolded, explaining, "I didn't write the music. I had a few ideas in mind and improvised practically the whole time. At the beginning it was supposed to be a recording of saz alone. But as I never go to the studio without the double bass, it was there, and I felt like making it sing over some saz rhythms."[6] The release of *Sazmorphosis* led to live television and radio appearances on popular shows, including *Les clés de la musique* and *Pop Club*. François's collaboration with Toulaï resulted in two recordings, *Toulaï et François Rabbath* (1980) and *Hommage à Nazim Hikmet* (1982).[7] Both albums were critical successes, and *Toulaï et François Rabbath* was awarded the 1980 Grand Prix du Disque. After this brief, intense love affair with the saz—the recordings and the concerts supporting the releases— François hung up the saz on his living room wall and returned his full energies to the double bass.

In May 1977 François made his London debut at Wigmore Hall. Moshe had arranged a double bill with the acclaimed guitarist Jean-Pierre Jumez. Like François, Jumez was a stylistic chameleon, comfortable performing in virtually any genre, from concerti with major symphony orchestras to jazz in small groups. Each artist played a solo set, and then the two came together for a few works. For this recital, François rescored his Concerto No. 3, sharing the themes between the double bass and guitar with piano accompaniment. While the London critics panned the work, they praised François's virtuosic performance of his solo pieces and Bach.[8]

Meanwhile, back in the United States, the bass community was slowly becoming aware of François. Frank Proto, bassist and composer-in-residence with the Cincinnati Symphony Orchestra in Ohio, had first heard François while a student at the Manhattan School of Music in the early 1960s. A cassette tape copy of *Bass Ball* had started circulating among the bass students. The recording quality was poor since it was a multigenerational tape, but the students could still make out that the playing was spectacular. Frank had long forgotten about the tape until he made a trip to New York to visit his former teacher, David Walter. Walter shared that he had attended an amazing concert by François Rabbath at Carnegie Hall and that he had stayed after the recital and befriended François, taking him to dinner. In thanks, François gave Walter several of his more recent albums as a gift. Walter was eager to share his new discovery with Frank. Upon hearing the LP recordings on Walter's stereo system, Frank was enthralled: "This time the sound was really good! The production quality was wonderful, and you can hear the brilliance of François."

Inspired by what he had heard, Frank dug out his old tape and played it for Barry Green. Barry was the president of the ISB,[9] the principal bassist of the Cincinnati Symphony, and a professor at the

Cincinnati Conservatory of Music (CCM). Frank suggested bringing François to the newly organized International School for Double Bass—an annual ISB summer course held at the CCM—as a special guest.[10] Barry didn't need any persuading after hearing the tape. In June 1978, François returned to the United States.

In the years before bassists were required to pack their instruments in huge trunks and check them as oversize and overweight baggage, it was possible to buy a seat for the bass and strap it in place using a seatbelt extender. So François boarded the plane in Paris with his bass. In scheduling the flight, Frank had tried to make the itinerary as direct as possible—a USAir flight from Paris that stopped for a brief layover in Pittsburgh and then continued on to Cincinnati. François spoke very little English, and when the flight landed in Pittsburgh, he asked the flight attendant if this was where he was to get off the plane. There was a misunderstanding, and by the time he had disembarked with his bass and figured out his mistake, the flight had left for Cincinnati without him. Thankfully, he had Frank's home phone number.

"So where are you?"

"I in Piss-burg."

"Piss-burg?"

"Oui, juste un moment . . ."

François handed the phone to an airline representative, who said, "We've got this man here. He seems to be lost, and he had your phone number."

"So, where is he?"

"In Pittsburgh."

"No, no. He was supposed to get off in Cincinnati."

"All right, we'll put him on the next flight."

It seemed simple enough—François would just arrive on a slightly later flight. Only the later flight didn't land in Cincinnati. It landed in Dayton. The Dayton airport is about 75 miles (113 kilometers) north of Cincinnati, and Frank was already on his way to the Cincinnati airport, which was quite a bit south, in Covington, Kentucky. In the meantime, a USAir representative called his home in Cincinnati and told his wife, Lise, "The plane with François Rabbath is landing in Dayton." Lise called the Cincinnati airport and had Frank paged.

Frank had always loved sports cars, but they had to be hatch-backs in order to fit his bass. At the time, he was driving a Nissan 260Z, a fast car with a long, aerodynamic nose. Frank recalls the trip in great detail: "I break all speed records and manage to avoid getting a ticket. I had no real idea where I was going. We had no cell phone, no GPS in those days. Nothing. I didn't even have a goddamn map. But somebody at the airport told me it was on I-75, and I got on it, boom! I get there in time, right around the same time as the flight landed."

Frank recognized François immediately—a "graying old man" (in truth, François was in his mid-forties), carrying his bass in one hand and a suitcase in the other, with a box of records wedged under his arm. Somehow they managed to cram the bass, records, suitcase, and themselves into the Nissan. Within a short time of arriving home, Frank discovered that François's bass playing was unlike anything he had ever heard. He wrote about his impressions for the *International Society of Bassists Newsletter*:

> Every now and then, just when you thought you had things all neatly arranged in their proper order, someone comes along and not only upsets everything you've done, but demands that you change your entire way of thinking before you can even begin to put them back together again. François Rabbath is one of those people.
>
> François Rabbath's uniqueness stems from his refusal to accept any traditional limitations. Whether [he is] perform-ing his own fascinating compositions, the music of others, or the classical repertoire, one is always moved by his profound musicianship and dazzling virtuosity. You quickly discover that he brings you such a sense of security that the most difficult passages sound effortless.
>
> The importance of François Rabbath to the develop-ment of double bass playing can be compared with that of Paganini to the violin. Since the early 1800s, when Niccolò Paganini established the violin as a virtuoso instrument, solo violinists have practiced the most brilliant of instru-mental arts. Meanwhile, the development of double bass playing had been seriously neglected. The great and popular

nineteenth-century composers did not consider the bass worth their attention, and in turn the bass repertoire did not attract potential virtuoso performers with enough genius to change the situation. It demanded an artist with the unique qualities of François Rabbath to break this impasse.[11]

The impact that François's appearance at the 1978 ISB summer bass course had on the United States bass community cannot be overstated. For the first time, François was playing for and teaching a large group of bassists. His career to this point had been performing for the general public. Almost without exception, when François performed in public, he was the only bassist on the stage, either accompanying a singer or performing as a soloist. Because of the attention his recordings and touring had received and the publication of volume 1 of his *Nouvelle technique* by the prestigious publisher Alphonse Leduc in 1977, he was aware that he had something special to share. The ISB now offered him the opportunity to perform and teach a large group of professional and pre-professional bassists and discover how his concepts would be received. Although the 1978 ISB summer course was only the second time the course had been offered, the event had attracted major teachers and players thanks to the interest generated by the ISB. Bassists came from as far away as Australia to attend, and among the clinicians were some of the most influential bassists from the United States at that time, including the principal bassists from the New York, Los Angeles, Chicago, and Boston symphony orchestras, as well as the esteemed jazz bassist Rufus Reid.

François was very active during the three weeks of the summer course. In addition to giving multiple masterclasses, he performed in a mass bass concert at Cincinnati's Fountain Square accompanied by a thirty-five-member bass choir, and he gave a solo recital in CCM's Patricia Corbett Theater. Critics were deeply impressed by François's performance at the ISB course, coming from as far away as St. Louis to cover the concert. James Chute raved in the *Cincinnati Post*: "It's not necessary to find a label for Syrian-French bassist François Rabbath and the music he plays. Suffice it to say that his command of the instrument is phenomenal and that his imagination—sponge-like in its absorption of jazz, rock, East Indian, and

Classical elements—is one of the most astounding this reviewer has ever encountered."[12]

Frank and Barry were thrilled by the response of the Cincinnati music public and collaborated with QCA, a local record label, to lease the recording of *Multi-basse* from Moshe for distribution in the United States. The *International Society of Bassists Newsletter* ran a review in early 1979: "At first, when you encounter QCA's recording of François Rabbath's *Multi-bass*, you'll wonder how it could be that America hadn't heard of him before. . . . To the classically trained musician, Rabbath's music is first of all a shock. It is Eastern, it is jazz, it is modal, it is foreign, but it is also immediately, and obviously, the product of a bass player whose technical command is nothing short of exceptional. Rabbath just isn't fighting the battles most bassists fight. Nowhere on this recording is there any sense, for example, that the distance between notes causes his hand any more difficulty than it does the average violinist."[13]

Frank was eager to collaborate with François and made plans to travel to Paris in 1979. He invited his friend Jack Goldzweig to join him. Currently living in London, Jack had first met Frank when they were music students in New York. Frank wanted to compose something for François, and Jack, familiar with François's recordings, was excited about the opportunity to meet him and potentially present him in London. The two men stayed with François and Martine, where they also met Moshe Naïm. Frank spoke about his trip to Paris in an interview with the *Cincinnati Enquirer*: "We were all sitting around talking about Bach's cello suites and François picked up the bass. He rattled off a couple of movements of one cello suite on the spot, which was impressive enough, but he didn't play them the way most bassists do—an octave lower than the cello. He played them in the normal tessitura, which is for us an octave higher, and we just sat there not believing what we were hearing, except that we were seeing it, so we figured it must have been happening."[14]

Frank asked François to create an edition of Bach's First Suite for Liben Editions, his publishing company, and invited him to record Bach for his new record label, Liben Music. François had previously recorded Bach in 1968 for Moshe's Emen label, but neither Moshe nor François was completely happy with the result, and consequently it was never released. Frank arranged for the new Bach recording to take place at the Cathedral Basilica of the Assumption in Covington, Kentucky, following the 1980 ISB summer course. François recorded the complete First Suite on one side and the Allemande from the Sixth Suite, the Gigue from the Third Suite, and the Sarabande from the Fifth Suite on the other. It was virtually the identical program he had played a decade earlier in Paris at Sainte-Chapelle. Frank released the recording in 1980 and went on to publish François's edition of the First Suite in 1982 and the Second Suite in 1986.

François's reputation as a teacher began to draw the attention of European bassists. Johnny Sølvberg, a former student who had met François shortly before his concerts with Paco Ibáñez at the Palais des Sports in 1971, arranged for François to come to Sweden and Denmark in 1979. A major European bass event was taking place in Stockholm with Knut Guettler (Norway), Klaus Stoll (Germany), and Frantisek Posta (Prague). Posta, a quiet, distinguished gentleman, was asked to moderate François's clinic, where François demonstrated his pivot and crab techniques.

At one point Posta asked, with sincere concern, "How is it possible for a bass section to play in tune with this kind of fingering?"

François joked, "Have you ever heard a bass section actually play in tune?"

His comment was welcomed with a hearty laugh from Posta and the audience, and François found they then became more receptive to his ideas.

Johnny had also arranged a pair of concerts in Copenhagen at the Vendsyssel Festival, the second of which was broadcast on Danish national radio. The following year, François was invited back to Denmark to appear on a popular live variety show on Danish television, and he performed *L'odyssée d'eau* with the Danish pianist and composer Jens Vilhelm "Fuzzy" Pedersen.

In 1980 Jack Goldzweig was successful in arranging a solo recital for François at London's Wigmore Hall. While in London, François was also invited to give a masterclass at the Royal College of Music, hosted by Rodney Slatford. By his own admission, Jack knew nothing about producing or promoting concerts, but through a stroke of luck, he managed to get François a spot on a very popular morning news program on the BBC. François performed unaccompanied Bach live on-air and greatly impressed the hosts. The Syrian embassy, hearing the radio broadcast, contacted Jack and offered to host a reception in François's honor. At the time Jack was playing in the bass section of the BBC Symphony Orchestra and recalled an upsetting conversation with the principal bassist, who said, "If you tell any of the players in the section about the concert and they go, I will be very angry with them." He was adamant that what François was playing was not music and not how the bass should be represented in public. The principal bassist's opinion notwithstanding, the concert attracted a capacity crowd, and François received glowing reviews.[15]

François continued to find success in the United States in 1980. Frank's release of the *Multi-bass* recording on his new Red Mark record label was selling so well that he obtained the rights to François's 1971 live release, *Rabbath au Palais des Sports de Paris,* from Moshe. He supplemented it with additional recordings from live concerts and released it as *Live in Paris.* Alphonse Leduc published volume 2 of François's *Nouvelle technique,* and François was invited to return to Cincinnati for the fourth annual ISB summer bass course.

François's international career was blooming.

11

The Audition

Before leaving Paris to attend the 1980 ISB summer course in Cincinnati, François came to the decision that he would audition for an orchestra position for the sake of his family. He had been a freelance musician for thirty-five years—beginning at the Hotel Normandy in Beirut with his brothers in 1945, then moving to Paris and touring with Aznavour from 1956 to 1962, and finally freelancing as a studio musician and soloist since 1962. François had always prided himself on his ability to play a great variety of musical genres in almost any setting, and joining an orchestra would mean tying himself to a formal classical music institution. However, he was now fifty and still constantly concerned about money—his father's earlier words after the fall of Bally Bank weighed on his mind, and there seemed to be no end in sight.

In 1980 there were two bass section auditions open in Paris. The audition for the Nouvel Orchestre Philharmonique de Radio France was scheduled two weeks before the audition for L'Orchestre Théâtre National de l'Opéra de Paris. Since the Opéra Garnier was only a seven-minute walk from his apartment and he dreaded the stress of traffic jams, François decided to audition only for the opera. He believed that this decision would help him focus with a greater clarity and determination. It would be the Paris Opera or nothing.

The audition program for the opera had been established a month in advance: the Courante from Bach's Sixth Suite (transposed to be played in the lower positions), a short list of standard orchestral excerpts, and a new modern piece composed exclusively for the audition. Martine, now pregnant with Cyril and experiencing some complications, was forced to remain in bed for three months before the expected delivery date. It was a joy for François to know that she was in the next room as he played, and she would often call out to him to share her pleasure in feeling the baby's movements. Nevertheless, François was sensitive to her condition and careful to prepare for the audition without disturbing her. Practicing Bach and the orchestral excerpts was not a problem; however, he had barely begun to play the first notes of the required contemporary piece when Martine complained that the music was a nightmare. François's solution was to study the modern score in bed with Martine before going to sleep each night. He would read through the piece three or four times each evening and focus on choosing the best fingerings and bowings. One evening, while François was reading the score in bed, Martine remarked, "You know how much I admire you—you read the score like a novel!"

There were sixty bassists competing for the single opera position, and François was the only bassist to pass the first stage of the audition, the Bach Courante. The movement is composed in two sections, and each section is marked with a repeat sign. François, not aware that he was not supposed to take the repeats in the audition, took the first repeat and thought he heard a slight murmur in the jury. He was about to repeat the second half when Louis Guilbert, the orchestra manager and a member of the bass section, interrupted to say, "Stop, it is enough. You do not need to take the repeat." Several members of the jury later remarked that they were impressed that he had dared to take the repeat and risk making a mistake after such a fine performance the first time through. Louis later told François that just before the vote was taken, one of the jury members had said that François's interpretation of Bach was inappropriate. The opera director disagreed: "No, that is the way Bach must be played. It is a courante and must be played like a dance." François received a unanimous vote from all ten jurors to go forward to the second stage.

The second stage of the audition included the modern piece. François found that he was very focused, but also felt a quiet inner calm, as if he were lying in bed next to Martine. Even though he had never actually played the entire piece on the bass, he gave an accurate performance and ended with an audible sigh. The committee chuckled at his response. After the second stage, François received nine votes and became a member of the Paris Opera Orchestra in May 1980.[1]

Founded in the seventeenth century by King Louis XIV, the Paris Opera has been considered one of the preeminent European musical institutions since its inception.[2] François, on the other hand, was a self-taught bassist born in the Middle East in 1931 and had never been introduced to the classical music culture that permeates the Paris Opera. He had, for instance, spent only a few scant weeks in the conservatory, and having performed for so many years with his brothers and in studios, he had little experience with the culture of large classical music institutions or the rancorous politics that often accompany these ensembles. Unlike major professional orchestras, the popular music and studio recording worlds offer no tenure. Either you can play at the level that is expected—and you will continue to be called—or you cannot. Contractors who work to organize musicians for studio sessions have favorite "first-call" players, but if these musicians develop issues that impact their ability to perform adequately, then they are replaced by the next musician on the list.

Because of the vast number and length of operatic performances, the Paris Opera has a large stable of musicians who rotate performances—in essence, the opera's orchestra is a double orchestra. In 1980 the Paris Opera often presented two performances on the same evening, one in the Opéra Comique (built in 1714) and another in the Opéra Garnier (built in 1875). The bass section of the opera has a three-tiered order. The highest paid are the two premières contrebasses solos, or super soloists. Next in line are the two deuxièmes contrebasses solos, or alternate super soloists. Following these are the regular section positions, of which the orchestra typically has nine or ten. François was hired as a member of the regular section. These positions do not have the same attendance requirements as the soloists, and consequently it was easier for François to request leaves of absence to pursue outside projects. From time to time, due to the nature of the music, François was asked to serve as principal bass. For instance, the Paris Opera Ballet conductor would occasionally request François as principal bass for works that had a jazz influence and required a smaller bass section.

Although the schedule in a professional orchestra is fairly routine, life behind the scenes can become stressful. Rank-and-file musicians who play in a large ensemble can easily become frustrated. After having worked diligently for decades to win such a coveted position, they find that the realities of the daily work can become repetitive and tiresome. Without the responsibilities of preparing a recital, be it solo or chamber, musicians can feel that continued intensive practice means little, resulting in stagnation. Furthermore, in the opera, instrumentalists serve to accompany the singers. They cannot even be seen by the majority of the audience. And then there are the personal insecurities that stem from measuring one's self-worth in musical terms against an impossibly high bar of perfection, and the petty jealousies of those who may not be offered the same performance opportunities as others.

Before joining the Paris Opera Orchestra, François was already well known to several of his new colleagues—some through freelance work in the recording studios of Paris and others by reputation. On one occasion he had been hired by the opera orchestra to play an amplified jazz bass part when the music director decided that no one in the section was capable of playing the part with the appropriate sound and rhythm. The work had a long, fast, intricate unison triplet passage for the basses, the celli, and the jazz bass. In the first rehearsal the opera's bass and cello sections came to the passage and stopped playing. François was so focused on sight-reading the part that he continued, completing the passage even though the rest of the orchestra had stopped. He then looked up to see what had happened and the bassists and cellists began laughing—they didn't believe that the passage was sight-readable.

François had already led a rich musical life full of myriad opportunities, performing as a soloist in front of enthusiastic audiences of thousands across the world. Having had these experiences, he entered the opera with a childlike view of the proceedings and became especially enamored of the singers. He had worked with singers his entire career, but operatic singers are creatures of another ilk, their highly trained and powerfully expressive instruments light years apart from the cabaret singers he had worked with for so many years.

And so François was lowered into the opera pit.

12

Frank & Paul

You must dominate everything.

rançois's appearance at the ISB summer courses had made a stunning first impression on the American bass community. Certainly many bassists in attendance weren't sure what to make of him—his effortless facility so vastly surpassed anything they had ever encountered. And then there was the music itself, peppered with strange and exotic influences, melding the sounds from Middle Eastern, jazz, and classical genres into an intoxicating bouillabaisse. They found him fascinating but couldn't quite see how his virtuosic techniques might apply to them. His virtuosity did not seem to offer them anything that would help them win an orchestra audition, for instance. What he was doing on their chosen instrument was simply beyond their comprehension. Others were deeply transfixed, however, and wanted to know more, to get closer to François.

Frank Proto was inspired. More than anything he wanted to compose a major work for François and the Cincinnati Symphony Orchestra (CSO). But his dream would require creative planning. In the past he had been asked by the CSO to write numerous works for guest artists, from opera star Sherrill Milnes to jazz legend Doc Severinsen. Typically, a major symphony orchestra will hire guest violinists, cellists, pianists, or vocalists, but they will use the principal player from within the orchestra to perform a work written for viola, double bass, or anything from the wind or brass family. Barry

Green was just as interested as Frank in seeing François return to Cincinnati and perform with the CSO, and the two began to brainstorm. They asked Paul Ellison, the Houston Symphony principal bassist, to join them in an effort to expand the ISB summer bass course into an International Society of Bassists convention featuring a double competition, for jazz and for classical bassists. Barry was persuasive and convinced the CSO management that the convention would attract a large number of attendees from around the world, and that the world premiere of a new concerto featuring François Rabbath would have a built-in audience. Frank then pitched the concept of writing a new piece for François to the orchestra's artistic administration, and David Stahl, the CSO's brilliant assistant conductor and winner of the Exxon/Arts Endowment Conductors Program, agreed to conduct. But François was unknown as a soloist in the United States, and the creation of a new work would require significant funding. Longtime CSO supporter Marion Rawson came forward at a fundraising event and made a significant donation toward the creation of a new work to be composed by Frank and featuring François. With all the pieces finally in place, the four-day event was officially announced as the 1981 ISB Frederick Zimmerman–Charles Mingus Competition and Workshop, with François Rabbath as the special guest artist. Sixty classical and jazz competitors would perform for a dozen of the most distinguished classical and jazz bassists from across the United States.[1] Two days of workshops were planned on a vast array of topics, ranging from performance techniques to bass repair. And then, finally, François would premiere Frank's new work with the CSO.

Frank completed the work, entitled Concerto No. 2 (he had composed an earlier concerto for Barry), sooner than expected. This allowed Johnny Sølvberg time to arrange an early, unofficial world premiere performance of the work by François in Copenhagen in July. François was accompanied by the Tivoli Symphony Orchestra (later to become the Copenhagen Philharmonic), conducted by Frans Rasmussen. The concert was an all-Rabbath affair. The first half featured François in a jazz trio format with the conductor playing piano and the famous Danish drummer Alex Riel (Bill Evans, Dexter Gordon). The second half of the program was given over to the new concerto. The critics were enthusiastic in their praise,[2] and Frank surreptitiously recorded his concerto and then made several adjustments to the score before the CSO premiere.

The official world premiere of Concerto No. 2 attracted the second-largest crowd of the CSO's 1981 season. The piece received a lively response from the large audience, and the reviewers were complimentary to both François's performance and Frank's composition.[3] Despite the overwhelmingly positive response from all corners, the CSO would never reengage François. This was painful for Frank: "So, all these bass players came from the ISB event. But in reality, it wasn't even that many. Because if every bass player who came to the bass convention at the time came to the concert, that would be I think four, five hundred people. The capacity of our music hall at the time was 3,800 people, and I know there were over 2,500 people there." Afterward, François told Frank that he had learned the concerto in only two weeks, a stupefying achievement considering the virtuosic level of the piece. Sadly, Marion Rawson had died shortly before the concert.

———

François's performance with the CSO was transformative for Paul Ellison. After hearing the concert, he knew he had to find a way to travel to Paris and study with François. Concerto No. 2 featured several groundbreaking techniques, but there was one extraordinary passage in particular that caught Paul's attention—an extended descending passage of harmonic trills on two strings simultaneously. After the concert Paul was in conversation with several of the other faculty and guests, including David Walter, Stuart Sankey, Eddie Gomez, and John Clayton. None of them had any idea of just *how* he was doing it, or even of exactly *what* he was doing. The experience affected Paul deeply. He recalls, "I couldn't sleep after witnessing that." Paul called François shortly after the 1981 ISB convention and reminded him of how they had met and how much he had enjoyed hearing him play.

"I must leave my current positions and come to study with you as soon as possible," he told François.

François replied, "No, I don't know what you're thinking. I've heard you in your orchestral repertoire classes and they are very good."

He was very complimentary and went on for a little bit and then added, "You have no need to come and see me."

Paul tried to explain what he had experienced hearing François's performance. "I cannot call myself a bass player or a bass teacher without coming to find out more about how you do what you do. How you've learned that. And to learn from you. And that's what I wish to do."

Long pause.

Paul remained silent for a minute and then said, "I don't hear you say yes?"

François again said no.

Paul was insistent. "François, I tell you, I will sell my bass and my bows and become a conductor if I can't come and work with you."

Silence.

"You are kidding, man?" François finally replied.

Paul was defiant. "No, man, I am not kidding! I am very serious, and I will be there by January, by New Year's Day, or the day after. And I will stay as long as possible. If it's a year, fine—if it's six months or eight months—whatever it takes."

Again, another long pause.

"You are how old?"

Paul said that he was forty and joked that it might well be a midlife crisis.

"You must do this?"

"Yes!"

Paul recalls François's precise answer: "Then how I can say no?"

"I just wasn't taking no for an answer," Paul says. "I just wasn't having it any other way. I didn't know how it was going to work out, but I knew that I was going. That was the beginning."

It was a good thing that Paul was singularly focused on studying with François in Paris and determined to learn everything he could from him no matter the obstacles. While it was certainly challenging to coordinate leaves of absence from his positions with the Houston Symphony and Rice University, achieving permissions was only the prelude to the journey. The act of living in a foreign country with no knowledge of the language and customs can be stressful. To then place yourself in the hands of someone whom you barely know, who has little teaching experience, and who will challenge your most basic skills and understanding of an instrument that you are already an acknowledged master of—at the age of forty?

Paul might have anticipated that François's teaching style could be a little rough. He had arranged for several students to play for François at one of the ISB summer courses and had saved his former student, Hal Robinson, assistant principal bass of the Houston Symphony at the time, to play last. Hal played an Eccles solo piece and François said some very kind words—the piece was nice, interesting. Hal didn't play the Eccles in the appropriate baroque style, but François liked the performance and was complimentary.

And then out of nowhere he exclaimed, "And if you don't fix your bow, I will kill you!"

Immediately whirling around, he looked at Paul and said in front of the whole room, "And now where I can make a pee-pee?"

François knew he had just challenged a fine bassist in front of his peers, and this was his way of deflecting the impact of what he had just said.

The class took a break and François, Paul, and Hal went to lunch. Hal was quick to ask, "What did you mean about my bow?"

François responded, "You can do what you do and use that for orchestra, but when you play Bach or play other things, you must have other ways to use your bow."

Paul's first lesson in Paris echoed Hal's masterclass experience.

He stood with his bass in François's living room and François asked, "Play for me your D string."

So Paul played.

"Why do you sound like shit?"

Paul looked at him and thought he must not be getting enough sound, so he pressed down with the bow and played harder and louder.

"Now you sound even more shitty—give me your bass."

Paul handed over his bass and bow. François flipped the German bow to play it overhanded with a French bow hold, and his signature open, resonant sound filled the room.

He then handed Paul back his bass.

Paul proceeded to try even harder and got an even more pressed sound.

François shook his head and then demonstrated again.

This time Paul closely observed François's physical posture, seeing where his bow arm was in relation to the bass and taking particular note of the movement of his right arm. He realized that he would need to adjust his arm position to obtain François's movement, regardless of his bow hold. It was the beginning of Paul's understanding of how to use any bow, overhand or underhand, and obtain a free, ringing sound.

François would call Paul his first "serious" student. He was aware that Paul wanted to know as much as possible, and he tolerated him trying to catch every angle, from crawling around on the floor to see his hand from below to walking behind him to observe his shoulders. Paul had permission to prod and probe in his quest to clearly understand how and why François was capable of playing the way he did. As patient as he was, François was also effective at managing Paul's impatience, which by Paul's own admission was not always easy to accomplish. François could sense if a storm was brewing beneath Paul's outer demeanor and would interrupt the lesson, saying, "That's enough bass. Let's have coffee." And either he would then make the pair some Turkish coffee, or they would go across the street to the L'Étincelle café. Paul relates that they would chat about whatever there was to talk about and "maybe we would go back to the bass or maybe not—which was always exactly the right thing to do."

Paul would occasionally accompany François on trips to local shops where many people knew him by name. Some of this was due to François's loquacious and irrepressible personality, but it's also likely that older shopkeepers recalled François from his days accompanying Aznavour. Chances are good that if you heard a chanson on the radio or saw a performance on French public television from those years, François was playing. Despite the frustrations that Paul faced during his time in Paris, the public acknowledgment of François helped to validate his importance. Paul recalls an experience that brought this particular point home: "One of the funniest stories from my early time in Paris was from the movies. I was in one of those American movie houses on the Champs-Élysées that showed American movies with French subtitles. I would do that to just clear my head, to avoid listening to any French and just go to the movies. During that period, they cut the movie and created an intermission to have some time to sell popcorn and candy and ice cream.

It was a normal thing in Paris. Then, before the film came back, there was always an advertisement. This particular day I was frustrated. I was angry at Paris. I was angry at François, at Bach, at the bass, and just about everything. Then the intermission cartoon comes on and it's a little animated Peugeot running down the street with smoke coming out of the back, and guess what's playing in the background? François playing one of his pieces in descending fourths, and I just did a face-plant. Oh, my God—I can't even get away from him in a movie house! It just gave me yet another jolt—holy shit, Rabbath is everywhere and I'm not getting away from this. It was a strong message."

During Paul's time in Paris, François had him perform the exercises and pieces from the yet to be published volume 3 of his *Nouvelle technique*. François would dole out various pages piecemeal, choosing material he wanted Paul to practice, both for Paul's benefit and to gauge the effectiveness of the method. Paul had played through the entire book by the time his stay was over. In his opinion, there simply was no pedagogy that existed that offered as many concepts and options.

Paul kept a journal during his trips to Paris, between December 1981 and June 1982. The journal outlines the repertoire and bass material he was working on, alongside intimate reflections on his struggles and successes from that time. One particular entry gets to the core of François's teaching philosophy: "I don't want to write this, but it's true—I was practicing Bach before—like an étude—not *playing* it, like music. The word *practice* has new meaning now—I will not practice—practice wastes time."

The impact that François had on Paul was indeed profound. Beyond bass technique and musical ideas, Paul was adamant about the gifts that François shares with those who come to him with an open mind, declaring that "among the wonderful gifts we receive from François" are

the gift of his humanity,
and his philosophy,
and his gift of the idea of family,
and of the support for one another,
and that, as bass players, we need to care for one another,

that we not only love the instrument, but that we also love
    and care for each other,
and that the idea of competition is unnecessary,
and that the composite player of all bass players would be
    an incredible bassist,
that each one of us has something unique to give,
and that we should appreciate each other's uniqueness,
and the idea of competition is only for oneself to see what
    level each of us can get to on our own,
and this is the kind of philosophy and a kind of humanity
    that not just the bass world,
but the entire music world could profit from.[4]

13

A Fantasy, a Film & Other Dramas

If he don't exist for you, you don't exist for anyone.

*I*n Paul Ellison, François had found a receptive professional—a seasoned orchestral principal and university professor who was willing to leave his professional responsibilities for months and immerse himself in the *Nouvelle technique*. Paul came away exhilarated by how his work with François was transforming his playing. He would begin to share François's technique in his own teaching, and he devoted himself to creating additional opportunities for François to return to the United States. He had become a disciple.

Once home in Houston, Paul set out to persuade the Houston Symphony to commission another world premiere to be composed by Frank and performed by François. After Paul's passionate recommendation, the artistic management at Houston Symphony agreed to engage François as a soloist. However, as in Cincinnati, the symphony's artistic management had a few reservations. In order to come to an agreement, a compromise was reached. François would perform the Vivaldi Concerto for Violin in D Major, op. 3, no. 9 accompanied by strings, to be paired with a new, less ambitious work, commissioned from Frank. Wanting to appease the Houston Symphony, Frank was mindful of keeping within the boundaries of their commission. They had requested a "short piece," and Frank was proud that he was able to create a compelling fifteen-minute work. Entitled Fantasy for Double Bass and Orchestra, the work was heavily influenced by François's Middle Eastern roots. The *Courier-Mail* in Brisbane, Australia, gave an apt description of the work: "The Fantasy, scored for strings, flutes and percussion, has two sections: one with sinuous melodies of a Middle Eastern turn, the other a wildly turning devilish dance that subsides into an extended raga-like improvisation with percussion."[1]

Sergiu Comissiona, the Houston Symphony's music director, was a highly respected conductor who had decades of experience conducting major symphonies and operas, including the New York City Opera. But Frank's musical language combined both classical and jazz vocabulary, and Comissiona, trained as a classical violinist in Romania from the age of five, had no experience with American jazz. The primary problem was the interpretation of rhythm and tempo. Playing a fast tempo in Schubert or Brahms is not the same as playing a fast tempo in the jazz world. Generally, in the classical world, the concept of tempo is more elastic than in jazz, and to complicate matters, Frank had written complex changing meters that had to be played precisely. The orchestra needed to stay on the front edge of the pulse in order to play with François. As Frank observed, "When François learned a fast phrase, he wasn't taking any prisoners!"

There was also an issue with the percussion section. The slower first movement had been inspired by *Poucha-dass*, François's raga for bass. The fast second movement features an extended improvisation for François accompanied by percussion, and Frank had originally envisioned using tablas to match the Indian musical lexicon. Unfortunately, a tabla player could not be found in the Houston area. Jimmy Simon, the principal percussionist of the Houston Symphony, was an experienced hand drummer and made the suggestion to use a doumbek, a goblet-shaped drum from North Africa. The single-headed drum has a bright sound, and although it doesn't offer the same range of pitches as a pair of Indian tablas, the doumbek's tight head allows the drum to respond quickly to various intricate hand gestures, including finger rolls and snaps. These were the same drums that the Rabbath Orchestra had used at the Damascus cabaret years earlier. François loved the sound of the doumbek, which brought back memories of performing with his brothers.

The performances took place on October 8 and 9, 1983. Charles Ward of the *Houston Chronicle* was effusive in his praise: "Rabbath's best work of the evening came with the Proto piece. It is a two-movement work that gives the soloist plenty of showy passages, and he simply tossed them off with graceful ease. . . . And, in the second, fast movement, the soloist plays against and with a dombec, or hand drum, in writing that draws its spirit from the world of jazz and that idiom's interplay between bass soloist and drummer."[2] The album *Rabbath Plays Proto* was released in 1986 on Frank Proto's Red Mark record label with both the Fantasy and Concerto No. 2. David Stahl, the assistant conductor of the Cincinnati Symphony Orchestra, conducted both performances. The recording received great critical acclaim from international music publications.[3]

In 1980 the movie director Nicolas Roeg was working on a major motion picture, *Bad Timing*, starring Art Garfunkel, Harvey Keitel, and Theresa Russell, Roeg's romantic partner. Considered something of an iconoclastic director, he was known for presenting stories in a nonlinear fashion, emphasizing vivid imagery, and often interrupting scenes with abrupt, stylized cuts. Roeg and composer Richard Hartley (*The Rocky Horror Picture Show*, *Shock Treatment*) were in London to record the film's soundtrack when Roeg came across a copy of *The Sound of a Bass* LP. He was attracted to the wild virtuosity and powerful primitivism of the music and asked Hartley if he could compose something like it to accompany a particularly intense scene. Hartley replied that scoring such a freely improvised piece was outside his expertise and that it would be difficult to find a musician who could sight-read something that complex. He suggested contacting François directly.

Well known in the Parisian studio scene for decades by this time, François was relatively easy for Roeg to find. François accepted what he felt were generous terms and made the trip to London for the recording session. The plan was to have François improvise for about two minutes while viewing the chosen scene on the soundstage screen. François improvised to the film, and Roeg was ecstatic. The effect was just what he wanted. He then asked if François wouldn't mind trying another scene, and then another. François was given shared musical credit with Hartley.

Three years later, François was again contacted by Roeg's office to contribute to his film *Eureka*, starring Gene Hackman, Mickey Rourke, Joe Pesci, and Theresa Russell. François's friend Jack Goldzweig suggested that he represent François in negotiating the contract this time, since it was rare for an independent musician to work directly with a studio. The result was that François was offered almost twice as much money and a per diem. Although he was in London for only two days, François recalls the commissary lunch at Wembley Studios with fondness because a James Bond film was also in production and he met several of his favorite actors.

Eureka's music director was Stanley Myers, a well-known English film composer (*The Deer Hunter, Jarhead*). Jack described the relationship between the two men as somewhat discordant. The music director normally has the final say over the soundtrack. But François had numerous soundtrack credits and had been asked to perform his own pieces. For the *Eureka* score, he had been asked to make three contributions: improvise a few segments, compose one piece for an involved scene, and perform the melody of the movie's theme accompanied by the studio orchestra. Jack, having negotiated the contract, felt somewhat responsible and asked François if he had prepared his composition assignment for the next day's recording.

François responded, "Yes. Don't worry. I've got it all done."

But he hadn't written anything down.

Jack was floored. He recalls: "You know what he did? He didn't have any music. The scene came up on the large screen and he told the booth, 'Roll the recording,' and he started an improvisation on the bass. He stopped and then said, 'OK, roll it again,' and he layered one overdub over another. He made it up on the spot! And it's in the movie!"

For musicians in a high-pressure field such as creating and recording film scores, it can be alarming to encounter someone who works in a vastly different manner. Movie soundtracks are typically planned in great detail a month or more in advance. François was certainly capable of writing out a five-part bass piece to be used for the film, but he was also capable of improvising those parts—a process that might very well have yielded a better-suited score precisely because he was reacting viscerally, watching the movie as he played, rather than interpreting a previously written piece.

Sadly, the film's potential was ruined by Roeg's stubbornness. He decided to give Theresa Russell, now his wife, a twenty-minute monologue in a court scene at the end of the film. The Hollywood studio told him that he had to cut the excessively long scene. When he refused, the studio chose not to release the film in theaters, and instead it went directly to video.

———

In 1983 double bassist Thierry Barbé won a section position with the Paris Opera Orchestra, where he first encountered François. Thierry had just graduated from the Paris Conservatory, and his teacher, Jean-Marc Rollez, was one of the opera's super soloists. "I knew about [François]," says Thierry, "the same way the world knew of him, through his recordings. But of course, studying with Rollez, he did not share the same point of view as François, so we students never met him. It was not like today where we have more masterclasses and the world is more unified. I think probably the first piece I played with the new team was Verdi, and I sat with François—and then I shared a stand with him for ten years."

Thierry's first impression of François was of someone with enormous arms and a huge sound—round and clear. François was very welcoming and collegial. He loved to share his ideas about the bass and often made fingering suggestions, sometimes, Thierry felt, unnecessarily. But Thierry was fascinated that François seemed perfectly comfortable using his thumb to play pitches anywhere on the fingerboard, something far outside traditional pedagogy. The two bassists quickly became close. They spoke together during breaks, roomed together on tour, and shared the same point of view about the attitude in the orchestra. "We were not principals, we were in the section, but we were free, and it was a pleasure, a human pleasure to be with him," recalls Thierry. François generously shared the music he was working on with Thierry, including yet to be published works that had been composed exclusively for François.

After a conversation with Paul Ellison in which Paul extolled François's innovations, Thierry decided to take a lesson with his colleague. François had long wanted to share his method with a French professional bassist and was delighted that Thierry had approached him. Thierry initially took one lesson, which led to two, and then many. François was in the final stages of refining volume 3 of his *Nouvelle technique*—a text filled with scales, alternative fingerings, and extensive bowing variations—for publication. Thierry recalls that "coming from the classical tradition, we were obliged to use the bowings written in the part. With François, we were now free—you can imagine everything, you can change the bowings, you can imagine any kind of fingering. And that was fantastic for me—it completely changed my mind." Another major change for Thierry came from the way François approached the bow. Rollez had taught a French bow hold that required the first finger to wrap around the stick of the bow, limiting the flexibility of the right hand. The end result was that the sound was not as open, and the bow hold made off-the-string strokes significantly more difficult. François's approach, which insisted on the free flexibility of every joint in the fingers, helped Thierry develop a more open tone.

François had recently instituted a diploma system to reward students who excelled in studying his method. He created one for teaching and another for performance, based on a student's success in understanding and mastering the *Nouvelle technique*. Thierry was given the second set of diplomas, after Paul. This was significant because while François was seen as an innovator in the United States, where accomplished bassists were studying his new pedagogical concepts, he was not as well known in the European bass community as a serious teacher. Thierry became the first French professional bassist to embrace François's pedagogy and apply it in an orchestral setting. He later went on to become a professor of double bass at the Paris Conservatory.[4]

Hervé Le Floch, one of the Paris Opera Orchestra concertmasters, invited François to perform in a chamber music series sponsored by the Paris Opera in 1983. The concept behind the series was to give the super soloists of the opera orchestra an opportunity to perform in an intimate chamber music setting. Le Floch suggested the program: Bottesini's *Gran duo concertante* for violin and double bass, Schubert's

"Trout" Quintet, and a set of solo pieces of François's choosing. The concert was to be nationally televised from the Opéra Comique on the eve of the orchestra's departure for a South American tour. François chose to perform a handful of his most familiar solo works, including *La guerre et la paix*, *Poucha-dass*, and *Briez*, but began by performing the complete Bach First Cello Suite. François performed the Bottesini, Bach, and his unaccompanied works on his Quenoil bass in solo tuning, a whole step higher than normal, and then performed the Schubert on his large Bernadel bass in orchestra tuning with his colleagues from the Paris Opera.

François was not aware that all of the participating performers were supposed to have the opera orchestra's super soloist designation. He had agreed to play because Le Floch was one of the opera's two concertmasters and had asked him personally. When the announcement went out about the concert featuring François, a complaint was lodged by Jean-Marc Rollez. Letters were sent to François and to the opera's managing director, and posted on the musicians' notice board. Not wishing to cause a problem, as soon as he learned of the complaint, François went into the administrative offices to let the managing director know that he was willing to be replaced by one of the four double bass super soloists. But the director knew that ticket sales for the overall concert series were down and that François's name would be an audience draw. Furthermore, he was annoyed that Rollez would lodge a complaint over a petty jealousy. He told François that the hall had already been booked and paid for, and per the contract François had signed, if he were to back out of the concert for a reason other than illness, he would be liable for the hall's expenses. François agreed to play.[5]

More drama ensued in the moments leading up to the concert. The pianist who was to accompany the Bottesini saw the music for the first time at the dress rehearsal on the afternoon of the performance. After playing for a few moments, he got up from the piano bench and announced, "I am not going to play this circus music!" and walked out. Fortunately, Le Floch's wife, Bridgette Vandôme, was an accomplished concert pianist and agreed to play. She would come to François's rescue again that evening. He was wearing a new shirt with sleeves that required cuff links. Having never performed in such a shirt before, he realized that the cuff link on his left sleeve was hitting the side of the bass. Bridgette had a needle and thread in her bag and sewed François's shirt cuffs together so he could play without the links. It had also been several years since François had worn his suit, and he had not tried it on before he left for the hall. His waistline had grown and he discovered that he couldn't quite fasten his pants. Le Floch offered François his cummerbund to hold his pants up, and another musician lent him a jacket.

Then, just before the concert, as the musicians were relaxing backstage and quietly preparing, a young man burst into the green-room and shouted at François, "If you make it past the third bar of the Bach, I will castrate myself!" Le Floch furiously grabbed the young man by the back of his coat and threw him out the door. Given everything that had already happened, François took this all in stride.

The hall was filled to capacity. Despite one heart-stopping moment when the Bottesini score fell to the floor after an overen-thusiastic page turn, the concert was a great success. The opera had chartered a plane to take the orchestra on the South American tour, and the plane was being held until the musicians from the chamber concert arrived. As they boarded the plane, someone called out, "Were you brilliant?" Le Floch shouted back, "Of course. We were amazing. And now someone is a eunuch tonight!"

After his experience, François lobbied the Paris Opera management to consider starting a chamber music series open to all the members of the orchestra. This idea received support from many of the musicians, who would now have a motivating, intimate performance opportunity outside the confines of the orchestra pit. The result was the introduction of a weekly noontime chamber music series.

The following year, an American conductor arrived to lead the opera orchestra in a contemporary work.[6] The piece required only one bass, but the opera always assigned two for the rehearsals in case of an accident or illness. A recently hired super soloist was assigned to be the primary player, and François was chosen to be the second. François recalls that the work was complex, and although the principal played beautifully, he struggled with the rhythms. During a break in the rehearsals, the orchestra manager approached François and told him that the conductor wanted to make a change: "He said he prefers the bassist with the white beard." François knew that if he were to accept, this would be the end of the soloist's career in the opera because he was still under tenure review. François immediately went to the conductor's dressing room and respectfully requested that he reconsider the decision. François explained the situation and offered to help. He would sit next to the soloist during the rehearsals and the first two performances until the soloist mastered the part. Begrudgingly, the conductor agreed, so long as François assisted, but he reserved the right to make the switch if things did not improve. Fortunately, they did. The soloist offered François a ride home after the final rehearsal. Parked outside François's apartment building, the soloist quietly thanked François for what he had done. François responded, "Don't say thank you. Just do it for another bass player if the occasion presents itself."

The musical world is full of examples of jealousy and schaden-freude. Even after working diligently for a lifetime and knowing full well the dedication that becoming a professional musician entails, many become embittered and take pleasure in the failures or humiliation of their colleagues. François's insistence on support-ing another's humanity often feels more like the exception than the rule. Despite, or perhaps because of, his own history of rejections, if he sees an empathetic way forward, François does what he feels is right. He freely shares his opinions, some might even say to the point of excess, but always with respect.

14

The Opera Years

You cannot play to show your ambition.
You cannot share your love with that.

lthough there were those who found François's distractions annoying, few would argue that he hadn't brought a fresh perspective to the routine life of the opera pit. He enjoyed himself during the opera rehearsals and was never bored, in part because he never took the music home to practice. He simply preferred to make his mistakes in rehearsals and give rehearsal time his complete attention. As a result, rehearsals for François went by quickly. From a dedicated professional's perspective, this is an abhorrent attitude. The prevailing view is that each musician ought to have their part learned in advance of the first rehearsal so that rehearsals can be used to refine interpretations, not for musicians to learn their parts. François was, however, a remarkable musician. His technique enabled him to play the most challenging passages with ease, his memory was exceptional, and he had developed significant endurance due to his work ethic and athletic training. He had the skill set to remain focused over the course of a three-hour opera without flagging and claims never to have written in a fingering or a bowing because, as he says, "all that is in my head."

Occasionally his insights influenced the entire string section. François had been asked by the opera's music director, Myung-Whun Chung, to give his son bass lessons. During one lesson Chung abruptly interrupted the lesson to ask, "How do you make an accent at the tip of the bow?"

François responded, "Just do this," and simply raised his elbow.

Chung looked at François quizzically, not quite understanding, and asked, "What is this? What are you doing differently?"

François took his bow and placed the tip of the bow on Chung's leg. He then raised up his arm, bringing the weight of his arm onto the leg.

Later that same day in rehearsal, Chung encouraged the string section, "Attack at the tip, put your elbow up!"

In an orchestra, musicians often find comfort in numbers. There are moments when a score requires a solo voice to emerge from the orchestral texture, but it is rare for a musician to volunteer to perform or demonstrate in front of the ensemble, unbidden by the conductor. François had no such reservations and was unafraid to speak his mind or share a musical moment. Numerous anecdotes illustrate his fearlessness, candor, and childlike enthusiasm in the face of embarrassment or ridicule.[1]

On one occasion, during a break in ballet rehearsals, the master of the ballet opened the curtains and said to Chung, "Please give us ten minutes more time."

Chung replied, "If I tell the orchestra to go and come back, it will not take ten minutes, it will take another half hour." And then, addressing the orchestra, he made an unusual invitation: "Please sit down and we will wait. And now, perhaps someone would like to play for us something?"

He began to look around. The concertmaster looked to the floor. The viola, the cello, the woodwinds, the brass all looked away.

Louis Guilbert, François's stand partner that day, leaned over to him and whispered, "Play something!"

So François, without saying anything, began to play *Poucha-dass*, the evocative raga inspired by Ravi Shankar's sitar.

The orchestra applauded his performance, and Chung asked about the piece.

François was surprised by the reception: "Nobody dared to play. When a musician won't play, who cares? You must dare to play. Yes, it's your life. These people are playing all day every day, all night every night. But alone, in front of your colleagues, you are paralyzed. Why?"

Another time, the Paris Opera was in Italy on a European tour with Chung conducting. They had just finished a rehearsal when Chung announced, "We have thirty minutes left, so we will read the Messiaen." The work was the *Turangalîla-Symphonie*, a terrifically complex and challenging piece. The sight-reading did not go well, but François mistakenly thought that he was hearing the piece the way it was meant to be played. When the orchestra finished reading the piece, François couldn't help himself and shouted to Chung, "You're going to conduct this shit?"

Up until the performance, François was still not convinced that the piece was worthy of the orchestra. The long work ends with a series of chords played by the upper strings and winds. François watched Chung as he directed each chord—single sonorities, one after the other, each more beautiful than the last, finishing with a brilliant fanfare. François was completely taken in with the beauty of the ending and, forgetting himself in the rapture of the moment, shouted, "Bravo!" from the bass section. The audience immediately jumped to their feet. Backstage François sought out Chung to congratulate him. Standing nearby, the director of the theater said to François, winking, "I saw everything you did."

And on another memorable occasion, knowing that François rarely looked at his music before the first rehearsal of a new opera, one of the bassists in the section approached him prior to the first rehearsal of *La traviata* and told him, "Listen to me—the next conductor is Zubin Mehta. He is highly regarded and a bassist, and there is a famous passage in this opera that he will ask to rehearse the basses and cellists—and maybe just the basses alone. You should look it over before the rehearsal."

François looked at the passage. He tried a traditional fingering; the frequent accidentals made the passage very awkward and almost unplayable. Studying the part more closely, François noticed that the passage was a two-bar sequence that ascended chromatically. By placing his thumb on the lowest pitch of each sequence on the fingerboard, he could use the same fingering across two strings and just move his hand position up the fingerboard chromatically. The passage now became easy. As expected, when the passage arrived in rehearsal, Mehta turned to the basses and celli and asked to hear the passage. François interrupted him by asking, "You mean like this?"

And he played the first several bars of the passage using his chromatic fingering. Mehta smiled and said, "That's fine. We'll move on."

Of their many years in the opera together, Thierry recalls François fondly as a personality. "He was an individual, a character. He would say things out loud in rehearsal, suddenly. He likes that people like him, and he was not timid. Coming from Beirut and then touring with Aznavour, he does not have the classical culture, which annoyed some people." Laughing good-naturedly, Thierry continues, "When you get to know him, it's okay—you know, he's a child at heart."

Martine was delighted that François had won the opera position. He was home more often and under significantly less stress. The rotating chair system in the string sections of the opera gave François flexibility in his calendar, including vacations, although he often found ways to use this new "free" time to continue working on pedagogical projects and new compositions. The family traveled with Cyril to the South of France near Avignon for a summer vacation in 1984. It was very hot, and they had rented an apartment without air conditioning or a swimming pool. The temperature was the same at midnight as in the middle of the day, and Martine was miserable. She couldn't sleep and was ready to return to Paris. But Cyril seemed to be fine, and François was perfectly comfortable. While observing crabs scuttle along the beach, François came up with the idea of a "crab" technique, a way to traverse the fingerboard while always leaving a finger in place, like a bookmark. He became completely obsessed with composing crab exercises, writing day and night. The result was twenty-eight pages of new exercises that made their way into the final draft of volume 3 of his *Nouvelle technique*, published later that year. Martine was impressed by how François could be so engrossed in his writing despite the heat. Fortunately for her there was a change in the weather for the better.

The Paris Opera was willing to grant François additional leaves of absence since his international presence enhanced their reputation, but he had to forfeit his salary during these periods. He was given release time from the opera to perform extended solo tours on three continents—Africa, Asia, and Australia. Earlier, in 1982, he had traveled to Taipei and Manila, playing recitals in major concert halls to audiences numbering in the thousands.[2] In 1985 François was

sent on international tours by Action Artistique, a French government agency, to promote French culture as an artistic ambassador.
The tour took François to West Africa and included stops in Nigeria,
Benin, Côte d'Ivoire, Sierra Leone, Mauritania, and Senegal, where
he composed *Reitba*. They then sent him on an Asian goodwill tour.
François requested permission to travel to Canberra, Australia, after
he performed in Taiwan in order to visit his brother Jean, whom
he had not seen in years. Jean was teaching classical piano at the
Canberra Conservatory of Music and arranged a recital for François.
It was a joyous reunion, both personally and musically.

After the Canberra performance, François was invited to perform at the Queensland Conservatory in Brisbane. It was here that
he met Ken Poggioli, who had just graduated from the conservatory
and was a substitute musician with the Queensland Symphony. Ken
was so impressed by François's recital and masterclass that the next
day he purchased a plane ticket to study with François in Paris. Ken
would continue to travel to Paris to study with François for decades,
and he organized several tours of Australia for François, including
a major tour through the Australian Student Travel Association in
1989. The tour crisscrossed the entire country and featured concerts
and masterclasses in most major cities, among them Perth, Adelaide,
Canberra, Sydney, and Brisbane. One of the highlights of the tour
was François's performance of Frank Proto's Fantasy for Double
Bass and Orchestra with the Queensland Symphony Orchestra in
Brisbane, broadcast live on ABC National Radio.[3]

During the summer of 1985, François was called to play a movie
score composed by Philippe Sarde, one of the most prolific and highly
regarded French film composers. The contractor for the film was a
violinist for whom François had worked quite often before he won
the opera position. François was happy to get the call, but he had
been traveling extensively and was on vacation, relaxing with his
family in the countryside. The contractor was insistent, stressing
that "the sessions are beginning tomorrow and Philippe says it must
be you."

The film, *The Temptation of Isabelle*, was scored for violin and double bass soloists accompanied by a string quintet (two violins, viola,

cello, and bass). François was asked to play the solo bass part. The additional string players were scheduled to arrive in Studio Davout from London the following day: the London Symphony concert-master, Michael Davis; the Gabrieli String Quartet; and the London Symphony principal bassist, Tom Martin. François had worked with the members of the string quartet in the past and knew them to be exceptional players. Ken Poggioli happened to be visiting François in the countryside at the time and confirmed that the contractor had asked François to bring two basses to the session because Tom Martin was flying in from London without an instrument. So Ken and François stopped at his apartment in Paris to pick up both the large Bernadel bass and the Quenoil bass on the way to the studio. Originally from Cincinnati, Tom was aware of François, but the recording session was the first time the two met.

As the musicians were warming up, Philippe Sarde was working feverishly with his copyist, rewriting and refining the parts. Once the copyist completed the parts for a scene, the scene was brought up on the soundstage screen, and the musicians were given a single run-through before recording to tape. The soundtrack was, in essence, a forty-minute double concerto. Musical gestures were freely passed between the violin and the bass and had to be phrased identically and then synchronized with the images on the screen. The solo bass part was virtuosic, twisting and turning across the entire range of the fingerboard.

Tom said of the session, "The music that Philippe wrote for that film was not easy. I was really impressed and thought: Oh god, this guy can really play!" François was able to sight-read such a demanding part due to his meticulous exploration of the bass and his develop-ment of an unorthodox approach to the instrument. "The music of Sarde requires the bassist to have mastered many techniques to be able to play this music freely," François explained. "He is not a bass-ist—he was writing for the film." While a solo violinist or cellist is often heard on movie soundtracks, *The Temptation of Isabelle* is the first major release to feature a bowed solo double bass prominently throughout.

After traveling extensively in 1985, François stayed closer to home for the next two years, performing a wide range of music, pri-marily in Europe. His appearances in France included a performance of the Proto Fantasy with the Orchestre Métropolitain in Rennes, a pair of solo recitals at the Festival du Pays in Becherel, and an improvisatory concert with Indian classical flautist Hariprasad Chaurasia at the Espace Cardin in the Champs-Élysées Garden in Paris. Farther from home, François appeared at Wigmore Hall in London for a third time in April 1986 to perform a solo recital, arranged by Jack Goldzweig. The performance received a glowing review from Stephen Pettitt in the *Financial Times*—his headline read, "Astonishing Virtuosity."[4] François also gave a solo recital at the French embassy in Prague and enjoyed a reunion with Paco Ibáñez at an outdoor festival on the Plaça del Rei in Barcelona. His only trip of significant distance was to the Domaine Forget International Music Festival in Quebec, Canada, in August 1987. The four-week festival hosted an annual double bass session, and he would return frequently for over thirty years, joining Paul Ellison and a handful of artist-teachers.

François's first five years in the Paris Opera had been very fruitful. He was no longer subject to the stresses associated with freelancing—waiting for the phone to ring, taking every gig at any hour, and then worrying about driving across the city to arrive on time. He now had only one place to be, a steady income, and, most importantly, time. Time to continue work on his *Nouvelle technique*, time to pursue creative performance opportunities of his choosing, time to compose, time to teach and propagate his innovative pedagogy, and time to spend with his family. He was relaxed, content, and happy.

All photos are courtesy of François Rabbath unless otherwise indicated.

Undated photos of Georges Séyes
and Bahija Ballyan, François
Rabbath's parents.

Circa 1945. The Rabbath Orchestra at the Coupole. The initials
H. F. on the music stands indicate Henri Fleming, the Coupole's
music director. Back row, from left to right: François Rabbath
(bass), unknown (guitar, trumpet), Victor Rabbath (drums),
Esteban Gutiérrez (accordion, guitar, trumpet), Pierre Rabbath
(piano), unknown (bass, trombone). Front row, from left to right:
Elie Rabbath (violin, guitar, bandoneon), unknown (violin),
unknown (accordion, trumpet), unknown (violin, sax), Henri
Rabbath (violin, clarinet).

Circa 1950. François Rabbath at the beach in Beirut.

Circa 1955. The Rabbath Trio at the Hotel Normandy. From left to right: Pierre Rabbath (piano), François Rabbath (bass), Victor Rabbath (drums).

Circa 1958. After-concert reception. From left to right: Victor
Rabbath, unknown woman (actor), Charles Aznavour, François
Rabbath, Daniel Bruni (driver), Pierre Rabbath, Gisèle Robert (Pierre's
wife, actor), unknown (Aznavour's manager at the time).

1960. François Rabbath and Mauricette Guigni sign their wedding
certificate in Versailles while Victor Rabbath looks on.

1960. At the Nice airport, returning to Paris from the Cannes Film Festival just after *Tirez sur le pianiste* was released. From left to right: François Rabbath, Madeleine Morgenstern (Truffaut's wife), François Truffaut, unknown (possibly Nicole Berger).

1962. *The Sound of a Bass* cover.

1962. Ambassador reception for *The Sound of a Bass* at the Pavillon Champs-Élysées. From left to right: Mauricette Rabbath, unknown ambassador, François Rabbath, Peter de Rougemont (director of CBS Records in France), Jean Rabbath.

1964. François Rabbath receiving the 1964 L'Académie Charles Cros Grand Prix du Disque Awards for composition and interpretation for *The Sound of a Bass*. From left to right: François Rabbath, unknown, Georges Auric (director of SACEM, president of L'Académie Charles Cros), unknown.

1964. In the Philips recording studio with Barbara, working on "Nantes." From left to right: François Rabbath, unknown sound engineer, Barbara.

1965. Cover photo for *No. 2*.

Circa mid-1960s. François Rabbath and Ornette Coleman at François's apartment on rue des Fossés Saint-Jacques.

1971. François Rabbath performing *La guerre et la paix* on October 24 in Vallauris, France, on the occasion of Pablo Picasso's ninetieth birthday in front of a crowd of over 5,000. (Note the graphic image of Picasso in the background.)

1971. Santiago, Chile, at a reception following François Rabbath and Paco Ibáñez's performance at the Estadio Nacional for the first anniversary celebration of President Allende's inauguration. From left to right: two unknown Chilean artists, Georges Moustaki (singer-composer who wrote for Edith Piaf), Mercedes Sosa (Argentinean singer), François Rabbath, unknown.

1972. François Rabbath's unaccompanied Bach performance at the Eighth Paris Summer Festival held at the Sainte-Chapelle.

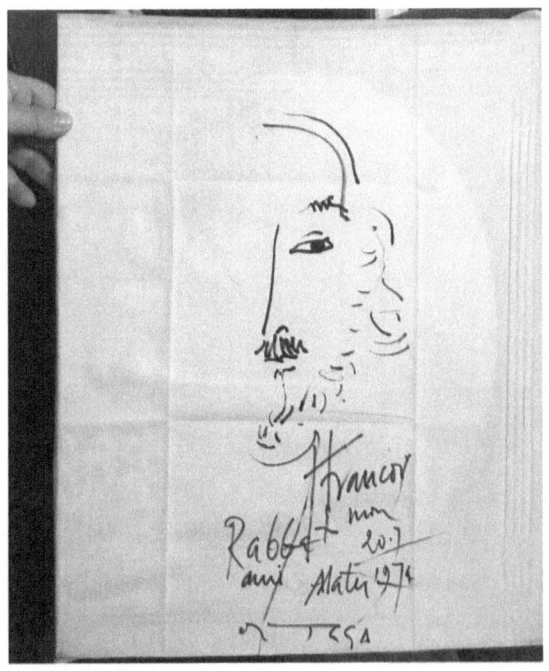

1974. François Rabbath's
portrait drawn by José
Ortega on a cloth napkin
while François was on tour
with Paco Ibáñez in Italy.

1975. First page of
the program for
François Rabbath's
Carnegie Hall debut.

1977. François Rabbath rehearsing with guitarist Jean-Pierre Jumez for their Wigmore Hall concert.

1977. François Rabbath performing on the saz with Toulaï in Avignon.

1978. ISB summer bass course. First row, from left to right: Dennis Trembly, Paul Ellison, François Rabbath, Barry Green, Teri Murai (conductor).

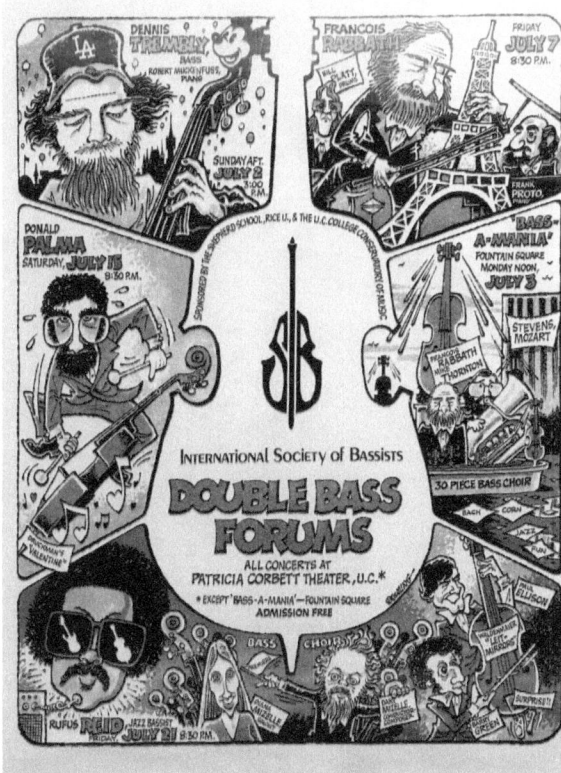

1978. ISB summer bass course poster. (Photo courtesy of Paul Ellison.)

1979. Stockholm, Sweden, bass masterclass faculty. From left to right: Frantisek Posta (Prague), Björn F. Holmvik (Oslo), François Rabbath, Klaus Stoll (Berlin), Tadeusz Pelczar (Warsaw).

Circa 1981. Members of the Paris Opera Orchestra. From left to right: François Rabbath, Louis Guilbert, Gérard Manley (Paris Opera Orchestra manager), Jean-Pierre Logerot (bassist).

1981. François Rabbath rehearsing Frank Proto's Concerto No. 2 with the composer, at François's apartment on rue de Clichy.

1981. François Rabbath rehearsing Frank Proto's Concerto No. 2 with the Cincinnati Symphony Orchestra.

Circa 1982. Rabbath summer workshop. From left to right: George Vance, François Rabbath, Barry Green, Paul Ellison, Hal Robinson.

Circa 1985. At home on rue de Clichy with his three sons. From left to right: Cyril Rabbath, François Rabbath, Sylvain Rabbath, Olivier Rabbath.

1985. François Rabbath on tour in Africa for the French government's Action Artistique program.

1996. In San Francisco performing with Ray Brown at the Golden Gate Bass Camp.

2001. With Martine Rabbath. (Photo courtesy of
Frank Proto.)

2004. With George Vance, at François's apartment
on rue de Clichy.

Circa 2005. With Moshe Naïm.

2007. *Art of the Left Hand* DVD motion-capture sessions. (Photo courtesy of Hans Sturm.)

2017. Sylvain and François Rabbath at the ISB convention in Ithaca, New York.

2017. Meeting Gary Karr at the ISB convention.

2017. With Paco Ibáñez performing at the Casino de Paris.

2018. With Michel Legrand in the recording studio for *Rabbath and Friends* (the last recording Legrand made, six months before his death).

15

Barry & Ray

> A single note in pianissimo will move
> one more than virtuosity.

François frequently speaks about the invaluable concept of finding inspiration to communicate with an audience, but finding an inspirational pathway is perhaps the greatest challenge a musician faces. From François's perspective, inspiration comes from the freedom resulting from technical mastery that then allows a musician to discover and express their deepest intentions and move an audience. Barry Green had heard François say many times that his goal in performing was to make an audience cry, but Barry didn't fully appreciate what François meant until he heard François perform *Reitba* for the first time at the 1988 Los Angeles ISB convention.

Following his studies in Paris, Paul Ellison had returned to teach at the ISB summer courses, and Barry noticed that he had undergone tremendous growth. Paul could now clearly teach and play François's technique, and Barry admits to becoming a little jealous. Although Barry had spent countless hours around François, he knew that he hadn't entirely embraced the *Nouvelle technique* for himself. François had been something of an enigma for Barry and many in the ISB community. On one hand, François performed concerts, to entertain and inspire, as well as to demonstrate a technique that no one thought possible on the instrument. On the other hand, François hadn't established a pedagogical connection with students of the bass. No format existed to show students *how* to do what François was doing—his technique was just too advanced for traditionally trained bassists to fully comprehend.

While Paul had been in pursuit of François's technique in Paris, Barry had begun his seminal work with Timothy Gallwey. The result was the publication of his best-selling book *The Inner Game of Music* (1986), devoted to overcoming the distracting critical internal voices that most musicians face.[1] By 1988 Barry's book had been in print for two years, and the first three volumes of François's *Nouvelle technique de la contrebasse* had become available in the United States. Once François's books appeared, the ISB summer course faculty could share François's pedagogy, but it was only Paul who had had the intensive personal experience with François.

After several years of devoting himself to *The Inner Game of Music*, Barry found that François's 1988 performance of *Reitba* gave rise to a longing to return to the bass and a determination to shift his focus—from seeking to play to impress an audience, to focusing on communicating emotion. Barry decided that he needed to start making trips to Paris to work with François. His wife was employed by American Airlines, so he could fly on standby at no cost, and François invited him to stay at his home. Barry began to request weeklong leaves from the Cinncinati Symphony Orchestra and would ultimately make some eight trips over the course of a year.

François welcomed Barry warmly and was prepared to introduce him to his techniques by beginning with the basics, as he had with Paul. But Barry had other ideas. In his mind, he had achieved the highest professional level. He had performed the Dvorak *Cello Concerto* at major symphony auditions and was the principal bassist of the CSO. He thought of himself as one of the rarefied elite, and truth be told, there were few of his colleagues who played at his level. But what Barry wanted to learn most from François, he wouldn't share—more than anything, he wanted to learn to play *Reitba*. François, however, had a singular path in mind. He needed to break Barry down and rebuild his technique from scratch, focusing on basics: adjusting his posture, developing flexibility in his bow arm, working on the mechanics of the pivot. For Barry, as an advanced professional, it was humbling and frustrating. "The most profound thing was more in the beginning, which is very personal and I've never shared. I was at his house and we were starting to work," Barry explained. "We worked a few days and everything he asked me to do, I couldn't do. And then I realized that everything had to be changed. And I went into his bathroom and I called my wife, Mary, and . . . and I cried on the phone. And, you know, everything wasn't working. I knew I had to let go of everything in order to get what it was that he was doing. So that moment, that was a realization. I was resistant, you know. I wanted all the things both ways. I wanted to keep my stroke, but was the bow straight? No. And everything I was working on I couldn't quite do yet. In light of those mounting frustrations and my inability to do what I thought I should be able to do, I realized that I felt just like Paul, who said he wanted take his bass and throw it out the window just like François had actually done when he was young."

Barry understood that he was not yet capable of doing what he professed to teach. He could read François's books and play the notes, but he still could not make the sound or express the style. One can learn from mastering the notes, but the magic of music exists between the notes, in the subtleties of interpretation made possible through precise technical mastery. "They'll hear you play once or twice, and then once they've heard it, they don't need to hear it again. But Rabbath, he can play the same thing over and over and over, and you still want to hear it because you're going to feel something. And you want that feeling—just like a popular song you love, it makes you feel a certain way."

Established professionals were becoming increasingly curious about the *Nouvelle technique*. Being active professionals, though, they were rarely in the position to devote the years necessary to fully adopt François's concepts. Adults have to overcome long-established ways of playing the instrument. Many, like Barry, were inspired by a performance. They desired to learn a particular technique or piece to add to their repertoire, not understanding the holistic demands of the *Nouvelle technique*, which requires countless hours of scales and arpeggios, physical alterations to posture, and adjustments to bow and left-hand techniques. It's a process that takes years for even the most talented and devoted professionals to master. François's method is not one that can be cherry-picked, and the process of rebuilding often engenders resistance.

Through the process of teaching Paul and Barry, François came to the conclusion that if his method was going reach younger students, he would need to teach bass teachers—people who would become expert in his pedagogy and then teach others, especially beginners. This created an interesting problem. François did not hold a teaching position, nor did he have the patience or the time required to teach the youngest students from the beginning. Both Barry and Paul were affiliated with major schools of music in the United States and could help to propagate François's pedagogy, but they were teaching collegiate students, not beginners. Barry took François's desire to heart and, beginning in the early 1990s, organized summer Rabbath workshops in Cincinnati for students of all ages. When Barry eventually retired from the CSO and moved back to his home state of California in 1995, he established the Northern California Bass Club and the Golden Gate Bass Camp. François would come to California and teach at the Golden Gate Bass Camp for four consecutive years.

In 1990 Action Artistique had created a domestic program to promote French artists. They created public events, pairing well-known musicians from France with ones from the United States. The pair would meet, exchange ideas, and perform for one another. François was chosen to represent the bass for France, and Ray Brown, the great jazz bassist, the United States. A few years later, Ray was planning a video series entitled *The Art of Playing the Bass*, and he had been so impressed with François that he invited him to participate. The series was filmed in Los Angeles in 1993 and featured Ray Brown, Milt Hinton, John Clayton, and François. All the bassists were in the studio at the same time, and François fell in love with Milt Hinton's marvelous slap technique.[2] François was very impressed and curious. He asked Milt to demonstrate, but François couldn't quite grasp what Milt was doing: "It seemed as if he had only one speed—fast."

François renewed his friendship with Ray Brown at Barry's Golden Gate Bass Camp in 1996. They were scheduled to share a concert—François would play the first half, Ray the second, and then they would perform a few pieces together to end the evening. Ray came to the stage at intermission to congratulate François, and as he was giving François a hug, he said to Barry, who was standing nearby,

"Don't bring this man anymore!" and laughed. François joined Ray to end the concert with a few jazz standards. During the performance of "I'm Beginning to See the Light," Ray took out his handkerchief and wiped François's brow, to the audience's amusement.

The following year in Paris, Joe Carver, one of François's American students, asked him if he would like to go to the New Morning jazz club to hear Ray Brown. Ray was one of Joe's heroes, and not quite believing that the two men knew each other, he purchased tickets at a front table. The trio came to the stage and began to play. Ray looked up and saw François sitting at the front table and smiled. At the end of the set, Ray sent the pianist and drummer from the stage. He proclaimed, "Ladies and gentlemen, I will now play for the greatest bass player in the world, who is here tonight!" and gestured to François in the front row. As the audience craned their necks to catch a glimpse of "the world's greatest bassist," Ray launched into a virtuosic twenty-minute pizzicato solo, darting across the entire range of the bass. When Ray was finished, François hurried back to the greenroom and exclaimed, "Man, you play pizzicato as if you are playing a bow, using your arm with all that incredible flexibility." Ray responded with a smile, "I never thought about that."

Recalling the evening, François said, "I was always a little embarrassed that Moshe had called me the greatest bassist in the world when he publicized Carnegie Hall, but it was one of the greatest honors of my life to hear Ray Brown use those words that night!"

16

Carmen & George

I take out the word "difficult."

Thanks to his affiliation with the ISB summer courses and the efforts of Paul Ellison and Barry Green, by the early 1990s François's pedagogical influence was spreading in the United States. He was delighted to see the increasing popularity of bass workshops and the inclusion of younger students. At the same time, he was also aware that the first two volumes of his *Nouvelle technique* had been written using the Nanny *Méthode* as a template. A question occurred to him: Knowing what he knew now, if he were to disregard all of his previous preconceptions, what would the earliest beginning method look like for young students wishing to pursue the *Nouvelle technique*? But François had little time to dwell on the matter. He was now in his sixties and had a full life—playing with the opera, keeping up with his sons, traveling to teach and perform, and occasionally finding a new composition on his doorstep.

Frank Proto began the process of composing *A Carmen Fantasy for Double Bass and Piano* in 1991 as a surprise sixtieth-birthday present for François. François had been looking for something new to feature at his recitals, and knowing François's style and temperament from their former collaborations, Frank thought he would enjoy a version of Bizet's opera *Carmen* reimagined with jazz harmonies and syncopated rhythms. He completed one movement, "Toreador Song," and sent it to François in time for his birthday. François loved the arrangement, and within two months Frank had completed the work.

The unaccompanied "Prelude" serves as a fantasy overture and is followed by the popular "Aragonaise," "Toreador Song," and "Bohemian Dance," all of which are featured in other *Carmen*-inspired suites (Pablo de Sarasate, Jenö Hubay, Franz Waxman, Vladimir Horowitz). Frank also incorporated "Micaela's Aria" from the third act, a lovely melody that is rarely heard outside the opera. François premiered the work in Cincinnati at the 1991 International Rabbath Institute in July, accompanied by Frank on piano. As it happened, he had received the music for the presto finale, "Bohemian Dance," only two days before the performance. François would continue his North American tour to Canada, where he received rave reviews,[1] and would return the following year to record *A Carmen Fantasy* with piano for Frank's Red Mark label, along with three of his own compositions: *Incantation pour Junon*, *Reitba*, and Concerto No. 3.

Due to the overwhelming success of the piece and the recording, François requested that Frank orchestrate the piece, and in November 1992 he premiered *A Carmen Fantasy for Double Bass and Orchestra* with the Toulouse Chamber Orchestra. In 1993 François toured *A Carmen Fantasy* in the United States, performing the work in solo recitals and with orchestras in Washington, DC, Chicago, Austin, Tucson, and Charleston,[2] where the orchestral version was recorded. The 1994 CD release of *Frank Proto: Works for Double Bass and Orchestra* features the 1993 recording of *A Carmen Fantasy* with the Charleston Symphony Orchestra in addition to the 1986 recordings of Fantasy for Double Bass and Orchestra accompanied by the Wolfgang! Chamber Orchestra and Proto's Concerto No. 2 accompanied by Les Symphonistes de Paris, both previously released on vinyl as *Rabbath Plays Proto*.

A Carmen Fantasy was embraced by bassists and entered the standard repertoire almost immediately. Neil Tarlton summed up the feelings of many bassists toward the work in his review for *Double Bassist*: "This is a really terrific addition to our repertoire since it's playable, showy and a vehicle for both emotion and technique. There's a lot to be said for the operatic fantasy, having saved many a performer from the awesome task of writing a hit. The tunes are tried and tested and understandably popular."[3]

François certainly shared Tarlton's sentiment, as he continued to perform *A Carmen Fantasy* frequently. In 1994 he would perform the piece another several times with orchestra, often pairing it with the Proto orchestration of *Reitba*. In March François appeared with the Tasmanian Symphony Orchestra in Hobart[4] and the Brisbane Conservatory Orchestra in Australia. In August he performed the work with the Orchestre Bilger in Avignon for the opening concert of Bass '94, organized by Barre Phillips. The concert took place in the Palais des Papes, one of the largest Gothic buildings in Europe. Following the performance, François-Xavier Bilger, the conductor, asked François if he would be willing to come to Apt, an hour east, to perform the piece the next evening, since their scheduled soloist had been injured. He also played *A Carmen Fantasy* with piano in the Taipei National Concert Hall that year, and again with a festival orchestra in Flaine, France, in 1995.

Just as Frank Proto had championed François as a composer, George Vance became a proponent of François's pedagogy. Recently retired from the military, George had relocated to Washington, DC, and was seeking work as a freelance bassist and teacher. The assistant director of the DC Youth Orchestra Program encouraged him to investigate the Suzuki method, a popular method for the instruments of the string quartet (violin, viola, and cello). George attended a Suzuki teacher training session, where he met Annette Costanzi, a cellist. She had recently returned from a Suzuki institute event in France, where several young bass players had shown up to her cello class. They were British bass students from the Yorke Mini-Bass Project, led by Rodney Slatford and Caroline Emery.[5] George realized that he first needed to find suitably sized instruments for young students with smaller hands. The next order of business was to consider a new way to introduce students to the notes on the fingerboard in a logical fashion.

Traditional bass methods begin students in the lowest register of the bass and make the assumption that as a student progresses into the higher positions, they are automatically able to understand and perform more complex music. There are two primary reasons why this is unhealthy from a pedagogical perspective. First, such a process instills in the student's mind that "high" equals "hard." And second, as students struggle with negotiating a new, unfamiliar position, they are required to perform more complex music at the same time. George's concept was that students should be introduced to a new position using simple melodies that would better allow them to become familiar with the position and discover how the new position affects other fundamental aspects of technique, such as bow placement and posture. He also believed that students would be better served by beginning to learn the bass from the middle of the instrument outward in two directions, rather than by starting in the lowest register and moving upward in one direction. The pitches are physically closer together and easier to reach in the middle register, and although there are physical adjustments that need to be addressed between positions, the lowest and highest registers are equidistant from the middle register, helping to alleviate a "fear of heights."

In the early 1990s George met Harold "Hal" Robinson, who by this time was the principal bassist of the National Symphony Orchestra. Hal had studied with Paul Ellison and attended an ISB summer bass course where he met François and learned about the *Nouvelle technique*. He felt that François's fingerboard concept was the missing piece of the puzzle. George recalls, "I found out about François Rabbath from Harold Robinson. And that was the key to how to continue from there. . . . François had already laid the fingerboard out along this line. . . . It turned out I didn't need to teach more places than the nodal points."[6]

George traveled to Japan to study with Shinichi Suzuki and made a striking observation: Suzuki's students were making great pedagogical strides by playing along with recordings. George recalled, "I realized that at his school, people were playing along with recordings constantly—and these were adults. They weren't children he was teaching—they were people who planned to go home to whatever countries and be teachers. . . . So, when I tell people, when I tell my students to play along with the recording, what I'm doing is giving them an insight into the musical imagination of one of the greatest string players of our time, because the reference recording for my books is made by Rabbath. . . . He was willing to play "Twinkle," and he played it beautifully."

François said of the Vance recording sessions, "Yes, George invited me to play his pieces. It was the people at Carl Fischer who produced the sessions to put a CD with his method. When I begin to play, I begin to play musically. George was concerned that my performance was not precisely in tempo. But the producer disagreed: 'François is just playing. We are listening to the music. We are not hearing an étude.' Normally, it was in pitch, everything, but my interpretation—I was feeling each piece, and I was expressing it. You play music. It's the same notes, but you begin to breathe."

While he was in the process of completing his method, George was invited to teach at Barry Green's early Rabbath workshops in Cincinnati alongside François, Hal, and Paul. He later joined Barry in California at the Golden Gate Bass Camp. George wanted to establish a summer course with François in Washington, DC, and created a weeklong L'Institut International Workshop that was held for thirteen consecutive years, from 1996 to 2008. It would be François's longest continuous teaching collaboration. George's *Progressive Repertoire* series, combining the Suzuki concept of graded repertoire with François's innovative technique, has become the most popular and influential beginning bass method in the United States.[7]

———

Prior to joining the Paris Opera Orchestra, François had spent much of his career accompanying popular singers—Aznavour, Brassens, Dalida, Barbara, Toulaï—tailoring arrangements to their voices and producing carefully crafted, award-winning recordings. He was a sensitive accompanist and learned from each singer how to best accompany them. But in the opera, François learned how to phrase lyrically from the finest classically trained singers: "I learned that we must imitate the voice with our bow. I feel that I must at least find a way to use the bow to make a continuous sound. Singers breathe when they need to take a breath. Often a change of bow can break a phrase. I didn't know that the opera could give me this beautiful knowledge. I say it works like another world, but I didn't know that I can learn how to imitate the voice, the human voice, with my bow. I learned that in the opera, and how they interpret." François also began to understand that instrumentalists are often afraid of using silence. But not the operatic singer. Taking their time to breathe, operatic singers use their breath in a meaningful way. A breath can cause a listener to wait for the appearance of a note, and then the singer places that note in the perfect moment for an optimal emotional effect.

François speaks with passion about the opera's influence on his interpretations: "When I play, the public cries. I know how to interpret musically each note because of the opera. Before the opera, a note was a note. I could play very virtuosically, but not like that. It was a happiness to play in the opera. At times I was distracted by the beauty of a singer's performance and sometimes forgot to play. My stand partner would gesture for me to play, but the conductor would look at me. He would shake his head quietly as if to say, 'Don't disturb him.' I was living each note. I would cheer my colleagues when they played a particularly beautiful solo. I didn't feel that I was not free at the opera—I had such a great time in the orchestra, I felt free. It was fifteen years of happiness, to accompany the world's greatest singers—Domingo, Pavarotti—and play for the world's greatest conductors: Chung for five years, Georges Prêtre, Zubin Mehta, Ozawa, and Barenboim."

Quietly, and without any fanfare, François happily retired from the Paris Opera Orchestra in 1995. He had won his position in 1980 at the age of fifty, when the retirement age for the opera was sixty. However, to receive the minimum pension, musicians had to play for fifteen years. The orchestra allowed him to stay another five years so that he could retire with benefits. The timing was fortuitous, since sixty-five was also the national mandatory retirement age. The Paris Opera had been a very positive move for François. He had a steady income for the rest of his life, and the worries of freelancing were behind him forever. The opera had given him permission to take leaves of absence and pursue international opportunities, allowing François to cultivate many deep, long-lasting relationships with musicians and educators who loved and respected him, and build an international network of projects and communities that continued to invite him back, many for decades.

17

Family Life & Picasso's Picassos

> To be a virtuoso, you must practice like virtuoso.

In Martine's eyes, François came from a different planet. She was fascinated by the stories of his childhood and how he had always followed his own path. At the same time, theirs was not always an easy relationship. Coming from the Middle East, François had been raised in a paternalistic culture—the man doesn't belong in the kitchen, for example. But Martine was clear from the outset: she had a career and creative interests and was not at all interested in being a housewife. Fortunately, François wanted more than anything to have a warm, loving, and strong family and would do whatever he had to do to keep his new family together.

By 1995, François and Martine's sons, Cyril and Sylvain, were teenagers. Martine had been working full-time, but changed jobs so that she only worked four days a week in order to have more time for herself and to keep an eye on the boys. Her new job as artistic director for *Marie Claire* magazine required fewer days in the office, but it had strict publication deadlines. This meant that François had to step into the role of parental supervisor more often—a role that he played in a very different manner than Martine.

Early in their relationship, Martine and François were traveling on their way home to Paris from a bass workshop and stopped in Belgium to visit François's brother Victor. Victor's eight-year-old was at home with a runny nose, and Martine was shocked to learn that they had left him at home in front of the television for several days in a row. She expressed to François how awful she thought the situation was and that when they had children, she would insist that they go to school. François's noncommittal response was prescient.

Cyril was good about attending school, but Sylvain was more problematic. From time to time he would complain that he didn't feel well, so Martine would check his temperature, which would be fine, and then tell him to get up and go to school. François would take him to school and Martine would go to work. While Martine was at work, François would return to school and bring Sylvain back home with him. If Martine happened to come home unannounced during the day, she would occasionally return to find both Cyril and Sylvain. François would say, "Ça va. Look at me. I succeed very well and didn't go to school. They will be fine." But this was a significant issue for Martine. She knew that François's life experience had been exceptional—but living in contemporary Paris, you couldn't skip school regularly and expect to be successful. The truth was that François just enjoyed being at home during the day with his sons. He missed them when he had to work in the evenings and did not want to miss out on their lives, as he had with Olivier. Martine increasingly felt her role was to provide balance in the boys' lives as a disciplinarian. She was the one who attended school meetings and checked on the boys' homework, while François was the one who cuddled with them on the couch, watching a movie.

Occasionally one of the boys would get into trouble at school. It was never major, but Martine was the one who was called to come to the office and discuss what had happened. Working under the pressure of ongoing deadlines, she became frustrated by this pattern of behavior. She finally had enough, and when the next call came— about Sylvain—she told François it was his turn to speak with the director. So François went to the school office with Sylvain and, in his inimitable manner, charmed everyone. François shared fascinating stories about his education—something revealing for both the director and Sylvain. Because he had left school at such an early age and had to go to work, François had a perspective that was dramatically different from that of the typical parent. Even though he did not have an extensive formal education, François had developed a focused and determined work ethic that led to his success, and he could share something special and unique from his experience. Martine was impressed: "He often surprises me how he can manage in these situations. He never tries to take advantage by using his past—he is simply honest in who he is."

After François retired from the opera, Martine wanted to take the family to Aleppo, to show his sons where he grew up. But François didn't want to go. He was at home in Paris and felt uncomfortable with the idea of returning to Syria.

Martine was insistent: "If you don't come, I will buy the tickets and take the boys myself. They need to see your home."

François eventually agreed, but he hadn't been to Aleppo since he was a child. So much had changed. A busy shopping district had engulfed his beloved family home, Beit el-Samane. Signs and billboards had been affixed to the outer walls, windows on the upper floors were thick with grime, and some were even broken. The house had been divided, with a shop on the ground floor and apartments above.

François entered the shop and introduced himself.

The owner asked, "But you are Rabbath, from the family Rabbath?"

François replied, "Yes," fully aware that the man likely knew the Rabbath name because of his father and Bally Bank.

The owner then asked, "But where do you live now?"

"In France."

"Why do you live there? Come back, come back to your country."

But Syria wasn't François's country. In truth, he had no national ties, felt no allegiance to borders. The house had been a wonderful place to grow up in when he was a young boy, but it was only a place—a meaningless box filled with pleasant memories. What had made Beit el-Samane special was his family.

Seeking new challenges, François asked his longtime friend and colleague Michel Legrand to write a concerto for him, something beautiful. "After all, he was the composer of 'The Windmills of Your Mind' and 'What Are You Doing the Rest of Your Life?,'" François enthused. "But what he wrote was something else again." Michel completed the score to *Contrebande pour contrebasse*, mounted his motorcycle in the east of France, and drove halfway across the country to Paris, the score tucked in his saddlebags. The spry, bespectacled composer strode into François's salon, placed the full orchestral score on the piano, and began to play all the parts at once. Michel loved the rich, sonorous low register of the bass, but knowing what François was capable of, he had created a terrifically virtuosic piece. Many of the melodically complex solo passages traversed three octaves at a brilliant clip. François found it so challenging that while they were reading the piece for the first time, he asked if it wasn't better suited for the violin. Michel's response was terse: "I wrote this for Rabbath! Just play." Eager to get on the road before the Parisian rush hour, Michel rushed down to his motorcycle to discover he had been given a parking ticket. He handed the ticket to François and, with a smile, told him it was his fee for the commission.

François performed *Contrebande pour contrebasse* twice. The world premiere performance with the Quebec Symphony Orchestra took place in December 1996 on a marathon program that also featured *A Carmen Fantasy* and *Reitba*. In January 1997, the Danish Bass Club arranged a masterclass and recital for François in Copenhagen. The first half of the recital featured his solo works accompanied by the conductor and pianist Frans Rasmussen, and after intermission, he performed Legrand's concerto accompanied by the Light Orchestra of the Danish Broadcasting Corporation. François would perform two encores, the second of which was a duo with the superb Danish jazz bassist Niels-Henning Ørsted Pedersen, who had developed his own unique virtuosic techniques. The concert was broadcast on Danish Radio Program 2.

Legrand's work is a paradoxical masterpiece: lyrical, yet harmonically complex; accessible, yet requiring an Olympian technique. The unreleased Danish Broadcasting Corporation recording of *Contrebande pour contrebasse* is a jaw-dropping demonstration of François's virtuosity. It is difficult to imagine a more technically and musically demanding work, requiring from the bassist a high level of facility and precision and, at the same time, incredibly nuanced melodic shaping. François has called it the most exacting work he has ever learned. With Michel's death in 2019, the future of the work remains in limbo. Perhaps one day François's performance and Legrand's score to *Contrebande pour contrebasse* will be released.

———

Meanwhile, in the United States, Frank Proto was serving on the ISB's board of directors. Since the mid-1980s, the organization had grown exponentially and had held a convention every two years. The ISB board was seeking innovative ways to make each convention unique and exciting and was considering commissioning a new major piece for double bass and orchestra for the 1997 convention. Frank volunteered to write a new work for François—it would be their fourth collaboration, and he was as excited at the thought of working with François again as he was the very first time they met. Frank was vacillating between writing a purely abstract piece or a programmatic work when he came across David Douglas Duncan's book *Picasso's Picassos*.[1] The book contains Duncan's photographs of 102 paintings from Picasso's private collection, spanning his entire career, from age fifteen to eighty. Frank chose four of Picasso's paintings and treated each a little differently: "As a composer you write essentially two kinds of music, program music or abstract music. Abstract is the classic blank page, and programmatic is a photograph or story. I was trying to interpret the paintings I chose. I would like the concerto to work as an abstract piece, and to this end I've followed—though sometimes loosely—some rather conventional forms. Where the programmatic aspects are concerned, I attempted in some cases to make a literal translation of what I saw and in others to make an interpretation of what I imagined might exist beneath the surface. Where I did one or the other, I leave up to the imagination of the listener."

For several years Frank had been composing works inspired by political events. He discovered that Picasso had similar ideas. During an interview, Picasso famously shared a note he had written to Simone Téry that ended, "No, painting is not made to decorate apartments. It's an offensive and defensive weapon against the enemy."[2] Of the four paintings Frank chose to use as his inspiration for *Four Scenes after Picasso*, three were political works.

The first, *Cat Catching a Bird*, was painted in 1939 after Picasso's mother had died. The Spanish general Francisco Franco had overtaken the cities of Madrid and Barcelona, and was on his way to declaring himself dictator of Spain. The painting is often interpreted as Franco, a powerful, violent man, holding the fragile ordinary citizenry in his jaws.

The Weeping Woman portrays the weeping Virgin Mary, a traditional subject of Catholic artists. Picasso asks viewers to imagine themselves as the woman—in essence, to become a weeping mother, crying over the death of her son. The work was, at least in part, his reaction to seeing photographs showing the aftermath of the German Luftwaffe's 1937 bombing of civilians in the small Basque town of Guernica.

Powerful and disturbing, *The Charnel House* is stark, painted in black, white, and shades of gray. The term *charnel house* was used to describe places where violent deaths had occurred. Completed in 1945, likely around the time Paris was liberated, the work was created after Picasso learned about the charnel houses of the Holocaust. The subject appears to be a family in their kitchen, recently killed and in contorted positions, the table set above them drawn in simple lines. Frank's score reflects the subject matter—often dissonant and violent.

The sole painting that is not political, *First Steps*, was painted in 1943 and captures the precious moment as a little girl takes her first steps, gently guided by her mother. Picasso's models were his housekeeper and her young daughter.

Four Scenes after Picasso was premiered at the 1997 ISB convention on the campus of Rice University in Houston, Texas. Frank was able to get permission to project slides of Picasso's paintings on a large screen above the orchestra, as François had done in his Carnegie Hall debut. Paul Ellison had organized an orchestra composed of Rice faculty and advanced students, and Frank recalls that the conductor, Larry Ratcliff, had done a brilliant job learning the score. The recording of the piece took place the day before the premiere, during the dress rehearsals. After the premiere performance, François would never play the work again, with the exception of *The Weeping Woman*. Frank opined, "Because it's beautiful. *Weeping Woman* is beautiful, and François wants to play beauty." The recording of *Four Scenes after Picasso* was released on Frank's Red Mark label as a CD-Plus in 2001 and includes several lengthy interviews about the collaboration, photos of the paintings, and links to explore Picasso's life and works. The recording project received rave reviews from the international music press.[3]

The beginning of the new millennium found François traveling to the far reaches of the globe. In June 2000, Peter McLachlan hosted a masterclass and recital for François in Adelaide, Australia.[4] Peter had first heard François play and teach during his 1989 Australian tour and was inspired to organize bass workshops. He founded Bassworks, a project catering to young student bassists, and organized three annual events for François between 2000 and 2003. In September 2000, Myung-Whun Chung, the former music director of the Paris Opera, invited François to perform *A Carmen Fantasy* with the Tokyo Philharmonic Orchestra. It was the most luxurious performance experience of François's life. He flew first class to Japan, stayed in a five-star hotel, and was paid extraordinarily well. Had he been a virtuoso violinist, this likely would have been a regular occurrence.

Martine acknowledges that unlike many musicians, François normally manages his feelings before a concert, but he often gets anxious before he travels. She believes his travel anxiety is likely related to the year he spent separated from his family while attending the Antoura School in Lebanon when he was very young. She noticed that he would start to feel sick as early as three weeks before he had to leave, but as time went on and he traveled more often, the sickness might appear only a week before. Once he got onto the plane and arrived at his destination, the sickness seemed to magically disappear. Sometimes he would have a slight fever, but at other times his sickness could be more serious. He once had frequent bouts of heart palpitations, and Martine took him to see a cardiologist. The doctor found nothing physically wrong, except evidence of panic attacks. He confided to Martine that his wife was a musician and experienced many of the same symptoms prior to a performance.

François had turned seventy in March 2001. At this stage of his career he was continuing to explore and develop new concepts, aspiring to even greater virtuosic and interpretive freedoms. His reputation, established through a long history of creative contributions, inspired composers to write more-adventurous pieces for the bass. Michel's *Contrebande pour contrebasse* and Frank's *Four Scenes after Picasso* were complex and challenging—technically, physically, and musically—and while both pieces were capable of helping to set a new standard for solo bass repertoire, they have remained obscure. In contrast to these more recent works, Proto's *A Carmen Fantasy* had become very popular. Its appeal was not entirely surprising since the work was technically accessible and the themes from Bizet's opera are familiar and tuneful. A symphonic concert featuring a solo bassist has always been a rarity, and from an orchestra's perspective, it is more tempting to program a piece that has familiar themes when featuring an unfamiliar instrument. It would take a special piece to merge the highest levels of François's virtuosic technique and artistry with a compelling and engaging musical story that would prove attractive to orchestras.

18

Bach

There is no difference between
scales and Bach.

I t was a perfect circle.

François says that, without a doubt, it was his former student and close friend GP Cremonini who came up with the idea. GP insists it was Minas Lourian, president of the Union of Armenians in Italy, who made the suggestion to François. And of course Minas recalls quite clearly it was François himself who, upon playing for a short time in the Biblioteca Zenobiana of the Palazzo Zenobio, expressed his joy at the acoustics of the gorgeous seventeenth-century room and suggested he would love for Minas to consider hosting an ambitious recording project—the project of a lifetime. Certainly, all three played their part, for without any one of them, the project would never have taken place. François had played movements from the Bach Cello Suites for years, but to be presented the opportunity to record all six suites remained a wishful, illusory dream.

The Palazzo Zenobio was built on the remains of a fourteenth-century building in central Venice. The large rooms on the ground floor are decorated with exquisite works of art embraced by gilt frames.[1] Tall doors open out onto a large, central, French-style formal garden. Situated at the far end of the garden are two smaller structures. To the right is a small apartment building used as living quarters for the Zenobio staff. It was on the top floor of this building that François stayed during his visits to Venice. Next to the apartments, and symmetrically centered across the gardens from the palazzo, is the Neoclassical Biblioteca Zenobiana, now home to the Centro Studi e Documentazione della Cultura Armena in Italy, a center for Armenian research. It was on the ground floor of the pavilion where François's Bach recording would take place. The room might be best described as a grand foyer, whose high, cornerless arched ceiling gives the space its unique acoustic properties.

The story of how François came to make the Bach recording in these historic surroundings can be traced to Giovanni Pietro Cremonini, known as GP. Born in Venice, GP was a talented bassist who had moved from Venice to Paris to further his career. He discovered François in 1994 through his friend Roberto Torno, an Argentinean bassist who had shown him a copy of one of François's method books. Fascinated by François's photograph, GP recalls thinking, "I have to meet this bearded Santa Claus of the bass." GP looked up François's number in the phone book and called. François answered and after the briefest of conversations invited GP to come to his house.

GP's ebullient personality, tremendous work ethic, and unique presence—his cutting-edge Italian style, waist-long curly hair, and distinctively chiseled face framed by large red glasses—made him irresistible to numerous popular French singers, who were concerned as much with image as music. During the early 1990s GP toured frequently, returning to Paris when he could. By mid-1996 the constant touring had begun to take a toll. There was a strong cocaine culture among the musicians he was working with, and once GP decided that he needed to take a break from the drug, he found that they were no longer interested in hiring him. He decided to remain in Paris and devote himself to the study of François's *Nouvelle technique*. Eventually he had the idea of organizing a Rabbath workshop and recital in Venice.

Minas always had a passion for unique music. In addition to his work with the Armenian center, he had partnered with various music societies in the Veneto region, producing concerts and festivals of both new and ancient music. Aware that these concerts might be the only occasion when many of these pieces would be performed in a lifetime, Minas felt compelled to document the music. He started a small recording company and hired Ermanno Velludo, an uncompromisingly brilliant sound engineer who brought with him several classic high-end microphones and a state-of-the-art 1969 Telefunken mixing board that he referred to as his "Stradivarius."

GP met Minas through a mutual friend and asked if Minas might be interested in hosting a Rabbath masterclass at the Palazzo Zenobio.[2] Minas readily admits that the double bass was not of interest to him, but he was intrigued by François's story. The parallels between the lives of the two men were uncanny. Both were of Armenian descent (François's mother, Bahija, was Armenian), both were born in Aleppo, both grew up in Lebanon, both studied music, and both settled in Europe. Minas was swayed by GP's enthusiasm, and the two organized a masterclass with François in April 1999. The Venetian masterclass was a great success. The event attracted bassists from across Europe and the United States, and François performed a recital in one of the palazzo's great rooms, accompanied by his son Sylvain, for a standing-room-only crowd.[3]

After François's recital, Minas shared that he had a small studio in the Biblioteca Zenobiana with exceptional acoustics and a brilliant recording engineer. He asked if perhaps François might be interested in a tour. François wasn't at first, but at a break during the next day's masterclasses, he asked to see the studio. Once he entered the room, heard the acoustics, and saw how Ermanno had arranged his microphones in a classic X/Y configuration, he asked GP to fetch his bass in order to hear how his instrument sounded in the space. François played a few pieces—one or two original works, and a movement of Bach. Within moments of beginning to play, he became enraptured with the sound. François had spent decades of his career recording in acoustically dead studios and then having artificial reverb added in post-production. The natural reverberation of the room enabled François to hear his sound in a warmly reverberant space as he played. He felt that playing in this acoustical environment was like a dream come true. He entered the control room, where he met Ermanno and heard the playback. François invited GP and Minas to lunch.

It was over lunch that Minas asserts that François leaned over and said, "Minas, I would like to propose to do together the 'will' of my musical career. I want to record a very ambitious project in this place, something I have dreamed of doing for a very long time, and I think this is the right place. But it is a big project. Do you agree to do this together?"

When Minas learned the details of what François was proposing—to record all six Bach Cello Suites on the double bass in the same tessitura as the cello[4]—it seemed to him to be such an epic and heroic undertaking that he couldn't say no. Both GP and Minas confessed that neither one of them was entirely prepared for the challenges they were about to face.

It was January 2000 before their schedules would align and the recording could commence. In the intervening period, Minas and Ermanno had been deeply involved in recording chants for the Armenian music archive, and François had been touring the United States and Canada, giving masterclasses and performing. Given these distractions, it is understandable that François was not entirely prepared for what was to come either. Nevertheless, it came as a major surprise to GP, who had made all the arrangements for travel, lodging, and food, when François arrived in the studio with his bass and said, "You must tell me what to do."

GP had no experience as an artistic director and producer and was feeling overwhelmed. But in the end, François was his teacher, his mentor, his friend, and so he accepted the task. What choice did he have? As the recording process began to unfold, he quickly realized that he had to become very organized and honestly critical, a task he did not relish. It was a trial by fire—to carefully keep track of each take, listen back every evening, and then make recommendations for what needed to be recorded in the following sessions.

There were additional complications. Ermanno, the recording engineer, was chronically ill. He had undergone two kidney transplants and, during an earlier rehabilitation process, had received a transfusion of bacteria-infected blood. He required dialysis every other day and was wheelchair bound. Travel in and out of the heart of Venice by wheelchair is enormously challenging. The cheapest and most efficient way to move across the city is by the vaporetto water bus system. Unfortunately, the Palazzo Zenobio is on a smaller canal, some distance from the nearest vaporetto stop. The "streets" in the center of Venice are narrow walkways, and Ermanno's route required crossing several small bridges, all of which had steps.

Every other day, recording ceased, and GP and Minas would assist Ermanno with his travels.

Ermanno had been working with Minas at the palazzo for some time, so he was familiar with the travel routine. But he was not a patient man by nature, and the trip made him irritable. Furthermore, he had very strong feelings about how the sonic environment of the Biblioteca Zenobiana should be captured. Because the building is a seventeenth-century historic landmark, the room can never be remodeled as a formal recording studio. And while the walls are quite thick, the windows are only single panes of glass. Consequently, sound interruptions would occur—from the ringing of neighboring church bells to the chirping of swallows nesting in the rafters of the building. The temperature and humidity also varied from day to day, affecting the sound and responsiveness of the bass. Ermanno, always seeking the ideal sound, would alter the position of the microphones from session to session to adapt to the changing acoustics, greatly complicating how the recording could be edited. It was virtually impossible to combine different movements from the same suite recorded with alternate microphone configurations.

And then there was François. GP adored and revered him. And he was capable of performing effortless miracles on the bass—superhuman, gymnastic feats. GP wanted the recording to be everything they both aspired for it to be, François's "will" on the bass. A heroic accomplishment. François had played many of the movements from the suites over his career. He had performed movements from the First Suite in the Palais des Sports as early as 1971 and recorded the entire First Suite along with movements from the Third, Fifth, and Sixth Suites a decade later for Frank Proto's Red Mark label.[5] He had also created complete editions of the First and Second Suites for Liben Publishing. But despite all his experience with Bach, there were movements François had never seriously studied or performed. To record the entire set of suites would require tremendous focus and dedication.

François candidly admits that he was never one to practice studiously. He often says, "I play a piece until I find a measure or two that speaks to me. I work to shape this gesture and then it tells me how the rest must be played." He acknowledges that he is an intuitive player, at heart an improviser, seeking inspiration. He feels that what inspires him will, in turn, inspire his performance and resonate with an audience. And this is his singular goal, to reach his audience. Playing instinctively and not being entirely prepared created tension in the studio. GP wanted to capture more than the correct notes and rhythms. He wanted a transcendent interpretation—they both did. Minas said of the process, "He was not always prepared. I think perhaps he is a little lazy." François understood that he was undertaking an ambitious project, and yet he was relying on his long history with Bach, and his instincts, to carry him through.

To capture all thirty-six movements, they recorded for a total of twenty-one days in three separate weeklong recording sessions: in January and November 2000 and in April 2001. During the early sessions, GP kept a detailed log of takes—first as handwritten notes and later on the computer, where he found he could more easily organize his plans. He would take notes as François played and then review and annotate them when listening back to the day's takes in preparation for the following session.

The January sessions covered familiar movements and went fairly smoothly. They had captured most of the First, Third, and Fourth Suites and two movements of the Fifth Suite that François had performed before, the Sarabande and Gigue. GP's notes indicate that, aside from an occasional false start, by and large François was performing either complete movements or half a movement in a single take. The pace of the recording was brisk, a day devoted to each of the three suites and a couple of days devoted to recording alternate takes for security. This is not to say that there weren't challenges. GP recalls the recording of the Sarabande from the Fifth Suite: "It was pure magic—a glorious take. But Ermanno cut the recording before the resonance of the last note was complete. In another take, he failed to start recording in time to catch the first note and didn't stop the take."

The November sessions focused on the preludes. They are the longest movements of the suites and, unlike the subsequent dance movements, have a free, improvisatory character. GP had decided to focus on the prelude movements of all six suites, and the first day's sessions resulted in successful takes of the preludes from the Third and Fourth Suites, familiar material. GP recalls the recording of the Prelude to the Fourth Suite: "The first take was a series of hesitations—start, stop, start. And then, the second take was complete with the exception of a single chord." The logs show numerous takes of the preludes from the Fifth and Sixth Suites. And it was at about this time that GP began to realize that being artistic director meant that he would have to ask François to review and practice specific movements during their days off when Ermanno went for dialysis. François questioned the necessity of having to rerecord something he felt was acceptable, and GP had to push François to get him to listen carefully to the takes in question.

By the end of the November sessions, François had completed entire versions of the First, Third, and Fourth Suites, the preludes from the Second and Sixth Suites, and four movements from the Fifth Suite. He lacked all five dance movements from the Second and Sixth Suites and another pair from the Fifth. With the exception of the dance movements from the Second Suite, the remaining movements were the least familiar to François. The project had begun to feel like a struggle to GP. He resented François's resistance to his efforts and was looking ahead to the final recording session with a sense of trepidation.

The final sessions were scheduled for April 2001. By this time GP had been back touring with a handful of popular French singers and was feeling more confident. It appeared that François, too, was better prepared. He arrived in good spirits, and everyone was eager to complete the project. But after the first day of recording, it became apparent that François was *not* entirely prepared. GP found himself again asking François to listen back to the day's session and requesting that he spend time practicing. GP would leave the apartment to assist Ermanno on his trip to undergo dialysis and return to find evidence that François had, in fact, been practicing—a good sign. There were still some acrimonious moments, however. The Courante of the Fifth Suite was particularly troublesome. GP contends, "It was musically completely empty—he had the notes, but was making no music." What is fascinating about GP's tracking notes from these sessions is that they show just how quickly François could bring himself to perform some of the most challenging repertoire with strong interpretations. For any given movement that caused trouble on one day, the following session shows three or four interruptions and then complete takes. It was almost as if François had learned the movement in a single day.

After the recording sessions were completed, François requested a contract from Minas to make sure all the correct legal releases were in place. GP and Minas created a contract in Italian and GP translated it carefully into French. François reviewed the contract and suggested that it would be a good idea if GP were named in the contract as the artistic director. GP and Minas made the adjustments to the contract, and the three met again in Venice. As they came together to sign the contract, GP again read the contract in French to make sure that everything was clear, and François changed his mind and decided that GP did not need to be named in the document. This made GP furious, not because he would no longer be named in the contract, but rather because he and Minas had spent hours reviewing, editing, and translating the contract and Minas had been so generous in allowing them to record in his studio space and live in the apartments of the Zenobio at a nominal cost—all on top of the stress related to the recording process. At this point, GP desperately needed a break.

But now that the recording process was completed, the monumental task of choosing the takes and making the edits fell to GP, as artistic director. The upside was that he could do this alone and no longer had to confront François. On the other hand, now all the subtle nuances needed to be tended to: checking that the tempi between the first and second halves of each movement aligned, listening for a matched bass tone between takes from different sessions, making sure there were no extraneous sounds from birds or bells. It was a giant puzzle. Once GP completed editing a movement, he sent the file to François for approval. If François approved of the track, then he would work on refining the sound with his son Sylvain. GP had the right of final approval, yes or no, but for technical reasons only, such as balances and the sonic quality between movements.

The cellist Hubert Varron had been one of François's earliest inspirations to play all six Bach Cello Suites. Hubert was a super soloist in the Paris Opera Orchestra. François was playing a portion of the Prelude from Bach's First Suite before a rehearsal and stopped to ask Hubert which Bach edition he preferred.[6] Hubert told him and then added, "A bassist playing Bach at pitch successfully would be like jumping from the sixth floor and landing on your feet without hurting yourself."[7]

He then challenged François: "If you succeed to play an entire suite, I will give you my cello—if you do not, you must give me your gold chains."

In 1982, François came back from Cincinnati with the LP recording he had made for Frank Proto's Red Mark label.

Hubert responded dryly, "What about the rest?"

Sadly, Varron died only a month before François's recording of all six suites was released in 2012 by Solstice, an independent classical French label.

From conception to release, *Bach: Suites pour violoncelle seul à la contrebasse* had taken a dozen years to complete. Considering the time span, the recording process itself was relatively brief, a total of twenty-one days spread out over sixteen months. Due to the complex nature of the recording, the editing process was lengthy and sporadic—files were sent back and forth between GP, Sylvain, and François over a five-year period. And then it took several years to find a record label willing to release a three-CD set of the Bach Cello Suites performed on the bass. In the end François was elated with the results—all six Bach suites, with the first five in the same register as the cello. His dream had finally come true!

The Solstice record label promoted the recording, leading to interviews on Radio France and extensive European airplay. François and Sylvain performed a celebratory concert on November 26, 2012, on the main stage of the Théâtre de l'Athénée Louis-Jouvert to a sold-out house. The program included movements from the Bach First and Fifth Suites, as well as original works by François; as had become his custom, he chose to end the evening with Cole Porter's "Night and Day." The first printing of the CD box set sold out within two years, a very short time for such a unique classical recording.

19

Paganini & Jazz

Don't try—do it!

Every time they embarked on a new collaboration, Frank Proto would call François and laughingly say, "I'm going to write you something that you can't play." In 2001, Frank and François were discussing their fifth major project for double bass and orchestra, and Frank suggested a set of Paganini variations. He loved the flexibility that the simple theme offered and had recently completed two successful versions, one for trumpet virtuoso Doc Severinsen and another for clarinetist Eddie Daniels. In Frank's words, "Niccolò Paganini's Twenty-Fourth Violin Caprice has inspired composers for many generations. The simple sixteen-measure tune lends itself both melodically and harmonically to myriad treatments, from styles classical to the avant-garde. If there were such a thing as a 'repertoire for composers,' this little melody would certainly occupy a prominent spot. Whether writing short variations on the melody or developing longer songs or movement-like segments using mainly its harmonic underpinnings, it is one of those challenges that—when all's said and done—is just plain fun."

At first François wasn't interested. He loved Paganini, but it was violin music. However, after hearing the Eddie Daniels recording, François warmed to the idea. Frank began by composing a set of variations for bass and piano, as he had done for *A Carmen Fantasy*. This served as an insurance policy. In the event François didn't like something about the piece, he wouldn't have to reorchestrate large sections. He called the new work *Nine Variants on Paganini*.

The work is an extraordinary tour de force, and François loved the challenge. Technically, rhythmically, and harmonically sophisticated, the piece brings the concept of a theme and variations into the twenty-first century—adorning Paganini's nineteenth-century theme with such disparate genres as Latin jazz and atonal expressionism—and demands exceptionally fleet virtuosity and derring-do from the bassist. It was a triumph. François's only criticism was that he wanted to contribute his own unaccompanied cadenza to balance the work—a short set of variations on the Paganini theme more in keeping with the original.

François was so pleased with the piece that he performed it in four international recitals in 2001: the world premiere in Honolulu, followed by appearances in Washington, DC; Adelaide, Australia; and Graz, Austria. François's connection to Honolulu came about through his appearances at the International String Workshops, where he met George Wellington. The former principal bass of the Honolulu Symphony Orchestra, George had taken a day job teaching strings in the public schools to help manage Hawaii's high cost of living. George was quick-witted and had been trying to convince François to come to Honolulu for several years. He approached François at a workshop—accompanied by his daughter and several students—to say "aloha" and give François a lei. George asked François for his autograph to give to his daughter and then turned over the paper to reveal that François had signed an agreement promising to come to Honolulu. Laughing at George's audacity, François finally agreed. Their relationship led to François coming to visit Honolulu six times between 2000 and 2014.

After having performed *Nine Variants* several times, François asked Frank to orchestrate the piece. Frank completed the orchestration in 2002, and François returned to Hawaii to premiere the work with the Honolulu Symphony Orchestra, a performance that was broadcast on the National Public Radio program *Performance Today*.[1] He performed it later that year with the Stavanger Symphony Orchestra (Norway). In 2009 he performed the work with the Syrian National Symphony Orchestra in Damascus while on a tour of the Middle East, and then in 2012 he went on a South American tour organized by Marcos Machado and performed *Nine Variants* with five orchestras in Brazil and Uruguay. After the tour, François flew to Cincinnati and recorded two versions of *Nine Variants* and *Reitba*, one accompanied by piano and the other by full orchestra.[2] François then asked Frank to arrange a third version of *Nine Variants* for bass and strings, to which Frank added a piano to help cover all the parts. He now says, "I'm glad I did because the piece gets played in all versions." Frank's concept was prophetic—the work has entered the standard repertoire of the double bass as one of the most demanding works that "is just plain fun."

One mark of a soloist's greatness in the classical world is for a performer to reach such heights that they inspire composers to write for them. Occasionally a composer will form a special bond with a performer and create multiple works, such as the relationship Brahms shared with the violinist Joachim. Frank and François enjoyed such a collaboration, resulting in five major works for bass and orchestra over a twenty-year period. Frank has always been candid about their working relationship. Early on he learned that to write for François, he needed to get past what François normally likes to do and push his boundaries. He began to understand that François is capable of playing almost anything, but needs to feel a strong connection to the music. If the project is a good fit—artistically, musically—and shows off his abilities, allowing him to connect with the piece and the audience, he embraces it. If a musical passage is challenging in a foreign way or the piece doesn't resonate with him rather quickly, he can be resistant.

From a performance perspective, Frank asserts that François is a quick study and can always move fluidly between the composed page and an improvisation. It is often the case that jazz musicians are not great sight-readers. The culture of improvised music generally expects musicians to learn repertoire and concepts by ear and play everything from memory, and François generally fits this profile. He plays recitals from memory, although he frequently reads Frank's pieces. Furthermore, he takes great care working out the moments where Frank has indicated an improvisation. François prepares his musical gestures in advance so his "improvisation" is similar in each performance. In this way, he is not truly improvising, but is free to shape and vary his ideas on a whim or for dramatic effect.

That said, Frank points out that François can be finicky. If he wants a change in the score, there is no negotiating, but it is usually something minor, such as a note change. Frank has no regrets: "So, he learned my pieces very accurately and I didn't have to spoon-feed him—unlike others I've worked with. And you have to realize that musicians like François are incredible—it's a privilege writing for them. And if they're going do 95 percent of what you write, hell, man, I'll take it. If they're just not going to play that one note, that's all right. Doesn't bother me. So, it's been a ball working with him. And it shows, because we're still great friends. And if it wasn't a ball working together and if either one of us were prima donnas—where he was the kind who would say, 'Nope, I'm not doing that,' or I was the kind that'd say, 'You've got to play every single last note the way I wrote it'—it wouldn't have worked."

———

Japanese producer Susumu Morikawa came to Paris to visit François in 2002 and asked if he would entertain the idea of making a recording for King Records. As François considered the offer, the Great American Songbook immediately sprang to mind. Ever since he was a teenager playing with his brothers, François had loved American standards. He had been inspired by so many singers whose expressive interpretations had thrilled him, and he was attracted to the music's unique combination of elements: the swinging rhythms, the sophisticated harmonic progressions, and above it all, the melodies—so different from the modal music he had grown up hearing. He would often play one or two of these standards as encores throughout his career. François saw Morikawa's offer as an opportunity to make a record of this music that he loved, and he pitched the concept. Morikawa was delighted by the idea.

In preparation for the recording session, François began to explore arrangement ideas with Nicholas Walker, an American bassist and pianist fluent in both classical music and jazz. Walker recalls that François demonstrated a keen ear and was quick to notice a voicing he didn't like as they explored a tune's harmonic progression. However, François was not fluent in harmonic jazz improvisation. He didn't feel comfortable improvising over a chord progression as a jazz artist would do, and instead wanted only to sing the melodies on the bass in the free manner he had heard listening to the great jazz singers and instrumentalists. He wanted to express these wonderful melodies in his own way, accompanied by an accomplished jazz pianist, someone who could provide him with the kind of creative support that would delight and inspire, and at the same time follow him through whatever twists and turns he wished to make at a moment's notice.

Through his former student Guillermo Benavides, François arranged a rehearsal with Manuel Rocheman, a highly respected French jazz pianist, and invited Morikawa to attend. Being a jazz fan, Morikawa loved hearing François's interpretations and was excited for the project. François asked GP to serve as the artistic director and arranged for the sessions to take place at Studio Ina, just outside Paris.

Each of the twenty tracks is quite short—the longest is under five minutes and most hover around the two-minute mark. Many, such as Victor Young's "My Foolish Heart," begin with a brief piano introduction, followed by François simply stating the melody in the upper register of the bass. He treats the tunes with respect and restraint, shaping the melody expressively and employing a colorful tonal palette. A few tunes, such as "Night and Day," "Good Morning Heartbreak," and "Unforgettable," feature François improvising over modal interludes. The title track, "In a Sentimental Mood," begins with an extended improvisation over a pedal tone, exploring different tonalities against the pedal and setting an evocative mood. Rocheman is a sensitive accompanist to François's interpretations, providing clear support and offering the occasional interjection and unexpected harmonic shift without distracting from the melody.

GP recalls one tense moment during the recording of Charlie Parker's "Ornithology." François had wanted to perform the work at a blisteringly fast tempo and then allow the performance to disintegrate into a high-energy free improvisation. Rocheman resisted. He wanted to hold to a classic jazz standard interpretation, in keeping with the rest of the recording. If there was to be an improvisation during "Ornithology," Rocheman argued, it should be over the chord changes and following the form. François capitulated and played the angular melody twice at a blistering tempo, finishing with a virtuosic flourish. François's son Sylvain was present at the sessions, and as an encore, the father and son recorded a version of François's *Le cri de Venise*. Since the piece was an original work and very different from the other tunes, François had intended *Le cri* to be placed at the end of the record, as a coda. But when Morikawa heard the final mixes, he was so moved by the performance that he chose to place François's piece first.

In a Sentimental Mood was a musical return to a beautiful time in François's life—to the warm evenings he spent playing with his brothers at the Hotel Normandy by the sea in Beirut, when Pierre would invite him to take over the melody with the bow in the upper register of the bass. It delighted François to finally record his favorite melodies from the Great American Songbook, tunes he had admired since he was a young boy seeing the American jazz artists in the films of the 1940s. *In a Sentimental Mood* was released in Japan in 2004 to critical acclaim.

20

Sylvain

> You must have all the technique in the world to play one beautiful note.

By the age of fifteen, Sylvain had learned the piano accompaniments to the majority of François's compositions and was performing full recitals with his father from memory, with the exception of Frank Proto's more challenging works, such as *A Carmen Fantasy* and *Nine Variants*. Within three years, he had mastered these pieces as well. Between 2002 and 2016, Sylvain performed with François on five continents, including dozens of performances in North America (returning multiple times to Minneapolis,[1] Kansas City,[2] and Quebec[3]) interspersed with several trips to England, Spain, and Poland; special appearances in South America, the Middle East, and Seoul, Korea; and a four-city tour of Australia.

In addition to touring with François, Sylvain had established a career in the professional recording industry. With the help of François, he created the Museum Recording Studio in Paris and produced numerous commercial projects for television, film, and advertising. He quickly developed a reputation as an excellent recording engineer, composer-arranger, keyboard programmer, and performer. His work came to the attention of recording executives at Universal France, who began to hire Sylvain to help develop songs and arrangements for up-and-coming singers. But no matter what professional opportunities arose, collaborating with François has always taken precedence for Sylvain, who explains, "I try my best to rearrange my schedule to go to Amsterdam or Korea with Papa. These are once-in-a-lifetime opportunities. Plus, we are composing together and still recording. I really want to be with him, because it will not last forever."

Sylvain grew up hearing François practice in the large living room in the center of their apartment, so the sound of François's bass was a constant presence in his life. Once Sylvain was old enough to take piano lessons, François played music with him daily, improvising bass lines to Sylvain's early piano pieces and later, when Sylvain was learning jazz standards, creating duo arrangements. The result of such an immersive environment was that as Sylvain began to learn François's repertoire, he became his father's musical shadow. It would only be a matter of time, though, before Sylvain began to have his own ideas and the desire to express himself in new ways.

Musical interpretation is often the cause of disagreements between longtime collaborators, and one recurring topic of discussion between father and son was the character of Sylvain's improvised piano solos. Sylvain knew that François was revered as a virtuosic bassist, and wanted to play more elaborate solos to match his father's energy. François, however, would frequently request that Sylvain play shorter, more melodic solos, and he would occasionally invent a counterline to play during his son's solos, a distraction for Sylvain. As Sylvain became older, he began to understand François's perspective. First of all, they performed for audiences who were there to hear François, but more importantly Sylvain's solos should reflect the qualities of the piece, especially when considering works like *Le cri*—such a simple, beautiful melody deserves a subtle treatment. These discussions and experiences helped strengthen not only the content of Sylvain's solos, but also his sense of musical time and artful rubato. Sylvain took his father's advice to heart: "He taught me how to share the emotional content of the music."

Performing with a longtime musical partner can be stressful under the best of circumstances, and traveling can magnify the pressure. In the moments leading up to a performance, François might feel a little unsettled and is reassured by Sylvain's presence. But while François travels with his own bass, Sylvain must always play on an unfamiliar piano. To complicate matters, François does not want to play more than a few notes on the day of a concert. He likes to get to the concert venue early and set up the stage, choosing the place for the piano and the bass podium. Then, perhaps, he will play a few notes to hear the sound of the bass in the hall. But aside from these few moments, he does not wish to practice or rehearse, saving his freshest energy for the performance. An hour before the recital, however, may be the only time Sylvain has the opportunity to touch the piano on which he is asked to perform that evening—less than ideal circumstances for him.

During the course of a recital, François has no problem stopping for any reason—for instance, to retune or if he has a memory slip. As he often says, "I am proud to be human and make a mistake." Yet Sylvain expresses that in rehearsals François won't necessarily accept fault for a mistake, especially as he has gotten older. "There was a period where it became a little difficult. He would blame me in rehearsals for a mistake that he would make, and then, some-times, he would blame his age. But," Sylvain points out, "he would not accept this excuse from anyone else." During one performance, François was feeling more anxious that usual and began to speak about his age, eighty at the time. In the car on the way back to the hotel, Sylvain spoke his mind, asking, "Do you want to be known as an eighty-year-old man who plays well, or as a bassist who plays well? Don't put your age in the mind of the audience—then they will say, 'He plays well for being so old.' Would *you* accept that from someone else? No." Reflecting later, Sylvain was in a more forgiving mood: "Look, there is the moment in the performance when the stress gives way to expression and is powerful. He always begins with *Poucha-dass* and that piece raises everything up. All the negative feelings dissipate once the music begins."

The role of travel coordinator would often fall to Sylvain, and flying with a bass inevitably causes problems. Bassists are all too familiar with stories of broken necks, lost instruments, and the refusal of desk agents to allow the instrument onboard during the check-in process. After the attacks on September 11, 2001, restrictions were added and tightened, making checking a bass even more difficult. The following pair of stories illustrate just how maddening it can be to fly with a bass.

Sylvain has often had to wrestle François's bass—in an over-size and overweight trunk—to the ticket counter and convince the airline representative to allow the instrument onboard at a reasonable cost. On one trip to Adelaide, Australia, in 2003, the clerk insisted on a fee of 1,500 euros for a one-way ticket to fly the bass in the cargo hold, the equivalent of a round-trip economy ticket. Sylvian was at a loss for words—they had to go, but the fee was exorbitant. François stepped forward and quietly told the clerk that he could not, in good conscience, pay such a high fee. It would, he explained, have to be reimbursed by his host in Australia, and since this was an educational workshop, they simply did not have the money. Therefore, François said he would call Australia and cancel his appearance. Since he and Martine had first-class tickets, the cost of their tickets was refundable, and he asked for his money back. The airline representative then quoted a lower price for the bass, but François was adamant—the fee was still too high. Finally, the clerk called a superior, and they agreed to fly the bass at no additional cost. Once they boarded the plane, the reason became apparent: the flight was almost empty. The airline was trying to make money in any way possible, and keeping a pair of paying first-class ticket holders was significantly more lucrative than making a little more on the transportation of the bass.

In the summer of 2013 François was scheduled to make three North American appearances. The bass trunk caught the eye of an overzealous customs official in Chicago, and François and Sylvain were detained for over three hours in a cubicle while the officer searched the internet, trying to determine if they were traveling for educational purposes or for a salary, which would require a work visa. François was exhausted from the long flight and exasperated by the way they were being treated. He finally told the officer to either let them leave so they could make their connection or put them on the next flight back to Paris—he was done being kept in airport purgatory. The officer allowed them to pass, but told François that he had flagged his passport, meaning François would be checked for the appropriate visa every time he entered the country in the future. The experience left him upset and discouraged about international travel.

Sylvain shared one particular story that weaves several of these stressful elements together and illustrates how he sees his father. François had been invited to perform as a headliner at the Dutch Double Bass Festival. The Amsterdam Andalusian Orchestra had been engaged to accompany François, and Sylvain had spent a few weeks creating full arrangements of François's modal pieces, tailored to the group's unique instrumentation—violins, ouds, and percussion. Sylvain was eager and nervous because they had only two rehearsals to put the concert together. Trouble began early, when the car carrying the bass from the airport broke down. Furthermore, unbeknown to both of them, the ensemble was a loosely arranged affair, and the members spoke a mix of languages, including Arabic, Dutch, French, and English, which complicated communication. Sylvain began to rehearse the ensemble without François, only to discover that the musicians could not read Western musical notation and played only unison melodic lines learned by rote. Once the bass finally arrived, François could begin to model the music for the ensemble. The concertmaster was very astute, and by listening closely to the melodies and François's interpretations was able to create an acceptable accompaniment. The concert attracted a large, enthusiastic crowd, and François and Sylvain were thrilled with the music and the audience response.

The organizers of the festival had arranged for two rooms in a five-star hotel near the concert hall—François occupied one room, and Sylvain and his girlfriend the other. A large reception followed the concert, and Sylvain and his girlfriend slipped out to buy some marijuana (legal in Amsterdam). Smoking in the hotel was not allowed, but Sylvain had taken a few precautions, draping one towel over the smoke detector and another under the door. They were still asleep when the maid came to the door and peeked into the messy room. Moments later the manager pounded on the door. Sylvain, barely dressed, answered it. The couple were evicted from the hotel and had to pay a 400-euro fine for smoking in the room. This complicated their travel plans because the festival wasn't over yet and François was expected to attend additional events with Sylvain. In the meantime, the manager of the hotel was so furious that he began calling everyone he knew at the festival, including François. A few hours later François called Sylvain and invited him and his girlfriend to have lunch with him. They anticipated the worst, but he said nothing about the events at the hotel—only how much he enjoyed traveling with them and how much he appreciated the work Sylvain had done on the music.

Thinking back, Sylvain reflects that François has lived such a rich life, and had so many experiences, that he has developed a great deal of patience and tolerance for almost any eventuality. For Sylvain, these traits are gifts that François has shared with him by example.

By 2016 François was eighty-five years old and found travel not only anxiety producing, but overwhelming. Yet he wanted to embark on a farewell tour and visit those former students and friends whom he considered his extended family. Needless to say, his longtime friends and colleagues were delighted to help make arrangements for masterclasses and performances across the globe. In July, he and Sylvain traveled to the United States and performed in Washington, DC, New York, Kansas City, and Minneapolis, followed by a week in Canada at Domaine Forget. In September they flew to Australia and performed in Brisbane, Sydney, Adelaide, and Hobart. François accepted an invitation from Nicholas Walker, his former student and president-elect of the International Society of Bassists, to perform as a headliner at the 2017 ISB biennial convention in Ithaca, New York. François gave a marvelous performance, and the capacity audience rewarded him with an extended standing ovation lasting several minutes. After his recital, François met Gary Karr, ISB's founder and a renowned bass soloist, for the first time. François had dedicated his Concerto No. 3 to Gary and performed it that evening.

Later that fall, François was invited to perform in Alba la Romaine, a small art colony in the South of France. He was surprised to see Louis Guilbert, his former stand partner and personnel manager from the Paris Opera, in attendance. Louis was there with two students.

After the concert, one of Louis's students exclaimed, "He blew me away!"

Louis responded with a grin, "He's been blowing me away since the sixties!"

On Friday, March 12, 2021, François Rabbath celebrated his ninetieth birthday by performing a forty-five-minute recital from memory, streamed from a recording studio outside of Paris. More than fourteen thousand people attended the virtual concert from all over the world. Immediately following the recital, he received a plaque from the ISB declaring March 12 François Rabbath Day. The proclamation extolled his performing, teaching, and generosity, and ended, "Whereas together we can make a positive change in our communities and the world by following his example. . . . Observe this day with playing, teaching, and acts of kindness that demonstrate and celebrate the life of Maestro Rabbath."

François was deeply touched and very emotional: "It is a big honor for me. It's never happened for me to have this—it's the first time." He concluded, through his tears, "I'm very happy."

Those in attendance shared countless emotional testimonials reflecting on their personal experiences with François. They thanked him for inviting them to embrace their humanity, play from their hearts, share their feelings, and accept their mistakes—in short, for giving them permission to be themselves. He was now being showered with the love he had shared with so many—the love of humanity, agape.

Coda

François Rabbath

When it's Bach, you play beautifully, but when you have scales and arpeggios . . . [*singing the Prelude from the Bach Fifth Suite*] Because it's Bach, you play it gracefully, but when you play scales, you play like a zombie. Because you are . . . How do you say? Training? No, I don't. I never train in my life. I never allowed me to train. My training, it's musical always. That's why. When you have that, you begin to form the note also. In this case, you touch the people. What is the music? It's to produce that. The music, it's . . . If I don't touch you with how I play, it's a disaster. Why should I play if you don't feel anything, why I'm going to play? For whom? For what?

But no, it's important to learn and to see that the communication must make a connection. You may stand on the stage and play perfectly and the audience goes from there and they will have forgotten your performance ten minutes later. But if you find a way in, to touch them in their soul, they will never forget. Sometimes I have some people see me ten years after a concert and say, "I remember your concert." Why? Because I touch him. I don't impress him. He was touched in his soul. He was crying or he was happy. They cried by happiness. After the concert, when they come and they want to say something, they say nothing. They just kiss you. They kiss you and they are happy. They don't say, "Oh, you are virtuoso." No, this is the worst thing that I can be told by somebody, "You are virtuoso." That mean it was perfect, and I don't touch him. It's very bad. When I say

195

you must have all the technique of the world to play one beautiful note, that mean you must master the bass, but never forget that all that to produce a beautiful note, the touching note.

Paris, 2020[1]

For the Future

François Rabbath

To reach this point I spent seventy-five years.

You can be virtuoso when you are young. I was when I was young, but my understanding of each note was not like that—to form the note.

But all that, it's to communicate with the public.

If you interpret something just for you, stay home. Because if you don't have the reaction of the public to say, "I understand what you do," or "I share with you your love," how you can share a love in showing your ambition? Your ability? No, you cannot share the love with that.

You share a love in doing a music—in using your ability to do the music—you can share that with the public in transmitting your love. If not, it's impossible.

So, it took me time. But I am so happy to say it. Because if I knew that young-young, it will help me to grow up more. I say that now for the others to permit them to grow up in this view.

You can find always somebody who can say something. And if he say it with love, you will take it. If he say it with aggressivity, you will reject it. Not, "I am and look what I do." No.

"Look how I love you. Look how I try to be in contact with you.

"Took my heart. In this phrase, took my heart. Come with me."

And the people react and they feel it. And that is the beauty.

I want to say for the future—for all the musicians, not just the bass players—love the rest of the people.

Don't stay alone. Don't be jealous.

You must know that you are unique. Definitely.

You must know that you must not compete with somebody else.

Compete with yourself. Be better than yourself. Love the other.

Because you must know that if the other don't exist for you, you don't exist for anyone.

Because you respect the other and you love them and you admire them, they will admire you and they help you to live—to grow up.

Don't make the other like enemy, because you are making a competition with them.

That's my meaning, because you will find out that you will be alone and you will fight with all the musicians.

Why you play the music, from the beginning, why?

Because you love it. Because you love to play the instrument. You begin to play because you love that.

When you begin, you are not jealous from anyone.

Little by little, you become jealous and you want to be better than the neighbors.

But the purpose you are fighting after alone, against everybody.

I think the love is the point of everything.

If you love the other bass players, the music, and you share with them something, they will share everything with you.

I think, what is the music?

It's when you play together. To share something. To say something one to another. And, together, to say something for the public.

I think the most important word, it's love. Love each other.

It's love each other and do in a way to don't stay alone.

To don't stay alone.

Atascadero, California, 2006[1]

Notes

All epigraphs are quotes from François Rabbath.

Preface
1. Henry Peyrebrune interviewed George Vance in 2002. Henry's wife, Tracy Rowell, helped arrange the author's access to the complete unedited version; Johnny Hamil and Christian Chesanek helped to transcribe the document. Excerpts of the interview are included with the permission of Martha Vance. A portion of the interview was published in the International Society of Bassists' *Bass World Journal* 41, no. 2 (2019): 37–43.

Chapter 1: The Early Years
1. Jennifer M. Dueck, *The Claims of Culture at Empire's End: Syria and Lebanon under French Rule,* British Academy Postdoctoral Fellowship Monographs (London: British Academy, 2010).
2. Hanna Batatu, *Syria's Peasantry, the Descendants of Its Lesser Rural Notables, and Their Politics* (Princeton, NJ: Princeton University Press, 1999).
3. Thomas Philipp and Birgit Schaebler, eds., *The Syrian Land: Processes of Integration and Fragmentation, Bilad Al-Sham from the 18th to the 20th Century,* Berliner Islamstudien, Band 6 (Stuttgart, Germany: Franz Steiner, 1998); William R. Polk, "Understanding Syria: From Pre–Civil War to Post-Assad," *Atlantic,* December 10, 2013.
4. Rabbat was the family name of Georges's maternal grandmother. The family later changed their last name to Rabbath.
5. Carmen M. Reinhart and Kenneth S. Rogoff, *This Time Is Different: Eight Centuries of Financial Folly* (Princeton, NJ: Princeton University Press, 2009).

Chapter 2: Introduction to the Bass

1. François and Martine still own an overlocker sewing machine. The overlocker is a complex professional sewing machine that uses multiple cones of thread, several needles, and special cutting blades. It is capable of creating refined edges on garments, giving them a professional finish.

Chapter 3: The Rabbath Trio

1. Samir Kassir, *Beirut*, trans. M. B. DeBevoise (Berkeley: University of California Press, 2010).

2. In 1963 François would move into an upper apartment at 26 rue de Clichy. This is the building where the violinist and composer Georges Enesco lived and taught out of a ground-floor apartment for many years. François would learn that Yehudi Menuhin was one of Georges's students there.

   In December 1998 the British ambassador invited François to attend an end-of-year chamber orchestra concert at the British embassy in Paris, performed by students from the Menuhin School. At the reception that followed, the ambassador introduced François to Yehudi Menuhin's daughter, Zamira. François asked Zamira to thank her father for the words of encouragement that had meant so much to him when he was young, and he sent her a few of his albums to share with her father. Yehudi wrote back, thanking François for his generosity and enclosing a signed photograph. Several years later Caroline Emery invited François to perform at the Menuhin School in London. He was delighted to see a portrait of Menuhin overlooking him as he played his recital.

   Also while playing at the Normandy with his brothers, François was encouraged by José Iturbi, the great Spanish pianist, conductor, and film star, who was staying in Beirut for a few days. Iturbi had become internationally popular after appearing as himself in several recent Hollywood films of the 1940s, and to avoid drawing attention to himself, he chose to dine in the hotel's private room. Upon hearing the music, Iturbi went into the main dining room to listen, standing in the back. When the trio took a break, he quietly came up and congratulated the group on their creative arrangements, and François in particular for using the bass as a melodic instrument.

3. See Marcel Rouet, *Culture physique athletique*, Sports SB (n.p., 1945).

Chapter 4: Paris!

1. The stories in this chapter were taken primarily from François's brief unpublished autobiographical document and expanded with material from hours of personal interviews with the author.

Chapter 5: Boussagol

1. Michael Greenberg, "François Rabbath: Sa carrière, ses apports techniques et son influence sur l'écriture musicale, au travers de la documentation éditée et inédite" [François Rabbath: His Career in Documents] (master's thesis, Université de Paris–Sorbonne [Paris IV], UFR de Musique et Musicologie, 1998), 13. Michael Greenberg's thesis shows that François's letter to be admitted as an adult student was dated October 3, and he was authorized to register on October 4. The first round of auditions took place on October 17 (the Bottesini) and the second round on November 7 (the Birkenstock and sight-reading by Jacques-Paul-Gabriel De Sauville de Lapresle).

Chapter 6: Fast Cars & Aznavour . . .

1. Picasso lived in his studio at 7 rue des Grands Augustins from 1937 until he was evicted in 1967. Paul McQueen, "A Travel Guide to Pablo Picasso's Paris," Culture Trip, June 21, 2017, https://theculturetrip .com/europe/france/paris/articles/a-travel-guide-to-pablo-picassos -paris/.
2. Frank J. Prial, "Charles Aznavour: A Story. A Passion. A Life of Song," At Lunch With, *New York Times*, August 19, 1992, section C, 10.
3. The exchange that François had with Brasco was a great disappointment. François holds the concept of family—not only his immediate family, but his larger family of students, collaborators, and friends—near to his heart. Being raised in such a large, loving, and dynamic home and then suddenly being isolated at the age of six to attend a foreign school had a profound impact on him. He would continue to seek the unconditional love and feeling of belonging that Bahija had showered him with, but he was ever mindful that events could change in a heartbeat. In a sense, that year of being deprived of his family gave him an understanding of what it feels like to be considered "foreign"— of the powerful emotions evoked when one is denied acceptance. He recalls his emotions: "What is terrible is that I came to Paris with the idea to find a family of musicians. When I was in Lebanon, they had an orchestra visiting from the United States. I met them and we exchanged ideas. And I met other musicians over the years, from Brazil, from Bavaria, 'How you do that . . . I do that . . .' And it was

friendly. I came here to France with this mentality. Here, in France, I must ask, For how long am I going to be a foreigner? They treated me like a foreigner, a stranger. Even if you become nationalized, it's always they reject you. I don't belong to any country. I have passports from Syria, and after, from Lebanon, and now France. But bass is my nationality. I help everybody, nobody helped me. [*crying quietly*] Comme ça. It's okay." Interview with the author, November 2018.

4. Impressed by their reception in Tehran, François composed a piece as a gift for the shah. The original score was placed in the National Library and Archives of Iran.

5. After Jacques Loussier replaced François and Victor for *Play Bach*, François was devastated. He recalls, "Whenever I am distraught, I take refuge in my bass, playing for hours. I cannot tell you the courage it took my bass on that day to console me." Interview with the author, July 2019.

Chapter 7: The Sound of a Bass

1. "Quincy Jones: Bio," NEA Jazz Masters Fellowships, National Endowment for the Arts (website), https://www.arts.gov/honors/jazz/quincy-jones.

2. François discussed the making of his first solo record, *The Sound of a Bass,* with Mike Johnston for the Canadian jazz magazine *Coda* in 1989: "Quincy heard me playing arco style and asked me why I didn't make a record. I told him I'd never been asked. So he asked me to make a demo and send it to him." Mike Johnston, "François Rabbath: The Sound of the Bass," *Coda*, June 1989, 37.

3. François describes *The Sound of a Bass* as his destiny. He feels that time and time again his life has been touched by a kind of magic, for which he is very grateful. He speaks this way when he describes the way his brother Elie gave him his first bass and his discovery of the Nanny *Méthode* in the tailor shop.

4. There were some early recordings featuring solo bass or the bassist as a leader. In the classical realm: Koussevitzky, *Master of the Double Bass* (1928); Gertovich, *Melody in the Old Style* (1952); Karr, *Gary Karr Plays the Double Bass* (1960); and Turetzky, *In a Recital of New Music* (1964). In the jazz world: Ellington/Blanton, *Sophisticated Lady* (1940); Pettiford, *Oscar Pettiford* (1954); Slam Stewart, *Bowin' Singin' Slam* (1956); and Paul Chambers, *Chambers' Music* (1956).

5. *The Sound of a Bass* (*Bass Ball* in the United States) garnered mostly positive reviews from the American press. John Wilson's review for *High Fidelity* was typical: "Rabbath bows and plucks his way through

a series of compositions so varied in style, approach, and melodic flow that they seem to reveal the potentialities of the string bass as if for the first time. He creates haunting, otherworldly pieces, warm melodic songs, strange electronic sounds, brilliant passages of bowing and plucking that are both astonishing and purposeful." John Wilson, *High Fidelity Magazine* 14, no. 7 (July 1964): 83.

Even though *The Sound of a Bass* was awarded a Grand Prix du Disque for composition, throughout François's career there were those who were critical of his writing, while acknowledging his mastery of the instrument. Such was the case in Harvey Pekar's *Downbeat* review of *Bass Ball*: "Rating this record would be meaningless, since it consists of performances designed primarily to showcase Rabbath's virtuosity. He wrote the selections, but while some are fairly enjoyable, they are of slight musical significance." Harvey Pekar, *Downbeat*, June 18, 1964, 26.

6. Barbara and François Rabbath were also filmed for a program entitled *Face au public* on July 17, 1964.

7. A comprehensive listing of recording projects and performances pre-1997 can be found in Michael Greenberg, "François Rabbath: Sa carrière, ses apports techniques et son influence sur l'écriture musicale, au travers de la documentation éditée et inédite" [François Rabbath: His Career in Documents] (master's thesis, Université de Paris–Sorbonne [Paris IV], UFR de Musique et Musicologie, 1998), 129–50.

8. François has said that it was two years from the time of the theft until he purchased Willy's bass. This is supported by his calendar, which shows a two-year period between November 1965 and October 1967 where he did not appear on live television. Furthermore, the instrument that appears on the cover of *No. 2*, released in January 1965, is not a Quenoil. The photo of him performing at Picasso's ninetieth birthday celebration in Vallauris in 1971 *is* the Quenoil, though, appearing to place the theft within this period.

9. Paco on François's artistry: "This is just one example of his brilliance, aside from being a virtuoso. Virtuoso because it's astonishing how he plays. To play a Bach suite on string bass, eh, to do that, you had to have almost been *born really early*.

"The sound, his sound! How do you achieve that sound?

"Because there are thousands and thousands of sounds. There are thousands of bassists and each one has their sound, but the sound of Rabbath—his sound is singular, unique. There isn't any other like it. Nobody else has this sound, this unmistakable footprint that he has. This sound that penetrates, that stays inside of you. It's not a sound that passes through you and then it's gone, but no, no. The sound that Rabbath has—it stays with you, inside you forever. This is François, François Rabbath!

"Then, as a person, he's very open, culturally immense, immense. And sometimes I think that Rabbath was born four thousand years ago, more or less like this. [*laughs*] He's as old as Abraham, as Hammurabi. And then he stopped off in Greece and he knew Socrates and Ramses—and all of these cultures he carries inside of him. And this surfaces, when you're with him—this wisdom he has inside. It comes out, it comes out, like how we're talking now. If François were here, he'd be spouting wisdom! [*laughs*] To sum it up, he's a musician, a wise man, and enormously intuitive with a keen sense of insight. This, this is François.

"And then, as a person, he's like a brother to me. On a sentimental [emotional] level it's a close human family relationship." Interview with Michael Weiss, May 2021.

10. François reflecting on his relationship with Moshe Naïm: "Believe me or not, Moshe produced ten records of mine and he never gave me one penny. Yes. When I asked him when I would get paid, he said always, 'Tomorrow.' But tomorrow never comes. That's me. It's not the money, for me. He was a foolish man. He had an idea and I liked him, but I didn't know he was a little bit screwed up. But never mind. Many times, I helped him to live. He asked me for money, because he doesn't have, so I gave him money." Interview with the author, December 2020.

11. Two weeks prior to the Palais des Sports concerts, François met Johnny Sølvberg. A student at the Royal Danish Academy of Music, Johnny had received a scholarship to study with Gaston Logerot at the Paris Conservatory for one month in May 1971. He also had hopes of meeting François Rabbath after hearing the record *Bass Ball*. At the time, Johnny thought François had used electronic synthesizers to create some of the exotic sounds on his first recording. Shortly after arriving in Paris, Johnny found François's address in the phone book and went to his house to express admiration for his playing. François was not at home, but Mauricette told Johnny to come back a few hours later. The two bassists met several times during Johnny's time in Paris, and François invited him to attend rehearsals for the Palais des Sports concerts. To his amazement, Johnny experienced firsthand that there were no electronic special effects on the record—François was capable of creating all those effects acoustically on the bass. In a pattern that would repeat itself numerous times, Johnny, like many other bass students, would find myriad ways to promote François.

Chapter 8: Picasso & Bahija

1. "Picasso Ignores Party for His 90th Birthday," *New York Times*, October 26, 1971, 48.

2. The reviewer for *La Opinión* in Buenos Aires was effusive in his praise for François's unaccompanied set: "The most surprising revelation for the entire audience assembled in the Gran Rex Cinema was, without a doubt, the appearance of the Syrian double bassist François Rabbath. . . . Rabbath is a true virtuoso of the instrument. . . . His intonation is impeccable, his tone excellent, with a vibrato of great expressive intensity. He attacked the most complicated passages with the greatest of assurance while maintaining the same tonal quality. The diverse techniques demonstrated in each piece allow him to extend the usual possibilities of the instrument and to perform as a soloist, a style of playing that is uncommon among bass players. His bow technique is supported by the speed of the fingers of his left hand, resulting in a touch that is particularly expressive and at times surprisingly rapid." "Revelación de Francois Rabbath, un contrabajista virtuoso y profundo," *La Opinión* (Buenos Aires), November 13, 1971.

3. The Estadio Nacional would become a prison camp after General Augusto Pinochet's coup.

4. Even with contracts in place, artists were often at the mercy of unscrupulous promoters while on tour far from home. Paco vividly recalls their issues with their South American promoter: "We were in Buenos Aires, where we played the Rex together. The Rex is a 3,000-seat theater, and we did two days there. And, well, it was a full house—the theater was packed to the brim. So, the Argentinean concert promoter came up to me after the show and says [*imitates Argentinean accent*], 'Hey man, I'm not even covering expenses.' Talking as if he was losing money. [*laughs*] It was packed, 3,000 people, sold out. [*laughs*] I told François, and he kind of laughs and says, 'How can he not be making any money?' But he took it like, whatever, and just figured it's no big deal. The next day it's another sold-out show, full house, 3,000 people, same deal. So, the guy comes up to me again and says, 'Hey, Paco, man, I'm not even making expenses . . .' [*laughs*] What the fuck! How can he not be making any money? What, we're going to fill a stadium, and he still won't be covering expenses!

   "We had another concert in Rosario, and then in Santa Fe, and then Córdoba. We get to Rosario, and the same thing—full house, packed—and 'I'm not making any money, not even covering expenses.' [*laughs*] Damn, when the hell are his numbers going to add up here? Santa Fe was the same deal—and then from Santa Fe we traveled to Córdoba.

We left in the morning by car, and on the way to Córdoba, François says to me with a straight face, 'Paco, I hope a lot of people don't show up tonight . . . that way we'll lose less money . . .' We only got out of there thanks to this Catalan painter in Colombia."

At the end of the tour, the duo was preparing to leave for France. As they were checking out of the hotel, the desk clerk informed them that their bill had not been paid and their instruments and suitcases would be held until the bill was resolved. Thanks to the crooked promoter, they had actually lost money on the tour and didn't have enough money between them to cover the final hotel bill. A Catalan painter friend of Paco's came by the hotel to see them off, and Paco explained that they may not be able to leave. "So he goes up to the front desk and asks how much money we owed, paid our whole bill, and we were able to leave . . . with François . . . If you run into him someday, he'll tell you all about it!" [*laughs*]. Interview with Michael Weiss, May 2021.

5. The reviews of François's performances in eastern France and Switzerland were universally exceptional. The Clermont-Ferrand critic highlighted the creativity of François's genre-fluid compositions: "The virtuosity is always stupefying, but is never gratuitous. It relies on a rich and stable musical material which is neither jazz nor classical nor avant-garde in the confining sense of each of these musical categories. . . . But it is perhaps when he asserts himself in a surprisingly faithful transcription of Bach's Suites for Solo Violoncello, a model the austere rigor of which does not permit [one] to fool oneself, that Rabbath reveals himself most eloquently." A. P., "Paco Ibáñez et François Rabbath: Une rencontre inespérée," *La Montagne* (Clermont-Ferrand, France), February 24, 1972, 4.

The critic in Geneva chose to focus on François's ability to shape and shade the vast sonic environment he has at his command: "François Rabbath with his instrument, the double bass, becomes a one-man orchestra through the extraordinary effects he draws from it. He has at his disposition a tonal palette that both seduces and surprises the listener. A prodigious technique serving a highly defined personality. . . . Finally, a true musician, François Rabbath performed with remarkable ease a cello suite by J. S. Bach." "Récital Paco Ibáñez," *Tribune de Genéve* (Switzerland), March 20, 1972.

Chapter 9: A New Life

1. According to an average from several historic currency conversion models, 80,000 French francs was worth about $16,000 in US currency in 1974 or about $89,000 in 2020.

2. François was often trusting and generous to a fault. During this period, he frequented the same small café, Le Cujas, and enjoyed joking with Jacques, one of the waiters. Jacques told François that his boss was going to retire and sell the café, and asked for his advice. François encouraged him to buy it and, in his words, take the chance. The café continued to do well under Jacques, and he asked François if he would hold some money for him. He explained that he was being inspected and didn't feel comfortable having so much cash on the premises. François agreed, so long as Jacques took an informal promissory note. François then put the money in a safe deposit box. Several weeks later, Jacques asked for his money back. Business was so good that he was opening a new café and needed the cash for renovations—and, by the way, would François be interested in investing in the new business? François declined the invitation to invest but told Jacques that he would be happy to loan him what savings he had. Eventually François stopped by the café to ask for a portion of his money, and Jacques gave him a check—but the check bounced. Thinking that there had just been a mistake, François returned to the café. Jacques apologized and gave François another check. It too bounced, and within days François learned that Jacques had committed suicide. He had been betting on the horses and gotten himself into trouble with bookies. François was crushed—the money meant nothing compared to a life.

   A short while later, François was contacted by an attorney. Jacques had kept records of his debts, and François's name was at the top of the list. There was to be a disbursement of his possessions, and François was given first choice. When François arrived at the home, he noticed that in addition to the officials and a handful of creditors, Jacques's widow and two young children were in the living room. She was clearly upset, and the children, not understanding what was happening, were crying. François made his way through the house and indicated he wanted the most valuable items, including the appliances and furniture. The other creditors were not left with much to choose from, and most left empty-handed. François waited until the process was completed, and then, turning to the widow, he said quietly, "It's all yours. You have suffered enough." Interview with the author, November 2018.

Chapter 10: New York, Cincinnati & London

1. The previously recorded *Les trois basses* and *Les sirènes d'alarme* were renamed *Pre-war* and *War* for the 1972 recording of *La guerre et la paix*.

2. *Multi-basse* would later be rereleased in 1979 as a collaboration between the QCA label and Frank Proto's Red Mark label in the United States. Nancy Malitz reviewed the recording for the ISB: "Rabbath has been performing his very own kind of music for 15 years in France, but it's as if he had been classified Top Secret there. Then, as you listen, you'll begin to think that maybe France had a good idea. This guy has something going for himself that is so unique, so individual, it deserves to be guarded carefully. . . . Rabbath isn't interested in restrictions—technical or otherwise. The conventions of stringed instrument playing, and of classical music, are viewed by Rabbath as a resource from which to draw. But he feels no more compelled by them than he feels compelled to make a living as a symphony orchestra musician." Nancy Malitz, "Rabbath's 'Multi-Bass,'" *International Society of Bassists Newsletter* 6, no. 1 (Fall 1979): 567.

3. Vittore Castiglioni was inspired to describe François's performance in extravagantly ornate language: "For those who get excited about pure virtuosity, last night at the Sforza Castle was exceptional. In fact, the bassist François Rabbath is an authentic phenomenon. . . . Cascades of notes are thrown in with such velocity, simultaneously caressing double chords and triple notes . . . Rabbath is a true phenomenon and alone sustained the weight of an entire evening with only the help of a very fine percussionist. The audience had a fine time and greatly applauded him." Vittore Castiglioni, "Contrabbasso straordinario—Rabbath al Castello Sforzesco," *Corriere della Serro* (Milan), July 24, 1974.

4. Peg McCreary, an amateur bassist and volunteer for the International Society of Bassists, wrote an insightful review for the organization's newsletter. In it, she extolled Francois's compositional skills, discerning his ability to meld diverse influences into powerfully expressive works that explore the entire range of the instrument, and enthused about his extraordinary virtuosity and unbridled joy in music making: "As a composer, his works are characterized by a synthesis of mid-Eastern modality and rhythms plus jazz, with the latter leaning into the post-tonal area associated with people like Coltrane. His opening composition, the *War and Peace*, written for a montage film on the Picasso work, was an immensely listenable amalgamation of these elements, but the power and the mood of the music, so far as I was concerned, far surpassed the painting. . . .

"Rabbath's use of the instrument's lower notes was especially impressive. Some of the virtuoso bass pieces which are played today tend to often neglect this lower range and instead exploit the uppermost octaves in an attempt to imitate the facility and sound of the cello. Rabbath, however, revealed no embarrassment about the natural warmth and sensuality of these notes, and frequently concentrated on them for the particular kind of evocative mood which is innate to no other instrument.

"The use of these lower tones also took the form of a 'drone,' which was particularly effective in works where the instrument simulated the sound of a sitar. Even more impressive, however, was his use of them as a pedal beneath extended virtuoso passages which employed the entire range of the instrument. The effect was that of hearing a complete string orchestra. . . . The techniques he employed was [sic] not as 'self-styled' as I had expected . . . [the] unconventionality of his playing consisted of its brilliance and facility. Using a French bow and a standard three-quarters instrument, he displayed a technique so sure and so facile that in other players the effect might be one of insouciance. Rabbath's personal style, however, was so obviously suffused with a love and respect for the instrument that one could not help but regard him as a serious musician." Peg McCreary, *International Society of Bassists Newsletter* 1, no. 3 Spring (1975): 68.

5. The *New York Daily News* and *New York Times* sent critics to review François's Carnegie Hall debut. Bill Zakariasen was effusive in his praise: "The agility of his fingers and bow, with trilled high harmonics, double and triple stops and the like, would shame the work of most cellists, let alone contrabassists. His intonation is dead-center and his tone is of uncommon richness from the grumbling depths to the plaintive top of his instrument." Bill Zakariasen, "A Mean Double Bass," *Daily News*, New York, March 15, 1975, 25.

Allen Hughes, in his *New York Times* review of François's Carnegie Hall debut, challenged the inclusion of so many guest artists. He suggested that the presence of larger ensembles, projections of paintings, and a duet with a mime served to distract from the purpose of the evening—to showcase the "World's Greatest Bassist." Having made his point, he went on to express his admiration for François's unique and effortless accomplishments on such an awkward instrument: "What traditionally trained double-bass player would venture so uninhibitedly into high pitch ranges, find ways to play the unwieldy instrument so that it sounds remarkably like a sitar or guitar, or even play the Sarabande and Gigue from Bach's Cello Suite No. 1 so lyrically and flexibly?" Allen Hughes, "Rabbath Plays in a Busy Concert," *New York Times*, March 16, 1975, 52.

6. Aline Montels, "Voix du saz, voix de la contrebasse," *Libération* (Paris), January 17, 1978, 14.

7. François's second recording with Toulaï, *Hommage à Nazim Hikmet* (Arion, 1982), was rereleased on CD as *Turkey: Song of Poets* (Arion, 2006).

8. The *Financial Times* sent critic David Murray to review the Wigmore Hall joint recital with Jean-Pierre Jumez and François Rabbath. Although the review was critical of François's compositions, Murray found François's virtuosity and interpretations to be quite impressive: "This work [Concerto for Guitar and Bass] proved to be heavily watered Michel Legrand, barbarously constructed. . . . His short pieces run neither to the academic nor to the merely outré; they conjure an almost orchestral richness and variety from his bass, often building around pungent little phrases with a Middle East flavor (Rabbath is Syrian by birth). One expects the bass to be ponderous, but in his hands, it is mercurially agile." David Murray, *Financial Times* (London), May 16, 1977, 3.

9. The International Society of Bassists (ISB) was founded by Gary Karr in 1967 at the University of Wisconsin–Madison, and he led the organization until 1972. Barry Green resurrected the organization in 1974 at the Cincinnati Conservatory of Music. "About Us: ISB History," International Society of Bassists (website), https://www.isbworldoffice .com/history.asp.

10. According to Anthony Scelba (*International Society of Bassists Newsletter* 5, no. 1 [Fall 1978]: 439), the clinicians who taught and gave masterclasses at the 1978 ISB summer course included some of the most influential American bassists of that time:
    Warren Benfield, principal bass, Chicago Symphony Orchestra
    Paul Ellison, principal bass, Houston Symphony Orchestra
    Dianna Gannett, professor, Hartt School of Music
    Eugene Levinson, principal bass, New York Philharmonic
    Henri Portnoi, principal bass, Boston Symphony Orchestra
    Rufus Reid, jazz great
    Dennis Trembly, co-principal bass, Los Angeles Philharmonic

11. "François Rabbath," Frank Proto, *International Society of Bassists Newsletter* 5, no. 4 (Spring 1979): 517.

12. Chute further enthused: "Rabbath demonstrated a unique compositional style, a rare improvisational ability and an awesome technical command of every facet of his instrument." James Chute, "François Rabbath Demonstrates Bass Virtuosity," *Cincinnati Post*, November 8, 1978, 15.

13. Malitz, "Rabbath's 'Multi-Bass,'" 567.

14. Nancy Malitz, "After Proto Writes It, Rabbath Will Play It," *Cincinnati Enquirer*, August 24, 1979.
15. London critic Dominic Gill clearly admired the remarkable relationship that François had forged with his bass in his Wigmore Hall recital, despite finding the original compositions lacking: "The double-bass player François Rabbath makes most other double-bass virtuosi sound like students. . . . For Rabbath is in love with the double-bass; and each piece is an exploration of one or more of its remarkable potentials, at once a brilliant tour de force and an affirmation of a passionate affaire. . . . As a composer, Rabbath is no Beethoven, more [sic] even a Dutilleux; but his passion, and his commitment, sweep through the concert hall like a breath of fresh and bracing air." Dominic Gill, "Wigmore Hall: François Rabbath," *Financial Times* (London), October 13, 1980.

Chapter 11: The Audition

1. His Paris Opera audition successful, François's employment was to begin with the fall season. It should be noted that he had not auditioned for the position of principal bassist. He was entering the orchestra as a member of the section. This would guarantee him a regular salary and keep him closer to home, since the Opéra Garnier was only a short walk from his apartment. While Rabbath's star was in its ascendency as a soloist and pedagogue, the opera now gave him both financial stability and the ability to have a healthy family life.
2. Patrick Barbier, *Opera in Paris, 1800–1850: A Lively History* (Milwaukee: Hal Leonard, 2003).

Chapter 12: Frank & Paul

1. The winners of the 1981 ISB Frederick Zimmerman–Charles Mingus Competition were John Clayton in the jazz division and Edgar Meyer and John Feeney in the classical division.
2. Hans Voigt, a critic for the Danish national paper *Berlingske tidende*, was impressed by Proto's concerto, despite its length: "Without Francois Rabbath as a fascinating virtuoso and captivating soloist, Frank Proto's Double Bass Concerto No. 2 (world premiere) would have seemed far too unreasonably long. But the solo theme (here, speaker-amplified) was effectively well balanced with the large, percussion-heavy orchestra and the jazz trio. . . . And thanks to Rabbath's formidable skill and artistic radiance, I still remember these 45 minutes for the good." Hans Voigt, "Utroligt kontrabas-spil," trans. Kristen Korb, *Berlingske tidende*, July 20, 1981.

Meanwhile, Hannahe and Walter Zacharias were most generous in their praise of François's solo portion of the program: "Just as a large acrobat seems to defy the laws of gravity, Lebanese François Rabbath, who played at Tivoli in Copenhagen on Saturday night, seems to have defied the laws of the double bass. But he has not. He has expanded the limits of the instrument's function in an incredible way: the whistling passages over all four strings, the sky-high-pitched figures, the rushing double-stops do not change the character of the double bass. We just never knew that the instrument could sound like that and yet still be a double bass. But behind this acrobatic virtuosity is a warm musical heart. We noticed its beat in Rabbath's beautiful performance of two movements from one of Bach's cello suites, and we noticed it in his own compositions—one of which Rabbath perceives as an appeal against killing whales. In his music, Rabbath merges elements from oriental music and from European music into an often very beautiful whole." (Hannahe and Walter Zacharias, "The Phenomenon Françios Rabbath," trans. Kristen Korb, *Land og Folk*, July 1981.)

3. The *Cincinnati Enquirer* sent critic Cliff Radel to review the premiere of Frank Proto's Concerto No 2. He left no doubt that François's performance completely transcended his preconceived notion of the possibilities of the double bass: "Rabbath educated the audience on how to listen to a string bass. It is safe to call him a nonpareil virtuoso. He does what all great instrumentalists must do. He places his music beyond the instrument. When he performs, he is not playing the bass, he is playing the music. No time is wasted in translation. The listener does not have to think 'bass' first, 'music' second. The two are one." Cliff Radel, "Rabbath Gives Listening Lesson," *Cincinnati Enquirer*, November 23, 1981, C-9.

4. Paul's final comment at the end of this chapter is quoted from the unreleased 1988 film *Bass Ball*.

Chapter 13: A Fantasy, a Film & Other Dramas

1. John Colwill, "Rabbath a Delight," *Courier-Mail* (Brisbane, Australia), September 8, 1989.

2. Charles Ward, "Soloist Is Uncommon Attraction for HSO," *Houston Chronicle*, October 9, 1983, sec. 3, 16.

3. Critic Joanne Talbot was taken with the creative collaboration between Frank Proto and François Rabbath after hearing the *Rabbath Plays Proto* recording: "Life would be dull without the colourful imaginations of artists such as Frank Proto, whose music fuses a heady mix of stylistic elements in a mesh of classico-jazz. . . . Nor is there any question of the

dexterity of François Rabbath, who nimbly travels the long fingerboard of the bass in flurries of exultant virtuosity. Perhaps the most effective work on the disc is the Fantasy for double bass and orchestra, where brilliant jazz improvisation merges with Indian-inspired folk music producing some original and fascinating sound combinations." Joanne Talbot, *The Strad*, https://www.liben.com/Reviews.html.

Edwin Barker, principal bassist of the Boston Symphony Orchestra, was impressed by the intentionality of François's playing: "François Rabbath's performances are at once sensitive and dynamic; it is the kind of playing that can easily inspire awe. His technical command is astounding. Rabbath's pronunciation of the phrases is done with exactitude and clarity, and his improvisational style contributes significantly to Proto's pieces." Edwin Barker, "Rabbath Plays Proto," *Bass World Journal* 13, no. 3 (1987): 57.

4. The process of bestowing a professorship in the Paris Conservatory is set by the French government. Two recognized experts in the field, one from France and the other from another EU country, are chosen by the government and are joined by three representatives from the administration of the conservatory to form the review panel. In the case of the double bass search, there were two open positions: a full-time tenure-track position and a part-time adjunct position. In an unexpected surprise, François was chosen as the French expert and was joined by Franco Petracchi from Italy. After the candidates had completed the audition process and the final vote was taken, François was shocked to learn that Thierry was not chosen for either position. In the judges' meeting, he asked Petracchi whom he had voted for—both had voted for Thierry. François confronted the panel and asked how they could possibly ignore the unanimous opinion of the experts in favor of bassists who, in their opinion, were not as qualified. At first the chair of the panel said that due to this development they would declare a failed search and repeat the process the following year. François's response was to say that he would not serve again, and as far as he was concerned, they would have to live with their poor decision. In a reversal, the chair took another vote, and Thierry was hired for the adjunct position. Within a short time, another double bass faculty member left the conservatory and Thierry's position became full-time.

5. In discussions with another musician familiar with the Paris Opera's chamber music event, it appears that there is another wrinkle to the story. It seems that Rollez, the author of the letter of complaint, had some time earlier performed the same Bottesini work at La Maison de la Radio with the acclaimed violinist Gérard Jarry, a faculty member

at the Paris Conservatory who was not a member of the Paris Opera Orchestra.

6. It was most likely James Conlon, who was the conductor of the contemporary work at the Opéra Comique.

Chapter 14: The Opera Years

1. Thierry Barbé and Louis Guilbert confirm many of François's stories, including those that follow: playing *Poucha-dass* during a short break in the ballet rehearsal while the orchestra waited in their seats (although Thierry does not recall Chung's invitation), shouting at the end of the rehearsal of Messiaen's *Turangalîla-Symphonie* in Italy, and demonstrating the crab technique for Zubin Mehta during the rehearsal of the famous passage in *La traviata* so the section would not have to play.

2. The Filipino critic Rosalinda Orosa was unprepared for the impact of François's recital: "Having fairly exhausted my superlatives for the Cleveland Symphony Orchestra, I thought I'd have no need of them so soon. . . . Rabbath unraveled, before an awestruck audience, not only the richness of the double bass as an instrument but also the integration of jazz and classical music for the unique enhancement of both idioms." Rosalinda L. Orosa, "A Phenomenal French Bassist," *Philippines Sunday Express*, March 7, 1982, 17.

3. François's performance of Frank Proto's Fantasy left a lasting impression on John Colwill: "Rabbath from France is one of the greatest string players of all time. His tone is incredibly rich and the nimbleness of his fingers matches the spring in his bow, a combination that creates pointed accuracy, more common to virtuoso violinists than solo bassists." John Colwill, "Rabbath a Delight," *Courier-Mail* (Brisbane, Australia), September 8, 1989.

4. While many critics are impressed by François's exceptional virtuosity on his chosen instrument, Stephen Pettitt was struck by the beauty of his tone and the ease of his playing: "Never have I heard the double bass sing as beautifully, and never have I encountered high harmonics, and indeed every sound-colour, produced so confidently and (usually) perfectly. . . . Still more uncanny, though, was the mellifluous ease and deep understanding with which Rabbath gave the slow movements from two Bach Cello Suites. Now that really was something incredible." Stephen Pettitt, "Astonishing Virtuosity: François Rabbath, Wigmore Hall," *Financial Times* (London), April 29, 1986.

Chapter 15: Barry & Ray

1. See Barry Green with W. Timothy Gallwey, *The Inner Game of Music* (New York: Doubleday, 1986).
2. Milt Hinton was the subject of a story on NPR's *Jazz Profiles with Nancy Wilson* in 2008. See "Milt Hinton: The Ultimate Timekeeper," *Jazz Profiles with Nancy Wilson*, NPR, November 12, 2008, https://www.npr .org/2008/11/12/96900242/milt-hinton-the-ultimate-timekeeper.

Chapter 16: Carmen & George

1. After François's recital in Winnipeg, critic Neil Harris wrote perhaps one of the more insightful reviews of his playing: "Rabbath is a phenomenon. He has been called one of the great string players of all times, and there was no one in the audience Tuesday evening who would doubt that. . . . In a few selections, it was if he was establishing that he could do anything that he wanted on this instrument, and, having established that, was anxious to move on to the effortless playing of extraordinarily beautiful music. . . . It would be fair to say that Rabbath is not a great composer, but he is a great composer for Rabbath." Neil Harris, "Rabbath Rewards Large Crowd," *Winnipeg Free Press*, August 14, 1991.
2. Charleston critic Claire McPhail came away from François's recital with a newfound appreciation for the double bass as a solo instrument: "I expected it to be rather dull, but to my amazement, I came away enthralled. . . . Not only did he give a remarkable display of talent as an instrumentalist, he gave the audience the added treat of hearing one of his own compositions, 'Reitba.' . . . Proto's 'A Carmen Fantasy for Double Bass and Orchestra,' in five sections, was heard first. It gave Rabbath even greater opportunity to display his virtuosity." Claire McPhail, "Double Bass Virtuoso Enthralls Audience," *Post and Courier*, April 4, 1993.
3. Neil Tarlton, "François Rabbath: Solos for the Double Bassist," *Double Bassist* 4 (1997): 79.
4. Echoing the sentiments of many critics, John Stafford's review from Tasmania was glowing: "The only word I can find to describe his performance is sensational. . . . Rabbath's technique is breathtaking; he plays with apparent ease, coaxing an amazing variety of sounds from the instrument. For example, playing melodies employing the harmonics of the instrument simply by use of the bow alone. In the midst of these original compositions, two exquisite pieces by Vivaldi and Bach." John Stafford, "Rabbath Proves Bass Is Sheer Beauty, No Beast," *The Mercury* (Tasmania), March 23, 1994, 37.

5. Caroline Emery first heard François perform in 1980 at Wigmore Hall and was taken with his complete virtuosity and ease of playing. Over the years, she heard him numerous times at international bass events, and she eventually went to Paris to take lessons. As she became an established teacher in London, she brought François as a guest to the Royal College of Music, the Bass Club, and—in an especially wonderful moment for François—the Menuhin School.

6. George Vance, interview with Henry Peyrebrune, October/November 2002.

7. Notable bassists who studied with George include Mike Kurth, member of the Atlanta Symphony Orchestra; Ted Botsford, member of the Los Angeles Philharmonic; Rex Surany, principal bassist of the Metropolitan Opera Orchestra; and Nina DeCesare, member of the Baltimore Symphony Orchestra.

Chapter 17: Family Life & Picasso's Picassos

1. David Douglas Duncan, *Picasso's Picassos* (New York: Ballantine, 1968).

2. "What do you think an artist is? An imbecile who only has eyes if he's a painter, ears if he's a musician, or a lyre in every chamber of his heart if he's a poet—or even, if he's a boxer, only some muscles? Quite the contrary, he is at the same time a political being constantly alert to the horrifying, passionate or pleasing events in the world, shaping himself completely in their image. How is it possible to be uninterested in other men, and by virtue of what cold nonchalance can you detach yourself from the life that they supply so copiously? No, painting is not made to decorate apartments. It's an offensive and defensive weapon against the enemy." Pablo Picasso to Simone Téry, *Les lettres françaises* 5, no. 48, March 24, 1945.

3. The critical reviews of Frank Proto's *Four Scenes after Picasso* recording praised both Frank's complex, evocative work and François's ability to bring the score vividly to life. British critic Alex Korda chose to focus on the composition: "Proto produces musical pictures in an effective and evocative work and although only using a chamber orchestra, is able to produce vivid, dramatic and violent textures when required. The music creates atmospheric and imaginative sound-scapes as he weaves the varying styles and moods together, and this work has more of a feeling of a tone poem than a concerto. The insistent use of snare drum produces a sinister and aggressive war-like feeling, and from 1939 onwards Picasso began voicing his thoughts through his art and reflected that painting is an instrument of war." Alex Korda, *British and International Bass Forum* (UK), 2001.

American bassist and critic Tom Knific was impressed not only by the piece, but by the transcendent synergy between Proto's piece and François's interpretation: "Rabbath's and the ensemble's performances are stunning throughout. The integrated nature of the music, which is not at all concertante in style, truly projects vivid images. This takes remarkable talent and execution from the performers, since they must collectively tell the story, something that is particularly demanding of the soloist, given the difficulty of his part. Rabbath succeeds in telling the story by bringing focus to the music and not to himself. *Four Scenes after Picasso* is perhaps the most substantial double bass orchestral project produced at the end of the twentieth century." Tom Knific, *Bass World Journal* 24, no. 3 (2001): 58.

The German critic Klaus Schruff, writing for the British publication *Double Bassist*, recalls François's historic relationship with Picasso and celebrates the creative musical relationship between Frank and François: "The relationship among the paintings which Picasso created in the years around World War II and the programmatic feel of the concerto is obvious. It was Rabbath himself who, on the occasion of Picasso's 90th birthday in 1971, wrote his composition *La Guerre et la Paix* (War and Peace) referring to the same cycle of paintings by Picasso, and here the circle closes again with the soloist meeting the composer with his new contribution to complete the picture [of sound]. . . . Rabbath is the perfect soloist for this music and many passages are obviously written into his hands with their unorthodox technique, reproducing much more than just notes—he seems to talk in music and is almost perfectly well accompanied by the orchestra." Klaus Schruff, *Double Bassist* (UK), 2001.

4. Jane Peters, concertmaster of the Rouen Philharmonic in northwestern France, came to François for lessons. She had learned about his bow technique from her husband, bassist Joe Carver, and wanted to learn more about the flexibility in his bow hand. François told her that he was scheduled to play a recital in her former home, Adelaide, Australia. After his recital was over and the audience was leaving, François could hear a woman speaking rather sharply with some students. François was a little nervous and thought she was not happy about something, maybe his playing. It turned out that it was Jane's former professor, Lyndall Hendrickson. She came up to François, smiling, and said, "Please forgive me, I was saying to them, the bow absolutely must be played like this!"

Chapter 18: Bach

1. The grand ballrooms at the Palazzo Zenobio can be seen in Madonna's 1984 "Like a Virgin" music video.
2. The Armenian Monastery of San Lazzaro, located on a Venetian island, was founded by monks who had fled persecution following the Ottoman invasion in the early eighteenth century. They purchased the Palazzo Zenobio in part to establish a center for the preservation of Armenian history. One of Minas's major projects had been capturing Armenian chants that had been historically passed down through an oral tradition. It had become clear that fewer young people were interested in the ancient chants, and many of the monks who knew them were becoming quite frail. The Biblioteca Zenobiana was endowed with special acoustic properties, and Minas began recording early Armenian and other ancient repertoire in the room. Minas and Ermanno were in the midst of a thirteen-year process to record and catalog over 150 eighty-minute audio CDs of ancient music, an archive that has since been recognized by UNESCO.
3. Also taking place at the Venice Bass Workshop were further refinements of the so-called "bent endpin." The French luthier Christian Laborie had the idea of drilling an angled hole in the bottom bout of the bass and using a straight wooden pin, rather than bending a traditional metal endpin. GP Cremonini and Nicholas Walker also collaborated on refining Christian's idea, and Walker was the first bassist to have an angled hole drilled in his bass to accommodate a straight wooden pin.
4. François recorded all the Bach Cello Suites at the same pitch as the cello with the exception of the Sixth Suite, which he played down a fifth so it would fit on the fingerboard of the double bass.
5. François's first recording of Bach was *Rabbath Plays Bach*, an LP released in 1982 on Frank Proto's Liben Music label.
6. Hubert Varron's preferred edition of Bach was made by Bazelaire.
7. After hearing Edgar Meyer's recital of the Bach First Suite at the 1984 ISB convention in Evanston, I had just such a conversation with Rodney Slatford. The great English bass pedagogue and professor at the Royal College of Music shared that a bassist could never interpret a Bach suite as beautifully as a cellist, so should seek alternate repertoire to perform. Fortunately, François never followed such advice.

Chapter 19: Paganini & Jazz

1. Honolulu critic Ruth Bingham was taken with François's mastery of the bass, heralding him as an intrepid protagonist: "François Rabbath took hold of the instrument on Sunday and transformed

it into a dashing hero a la Cyrano de Bergerac. Performing with the Honolulu Symphony, Rabbath was riveting, spell-binding, a poet with a lightning-fast touch (yes, on a string bass) and with dead-on intonation. . . . Rabbath performed the world premiere of *Nine Variants on Paganini*, the fifth concerto-like piece Frank Proto has composed for him. The performance was recorded to be broadcast on National Public Radio and was received with an enthusiastic standing ovation." Ruth O. Bingham, "François Rabbath Performs with Honolulu Symphony," *Honolulu Star-Bulletin*, March 29, 2002.

2. David Kettle was enthusiastic in his praise of the double recording of Frank Proto's *Nine Variants* and François's *Reitba*: "Two of the most eminent bassists around come together for what proves to be a thoroughly enjoyable, thrillingly played disc. . . . Rabbath is in the spotlight as soloist in all pieces, and also composer of the achingly beautiful, folk-inspired *Reitba*, which he delivers with a sense of freedom and spontaneity in its rapturous melodic line." David Kettle, "Double Takes from Two Leading Double Bassists," *The Strad*, January, 2014.

Chapter 20: Sylvain

1. François's recital in Minneapolis enraptured Pamela Espeland: "A near-capacity audience held its breath as the great musician, composer, and teacher François Rabbath played the double bass as if it were a string quartet: bass, cello, viola, violin . . . the music was almost unbearably beautiful." Pamela Espeland, *MinnPost Artscape*, April 17, 2012.

2. François returned to teach at the Kansas City Bass Workshops for several years and always gave a recital. Like Pamela Espeland in her 2012 Minneapolis review, Bill Brownlee heard François's virtuosity as if it were a string quartet: "The most impressive displays, however, were purely musical. Rabbath's bass sounded like two separate instruments as he played a call-and-response duet with himself. His rich tone and almost magical prowess caused his bass to occasionally resemble a full string quartet." Bill Brownlee, "French Bass Virtuoso François Rabbath Delivers a Masterful Performance," *Kansas City Star*, July 1, 2014.

Libby Hanssen likewise noted François's ability to create the illusion of more than one instrument, and was captivated by the breadth of his tonal palette: "François Rabbath's openhearted joy for playing the double bass transcends translation. . . . His style is so spontaneous and organic that it's difficult to tell where the written music leaves off and the improvisation begins. His technical ability is such that he sounds like a trio of one: bowing, plucking and hammering in an ever-flowing cascade of sound. He produces a range of timbres from raspy ponticello effects to a dark, resonant tone so profound it can be felt in one's own sternum at close range." Libby Hanssen, "Bassist François Rabbath Brings Spontaneous Joy to Parkland University Concert," *Kansas City Star*, June 24, 2015.

3. François's annual recital appearances at Domaine Forget became much-anticipated events in the region: "After yesterday's concert at the Sainte-Trinité cathedral, in the Classique & Compagnie series, it was obvious to everyone that François Rabbath is the greatest of double bass players, the one who knew how to raise his instrument to the level of the violin. His famous technique [is] so complete that it becomes a musical philosophy." Régis Tremblay, "Impressionnant François Rabbath!," *Le Soleil* (Quebec), May 6, 2003.

Coda

1. Although François rarely performs anymore, François and Sylvain have embarked on one last grand celebratory recording. The working title is *Rabbath and Friends,* and the project brings together many of the closest members of his musical family. The recording will feature famous collaborators such as Paco Ibáñez, Michel Legrand, and Benny Golson, as well as a long list of illustrious bassists that includes Ron Carter and Rufus Reid. As of this writing, a release date has not been announced.

For the Future

1. François, Randy Allen, and I were in California working on filming for the *Art of the Left Hand* DVD. We had just completed a stressful day shooting a set of live performances—François playing his virtuosic unaccompanied works in a San Luis Obispo recording studio—a day that had been interrupted by a computer failure and the loss of the morning's work. After a late night, we rose early and drove north in search of an interesting place to conduct an hour-long interview. We stopped at the historic Carlton Hotel in Atascadero for lunch and discovered that they had a nicely appointed back room we could use. François enjoyed flirting with the waitress, saying, "I can talk sweet to her, because I am old and she doesn't mind." She was kind enough to make sure we weren't interrupted, and she offered her pancake makeup to François to help reduce his forehead glare. He was relaxed after the large lunch and feeling talkative. After covering our scheduled questions, it occurred to me to ask François if there was anything he wished to say—perhaps something for the future.

Pedagogy

ncouraged by Jean Leduc to write a method book following his Maison de la Radio recital in 1973, François embraced the project with enthusiasm. His initial efforts were focused on his advanced techniques in the upper reaches of the double bass. Jean looked over his early submission and told François that the material was much too complicated to begin with. No one will understand what you are trying to do, he explained. You must start from the beginning.

It had been a decade since the release of his album *The Sound of a Bass*, and François knew that the techniques he had developed to play in the upper registers of the instrument were important and unique—no bassist he knew played like him. He had hoped to be able to bring his advanced techniques to the bass world to help bassists learn how to approach the upper register with ease. After careful consideration, François decided that Jean was correct, that "in order for me to bring students to play in this way, they must be brought up in this view from the beginning."

He went back to his well-worn copy of the Nanny *Méthode*, filled with his notes in the margins, and saw that like other methods he had seen, it began in the lowest register and then proceeded to introduce the higher registers of the instrument in a progressive manner. But François's aim was clear from the outset. In the preface to his *Nouvelle technique*, volume 1, he encourages bassists to strive to become soloists: "One must delve into the 'unknown regions' of the instrument and should shun any limitation to one's view of it. The instrument should set fire to the player's imagination."

Rather than the usual set of a dozen or so different positions found in the methods from the early twentieth century, François divided the fingerboard into only six positions, using the naturally occurring harmonics to define the lowest note of each position. It should also be noted that the earlier methods describe thumb position as a single position—the entire upper register above the octave harmonic is presented as a single position. The *Nouvelle technique* prescribes clearly defined positions for the entire length of the fingerboard.

François began in the lowest position and worked his way up the fingerboard, carefully labeling his positions and grouping notes according to the placement of the harmonic nodes. He divides the entire length of the fingerboard into six positions, three in the lower register and three in the upper register. Volume 1 of *Nouvelle technique de la contrebasse* (1977) is rather short—28 pages of music covering the lowest two positions, with scales, exercises, and melodic études and short pieces. Volume 2 (1980), significantly longer, is 55 pages of music and covers positions three and four, which includes the first thumb position above the octave harmonic. The volume covers the first thumb position with some rigor, requiring the left hand to extend the distance of more than a major third. In retrospect, François says that if he started the method today, he would begin students in thumb position. "The thumb position is in the middle of the instrument—it is the same distance up and down. Psychologically, this means that playing high is not difficult. You have done it already."

Volume 3 (1984) is the book that François had intended to write for Jean at the outset. At 122 pages of music, it is an intimidating text. In the preface he outlines his philosophy of movement, space, and time; the pivot motion; interpretation; the correct setup for the bass; posture; and more. Perhaps his most important point in the preface is "To be a concert performer, you must work like a concert performer." He shares that a concert performer must be able to play a two-hour recital; therefore a musician should develop endurance and focus in order to have the capacity to practice scales and arpeggios for two hours nonstop. The first half of the volume is devoted to some 120 scale fingerings for each key and over 200 bowing variations. The second half includes unaccompanied pieces, orchestral excerpts with advanced fingerings, and an introduction to the crab technique. As both Martine and Jack Goldzweig indicate elsewhere in this book, François was obsessed with this work.

Jack recalls that during his six weeks with François in the South of France, "He played for hours, working on every detail. He didn't get this from nothing." Rodney Slatford, the esteemed British bass pedagogue, reviewed volume 3 in the June 1985 issue of *The Strad*, noting that "perhaps, in the end, Rabbath's astonishing 'new technique' will influence, enrich and stimulate future generations of bass players. . . . For those who persevere and are open minded enough to adapt and absorb Rabbath's very personalized approach, the investment might prove one of the best they ever made."

Volume 4 (2012) revisits earlier études in higher positions and introduces challenging crab études. The balance of the volume is given over to a collection of unaccompanied works. Volume 5 (2015) is a collection of François's concert works for bass and piano. The original editions of volumes 4 and 5 feature François's original compositions—many of which were previously unpublished—and came with limited editions of the *Art of the Bow* and *Art of the Left Hand* DVDs. François completed volume 6, with additional technical studies, in 2018. However, the French publisher Leduc has been acquired by the Music Sales Group (now Wise Music Group), and there has not yet been a decision about its release.

Paul Ellison is constantly impressed by how universal the Rabbath method has become. "It all started with Rabbath coming to Cincinnati, thanks to Frank's idea and Barry making it happen. He had played his Carnegie concert, but the impact on the bass world from that concert was not anything compared to performing in conjunction with the ISB, where so many heard him. The kind of thing that happened in Cincinnati in the late 1970s impacted everyone. I mean, it's so pervasive and ubiquitous in everybody's concept. Only the most extreme dinosaurs are still playing the way they were in the '80s and even into the '90s. At first there was so much resistance. People were saying, 'You're going to hurt yourself' or 'That's only for soloists.' But that's gone now and François has become mainstream and is the father of modern bass playing in so many ways."

Pedagogy is often described as an instructional manual for teaching—the correct order of what must be done next to master technique. But the act of teaching, the way a teacher makes a student feel, is a more subtle art. At the 1997 ISB convention, Phillip Serna played in a masterclass for François Rabbath in the large Stude

Concert Hall at Rice University. Paul Ellison and François were seated on the stage, wearing lavaliere microphones in order to be heard in the room. The hall was packed with bassists from all over the world, and needless to say, Phillip was nervous. He began to play the Bourrées from the Bach Third Cello Suite, starting and stopping when he made a mistake or had a memory slip. After he stopped for the third time, François rose from his chair quietly, saying, "Just a moment, just a moment." And he went over to Phillip and gave him an amplified kiss on the cheek—the audience cheered and applauded.

François went on: "Everybody love you. Everybody." And then, gently: "But I think, I know that you play very good. I know that. I am sure about that, when I hear . . . but the position. You cannot play with the bass like this. You must have the opportunity to go here without problem and here without problem," he added, gesturing to areas on the fingerboard. "You have taken the bass in a way that has handicapped you."

Decades later, François recalled the moment: "Yes. And the more he made mistakes, the more he was stuck. I have a choice—to either save his life, because he is playing good, or I can be very powerful, I can take his bass and play perfectly and I show him like that? No, no. It's not the point. You must save his life because he is good. So what do I do? I kiss him. Yes. You see, all the people, you try to ignore them. They love you. They are not here to kill you. That means I show the people and I show him that we all know he was anxious and he was nervous. It's impossible to play like that. He must, in the future, learn how to relax and to play. That's all. But I proved to him and the other people that he is capable. He was nervous. But everybody in the hall was like that, anxious. Some people might be happy because they think they play better than him, but they don't think about being this man. He's playing for his life. So you must save him. How? You must approach each student differently. The role of professor is to help the people. It's not to kill them. Teach psychologically first; after, the rest. Each student is like a son. When your son is one year old and trying to walk for the first time, he falls down. You hate your son because they falls down? No, you help him, to teach him how he must walk. It's the same."

If François's unique performing abilities have completely altered the arc of bass history—to paraphrase Frank Proto, history will speak of the bass world before and after the impact of François Rabbath—then it is his compassionate and generous teaching that will cement his place in that history. François wrote and shared his ideas freely, not just from his own pen, but by assisting others along the same path, such as George Vance, whose *Progressive Technique* has continued to be the mostly widely used method in the United States and is frequently found in the bass studios of Europe and Asia. François traveled the world, sharing his insights, inspiring and nourishing young talent, from large groups of over one hundred bassists at a time to one-on-one lessons. He has given students the technical tools to enable them to play the bass freely, without encumbrance. His natural charisma and ability to temper much-needed directness with kindness to each student have helped establish a school of bass playing with a strong following among young students, amateurs, professionals, and teachers. It is these teachers of young bassists who will help ensure François's place in history.

I was studying with François during the summer of 2000, working on the bowing variations for scales in volume 3. I did not completely comprehend several of these strokes until I saw and heard François demonstrate. It was during my last lesson that François said, "This is my fear—that I will not be able to transmit my bow arm." I laughed and made a joke about the future potential for sharing his bow arm DNA for future generations, but his comment stayed with me.

I had made my way to the airport and boarded the plane. As I mulled over the problem, it occurred to me that if you look at a two-dimensional page of music, it is not as difficult to figure out what is intended for the left hand. Above each note, François gives you an indication of the finger to be used, and below each note, an indication of which string to play. It is possible to have an idea of what he intends, in the same manner that François used to teach himself where to find the notes on the fingerboard when he first started using the Nanny *Méthode* as a child. But there is no way for the page to truly indicate the motion of the bow or a sound.

Back on the plane, there was a mechanical problem; a part was needed. The pilot explained that it was the noon hour and the mechanics were on a lunch break. We could expect to wait for another forty-five minutes. I asked a flight attendant for something to read, and the only remaining magazine was a golf magazine. I don't play the game and was expecting to find little to interest me, but the magazine fell open to an article about a new Tiger Woods video game. There were numerous photos: Tiger on the golf course, Tiger in a skintight suit with reflective markers, and then the virtual video-game Tiger. The article claimed that the biomechanics animations used by the videographers had captured the realistic details of his stroke for the game. I had an epiphany: if they could capture Tiger's stroke, it would be possible to capture François's bow arm!

I returned to Ball State University and contacted the Human Performance Lab to see if they used biomechanics. They did. I brought my bass to the lab, and over a few months, they made a few preliminary videos that I could show François. On my next visit I excitedly showed François the normal videos and how the biomechanics animations transformed the video into a three-dimensional image that could be viewed from several angles. His response? "Why does your bow move like that? It needs to be more straight."

Fortunately François loves technology (he traveled then with two laptops and the latest Sony Ericsson cell phone; the iPhone wouldn't come out until 2007), and he was excited by the idea of making a DVD. I worked closely with my brother-in-law, Randy Allen, a videographer, and after five years of shooting, editing, and refining, the *Art of the Bow* DVD was finally released at George Vance's 2005 Rabbath International Institute in Washington, DC. The project features biomechanics animations, user-selectable camera angles, lecture demonstrations, live-performance footage, and interviews. It was as complete a study of François's bow arm as we could possibly envision within the limitations of the available technology and our budget. Our one regret was that we did not find a way to sync audio with the biomechanics animation system, so although there are many examples of him demonstrating strokes from different angles with audio, the biomechanics portion of the DVD is a silent motion study. François was thrilled with the DVD, and at the end of the workshop, when faculty, students, and parents were all gathered together, he announced, "This is fantastic!" and then, turning to me, "Now we must make the *Art of the Left Hand*!" The *Art of the Left Hand* two-DVD set took another five years to complete and was released in

2010. Both DVDs received critical acclaim. Sandor Ostlund reviewed *Art of the Bow* for the International Society of Bassists' *Bass World Journal* in 2006, shortly after the DVD's release, stating, "This DVD represents both a huge step forward for string pedagogy as well as an immensely valuable and inspirational tool for any double bass student or teacher." Cathy Elliott raved about both DVDs in the April 2012 issue of *The Strad*, declaring, "*Art of the Bow* and *Art of the Left Hand* are both packed with information delivered by an inspirational performer and teacher. Whether you are a keen amateur or a serious professional, no bass player's education is complete without having experienced Rabbath's demonstrations."

In the end, most importantly, François was delighted with the projects: "These DVDs explain my technique in a way a method book cannot."

Composition Stories

Dates are when the works were either published (written or recorded) or submitted to SACEM. Descriptions were either written by François (in quotes) or shared with the author.

———

À la Bach 1, 2, 3, 4, 5, 6 (2012; *Nouvelle technique*, vol. 4)

This piece is François's homage to Bach, to thank him for creating the six suites.

Basse en fugue No. 2 (Les gorgones) (1968; *François Rabbath No. 2* CD)

Basse en fugue No. 2 was for three bass parts and percussion.

Basses en fugue (1963; *The Sound of a Bass* CD)

Basses en fugue was recorded with two tracks for four bass parts. This was the theme for *Les tréteaux de la nuit* (Night Trestles), a radio show on Maison de la Radio in France, for more than twenty-five years.

Bitume (1963; *The Sound of a Bass* CD)

The famous detective author Auguste Le Breton asked François to write a piece called *Bitume*. Bitume is a crushed-stone covering on the street, like asphalt. It is also slang for "the streets." Le Breton said that he was a child of the streets. He coined the French term *rififi* (trouble) and used it in the titles of his books.

Briez (1972; *Multi-basse* CD)

The purpose of *Briez* is to produce (not imitate) the sound of a hurdy-gurdy (crank organ) or a vielle à roue. (François had one when he was six years old.) "Each Saturday we can go and see a movie. And I see a Spencer Tracy movie, *The Old Man and the Sea*. The sound of the movie soundtrack stayed with me. When I begin to work on double-stops, I begin to produce the sound in giving accents at each gesture like the crank. You must work to play the piece with an accent at the beginning of each bar. The vielle à roue is originally from Brittany, in the northwest of France. The name of Briez is the name of Britain in Brittany. I use the full range of the bass, with harmonics and double-stops. When you begin to play the natural harmonic in glissando on one string, we must hear each harmonic like fireworks (not an effect). Then, when the artificial harmonics appear, don't change the shape of the distance between the two notes as you glissando until the gesture repeats. The second time, use a smaller interval and a higher pitch will result. Keep moving your bow to different locations as you play the glissandi."

Chagall de basse (1973; Multi-basse CD)

Inspired by the painter Marc Chagall. The piece is dedicated to Ray Brown, and the opening is reminiscent of Mingus. It is for solo jazz pizzicato bass with percussion (Marcel Blanche, percussionist).

Chasse à cour (1990; Nouvelle technique, vol. 4)

Chasse à cour was written to protest against the morbid pleasure of the ancient tradition of the ceremonial fox hunt. The beginning illustrates several exchanges between two groups of hunting horns, one calling close by to announce the start of the chase, and the other responding from far way like an echo. Next, the dogs bark wildly as they run in pursuit of their quarry, and the horses gallop away as the hunting parties close in on their prey from both sides. François reflected, "Sadly, the animal is always the victim." The end of the piece quotes a phrase from the "Dragonetti" Concerto by Édouard Nanny (1872–1942), paying homage to the Paris Conservatory professor whose method François discovered and taught himself during his youth in Lebanon.

Classical Impromptu (1968; François Rabbath No. 2 CD)

Inspired by an impromptu of Chopin, but for the bass.

Clin d'oeil (1967; Nouvelle technique, vol. 4)

This piece is a collage of many musical ideas: short phrases, scales, and arpeggios, taken from a variety of sources. It is dedicated to Joe Carver, an American bassist now living and performing in France.

Concerto No. 1 (1967; Nouvelle technique, vol. 4)

Concerto No. 1 is an unaccompanied concerto. The work was originally used in the film *Salut á l'aventure*.

Concerto No. 2 (1973; Nouvelle technique, vol. 5)

"I wrote this piece for my Carnegie Hall debut in 1975. It was for piano, organ, drums, percussion, and double bass soloist. The piece is dedicated to the American classical and jazz bassist Hans Sturm."

Concerto No. 3 (1977; *Nouvelle technique*, vol. 5)

Concerto No. 3 was composed on November 30, 1977, and dedicated to Gary Karr in 2012. The piece takes its inspiration from the Concerto for Piano in A minor, op. 16 (1868) by Edvard Grieg (1843–1907). This work comprises two written-out cadenzas during the introduction and three continuous movements:

1. The first movement contains the exposition of the lyrical, singing main theme.
2. The second movement consists of a long improvisation in which the performer has free reign.
3. The third part is accompanied by various dance rhythms before the return of the main theme.
4. The second cadenza returns just before the final chord to finish this colossal work.

In the past, cadenzas were improvised by the unaccompanied soloist, but François wanted to change this tradition by giving performers the opportunity to express themselves over the piano's two chords.

Creasy course (1963; *The Sound of a Bass* CD)

Creasy course is a piece that mimics running "crazy fast" surrounded by lots of people.

Le cri de Venise (2015; *Nouvelle technique*, vol. 5)

"I composed this piece to express my concern when I learned that Venice is sinking a few millimeters into the mud each year. I later learned that government intervention was necessary to preserve the city. The beginning of the piece begins with a 'cry for help' of concern, followed by the melody which describes the beauty of Venice. I dedicated this piece to one of my students, GP Cremonini, who introduced me to this wonderful city, where I recorded six Bach suites in the small chapel in the Palazzo Zenobio. An unforgettable memory." The premiere was at a concert in Venice at the Palazzo Zenobio on April 21, 1999.

Cyril (1979; *Nouvelle technique*, vol. 3)

"I read in a medical journal that a fetus can perceive sound starting in the sixth month. I decided to attempt an experiment by composing a piece and playing it once a day beside my wife, Martine. So I made a recording of the piece to play softly during the birth. The experiment succeeded—when my son came into the world, he came smiling instead of crying. Thereafter, whenever he cried in his crib, I played him *Cyril*, which is the name of my son and also the piece, and while listening he immediately opened his eyes wide and stopped crying. This piece was composed around 1979, six months before the birth of my son Cyril. The harmonics of the beginning of the song, I played loud enough to catch his attention, and I play the double-stops pianissimo to create a rocking effect. The piece is a lullaby. The beginning of the piece must be played strongly to help the baby wake up (but not quickly)."

Désert (1963; *The Sound of a Bass* CD)
Désert is the first piece for bass and percussion composed by François for his first solo recording, *The Sound of a Bass* (1963). The novelist Auguste Le Breton chose this piece as the theme song for the radio adaptation of his popular novel *Rififi*.

Embruns (1967; *Multi-basse* CD)
"*Embruns* is a very beautiful piece for bass duo dedicated to Irena Olkiewicz, a Polish bass professor."

Emotion (1990; *Dialogues & Meditations* CD)
For solo saz. (The saz is a Persian instrument with three strings tuned in fifths: G, D, and A.)

Équation du temps (1970; *Multi-basse* CD)
"A student played the Koussevitzky concerto for me in a lesson and they had trouble with the end of the first movement. I felt I had to write something to help bassists to play the moving double-stops at the end of the first movement. I then built melodies around this theme. When you play the piece, it is important to think about the rhythm—it's not meant to be virtuosic, but very rhythmic. Remember it was composed with drums in mind. The piece was used in the film *Vaudou*."

Espoire (1990; *Live around the World* CD)
"*Espoire* is hope. I hope that one day they discover a cure (like penicillin) for cancer. My mother and father-in-law both died from cancer."

Étude de concert (Crabe no. 1) (1990; *Nouvelle technique*, vol. 4)
This is the first étude of a total of ten advanced études for the study of the crab technique. The piece is built around the crab system and is written in a more modern musical style. It is dedicated to the American bassist Sandor Ostlund.

Evasion (1990; *Dialogues & Meditations* CD)

"For three basses and saz. It begins with a sustained bass chord and the saz improvises above with choppy phrases. Once the groove is established, the saz accents the last eighth note of beat four to create an up feeling."

Exil (1963; *The Sound of a Bass* CD)

The piece is written from the point of view of one who is placed in exile, to have everything taken from them and not being allowed to return.

La guerre et la paix (War and Peace) (1971; *Live around the World* CD) (*Nouvelle technique*, vol. 4)

Pablo Picasso commissioned *La guerre et la paix* to celebrate his ninetieth birthday on October 24–25, 1971. He asked François to illustrate with a piece of music the two frescoes he had painted on the walls of a chapel in Vallauris in southwest France. Without being able to see the artwork because he lived in Paris, François envisaged the progress from war to peace in four contrasting sections:

1. The beginning depicts prewar negotiations: a conflict between two countries emerges, represented by two arguing voices, one accusing angrily and the second responding furtively.
2. The negotiations gradually disintegrate and the war begins. The metallic sounds of sirens announce a bombardment, an effect created when the bow plays sul ponticello near the bridge. The repeated sixteenth-note ostinato figure on the open A string that follows illustrates the sound of antiaircraft guns mixed with double-stops to show exploding bombs.
3. This cacophony grows in volume and intensity until finally stopping on a long harmonic A that announces the postwar mourning, with lyrical phrases that express grief and hope.
4. Since Picasso was Spanish, François imagined a grand finale, a celebration of peace, filled with Iberian songs and dances in addition to influences from the Middle East.

Alone in the chapel at Vallauris with the frescoes illuminated by candlelight, Picasso was moved to tears as he listened to François play the piece for the first time. *La guerre et la paix* received a standing ovation at its Parisian premiere at the Palais des Sports for an audience of five thousand people.

Hésitations (1963; *The Sound of a Bass* CD)

The piece is strong and gallops like a horse, but with hesitations—surprising places to slow down. François shares that the concept was to have fun with the drummer. The notes can always come a little after the beat—behind the beat.

Horda (1972; *Multi-basse* CD)

Horda was written for the movie *Vaudou*. The piece is used in one particularly striking scene. The villagers have a ritual where everyone in the village dances and one of the villagers goes into a trance. The piece has many overdubbed percussion tracks and as many as five bass parts, several playing the melody in unison and others creating the groove and adding special effects, including the howl of a wolf.

Ibérique péninsulaire (1970; *Live around the World* CD; *Nouvelle technique*, vol. 4)

François Rabbath performed this work for the first time at the Palais des Sports in Paris on June 1, 1971. This piece, dedicated to Paco Ibáñez (b. 1934), describes the story of a loving shepherd watching his sheep go to pasture on the mountain. In the first phrase of the piece, he shouts the name of his fiancée, but hears only his own voice returning as an echo from the mountainside. The second phrase is a beautiful melody played pianissimo in the low register of the bass, which describes his lovestruck state. The rhythmic phrase shows his joy as he dances like a whirling dervish, turning like a top until he falls to the floor, dizzy and happy.

Imagination (1990; *Dialogues & Meditations* CD)

For solo saz.

Impalas (1963; *The Sound of a Bass* CD)

"Inspired by the African animal the impala, running very fast."

Incantation pour Junon (1968; *Multi-basse* CD)

"Junon is a Roman goddess. The piece was used in the movie *La cage de Pierre* and is like a prayer."

L'infini Martine (2012; *Nouvelle technique*, vol. 4)

"This work was composed in 1986. I wanted to describe the beauty of my wife, Martine. I named the piece *Infinite Martine* because the piece is played with bariolage, with the bow constantly pivoting over the four strings, beginning and ending pianissimo."

Inspiration (1990; *Dialogues & Meditations* CD)

"For arco bass playing tag with the virtuoso Indian flutist Chaurasia, accompanied by tabla."

Kobolds (1963; *The Sound of a Bass* CD)

"The piece goes to many places. In mythology, a kobold is a small genie in the forest, like a leprechaun. The piece dances like a lively small wizard. Like a Gogol story. When I play this piece for young children, I am asked, 'Why do we become old?' and 'How do you deflate the bass to take it home?'"

Leitmotiv (2012; *Nouvelle technique*, vol. 4)

"*Leitmotiv* was inspired by the discovery that you can play a four-octave arpeggio without changing the position of your hand. It also explores the concept that you can use the same fingering for every scale in addition to many different fingerings for each scale and arpeggio."

Lise (1995; *Solos for the Double Bassist*, Liben Music)

"It is an homage dedicated to Frank Proto's wife, a wonderful pianist."

Maman Bahija (1975; *70* CD)

"A piece written for my mother. My heart goes out with her. The piece was featured in the film *Vanda Teres*."

Manteau de pluie (1967; *François Rabbath No. 2* CD)

"This is a coat for when it is raining, like a trench coat. In $\frac{5}{4}$, the piece features three bass parts: an arco melody, arco double-stop chords, and a pizzicato bass part with percussion."

Le mi dans le mille (2015; *Nouvelle technique*, vol. 5)

"*Le mi dans le mille* was composed for George Wellington, the wonderful bass teacher from Honolulu, Hawaii. I first met George at the International String Workshops when I was teaching as the guest of Gerald Fischbach. He was eighty years old and would come to my daylong workshops and ask me to come to Hawaii to give a masterclass. I always said, 'Maybe next year.' One day he asked me for my autograph for his daughter, Fumiko. He then took that autograph and wrote a letter above it on the same piece of paper saying that I agreed to come to Hawaii. It was so sweet, I couldn't refuse him. The piece is about hitting the bull's-eye."

Multiples facettes (1972; *Nouvelle technique*, vol. 3)

Formerly titled *Mouvement perpétuel*, *Multiples facettes* is a theme and variations, many ways of seeing the same idea.

Mutants d'eau pale (1973; *Multi-basse* CD)

For two basses and percussion. The piece was used in the film *Blood of the Voodoo.*

Nine Variants on Paganini (2001; *Premiere* CD) (2012; *Nouvelle technique,* vol. 4)

"Frank Proto wrote a piece for me entitled *Paganini Variants* using Paganini's famous theme. I noticed that after the opening statement of the theme, the variations went far away from the original. At the end I wanted to write a cadenza that would bring everyone back to Paganini and used the theme with a series of more traditional variations. I dedicated this to Dennis Trembly, the principal bassist of the LA Philharmonic."

Obsession (1990; *Dialogues & Meditations* CD)

For arco and pizzicato bass parts and two saz parts. It is modal music with an accompaniment of shifting timbres, with an effect almost like the folk instrument called a jaw harp.

Ode d'Espagne (1963; *The Sound of a Bass* CD) (2012; *Nouvelle technique,* vol. 4)

"Dedicated to Paco Ibáñez when I performed in the Palais des Sports. *Ode d'Espagne* shows that the bass can be played pizzicato lightly with the right hand like an Andalusian guitar by using all of the fingers of the right hand in order to produce a multitude of different sound." François also coined the word *progliato* to describe the technique of flicking the fingers in order and then lastly the thumb so that the nails hit against the strings, creating a percussive, rhythmic effect characteristic of flamenco dance music.

L'odyssée d'eau (1973; *Multi-basse* CD) (2015; *Nouvelle technique,* vol. 5)

L'odyssée d'eau for double bass and piano was written to protest against whale hunting. The piece was used in the film *Vaudou.* Even before whales were recorded underwater, François imagined the sound of their calls and imitated them with the high, whistling sounds of artificial harmonics on the double bass. When a recording of actual whale calls was released, the sound of the whales closely resembled the sounds he had imagined. The beginning of the piece depicts the preparation of the hunting boats with radar and sirens as the bass plays on its highest string. The boats arrive among a group of whales and begin to search out a victim. The hunters shoot a harpoon into one of the whales at the moment when the piano first enters with a pained pulsation that accompanies a singing melody in the bass, symbolizing the victim's suffering. Suddenly, the bass begins a fast, accented ostinato that represents the efforts of the other whales to save their wounded comrade from her agony by leading her away from the murderous boat; but they try in vain, and the harpooned whale dies with the last gesture of the piece. As François says, "Guess which animal is the most bloodthirsty of them all . . ."

Olivier (1976; 70 CD)

"*Olivier* is an homage to my first son. It is for bass and percussion. The glissandi in double-stops represent his crying, and the hesitations and blues phrases in the melody are the arguments, but the groove of life continues with a jazz feel in $\frac{12}{8}$ and the low notes are my feelings as a father—I understand."

Ordis (1984; Nouvelle technique, vol. 3)

"*Ordis* is an homage for Paganini in his style. I use a variety of bow strokes: sautillé, jeté, spiccato, portato, etc."

Papa Georges (1975; Multi-basse CD)

"*Papa Georges* is an homage to my father. It is an oriental piece for bass and percussion and was used in the film *Vanda Teres*."

Plus que perpétuel (2012; Nouvelle technique, vol. 4)

François's version of Paganini's *Perpetual Motion*. To work on the fingering, use a legato bow stroke and then play in sautillé.

Poucha-dass (1968; Multi-basse and Live around the World CDs, Nouvelle technique, vol. 4)

Poucha-dass, inspired by Ravi Shankar, imitates the sounds of the sitar and the tambura. *Poucha-dass* was originally published in 1979 by Liben Music Publishers in *Solos for the Double Bassist*. It has also been published by Leduc in volume 4 of the *Nouvelle technique*. Throughout this piece, the bassist plays against the normal physical aspects of handling the bow, by increasing the speed of the arm and by reducing its weight while still moving it close to the bridge to play sul ponticello in order to obtain harmonics above the fundamental notes.

Prades (1975; Live around the World CD, Nouvelle technique, vol. 4)

"*Prades* is an homage for Pablo Casals for solo double bass, but not in a classical sense. I like to thank him for letting us know about the Bach suites. He was the first for the cello to make the suites better known. They became famous and popular because of him."

Prelude á l'archet (1963; *The Sound of a Bass* CD)

"I wrote this piece for the shah of Iran after our trio played for him in the courtyard of his estate. Since it was a gift to the shah, it has been deposited into the treasury of the Iranian people. It is a duo for two basses, one playing bariolage and the other artificial harmonics."

Les quartes petit Suisses (2012; *Nouvelle technique*, vol. 4)

"Switzerland is so small. I once rented a house in Switzerland from a police officer. He told me that they won the war. I said, 'But you never fought.' His response was, 'We won because we did not accept any refugees.' It was a strange conversation. As we were talking, a supersonic jet passed overhead. Moments later, another passed in the opposite direction. I thought, maybe it was the same plane and Switzerland is as small as this man's ideas. *Les quartes petit Suisses* is dedicated to my dear friend and colleague George Vance."

Que c'est triste les vacances sans toi (2015; *Nouvelle technique*, vol. 5)

"It's a bass quartet. This piece came to me in a dream. I woke up and just wrote it down directly."

Que ferait Jacques (2012; *Nouvelle technique*, vol. 4)

"The children's song 'Frère Jacques' used to drive me crazy, so I created a set of variations to create a nightmare and remove the angst of playing difficult pieces on the bass. I end with the theme in minor, like the Mahler solo. It's a very virtuosic piece."

Refexion (1990; *Dialogues & Meditations* CD)

For solo saz, with a strong Indian influence of the sitar with quarter tones.

Reitba (1990; *Nouvelle technique*, vol. 5; *Two Miniatures*, Liben; *Carmen!* and *Live Round the World* CDs)

"*Reitba* was composed in Africa during a concert tour. A few kilometers from Dakar there is a salt lake called Reitba with a distinctive pink color. Because of the wind, it forms around the lake a foam two meters high and one meter wide. Seen from afar, it looks like snow and it's like a mirage. At the beginning of the song, to illustrate the movement of the waves, I used the two bass strings of the bass alternated with a fundamental phrase of the piece. The second part consists of two different melodies, accompanied by arpeggiated chords and improvisation that will be supported by an unchanging piano rhythm and which illustrates the beauty of the lake. The third part, resulting in the rise of a phrase that ends in the extreme low register, illustrates the short sandstorm raging unexpectedly for thirty seconds and suddenly disappears. The song ends by playing again on the two bass strings, but this time supported by a repeated note played in the bass of the piano, to illustrate the clinking of a bell in the distance. The track ends with the lowest note of the bass supported by a final chord. *Reitba* is dedicated to Australian bass professor Ken Poggioli."

Requiem for Goa (1965; *François Rabbath No. 2* CD)

A piece for a mythological god.

Rhapsody for Double Bass (1964; *François Rabbath No. 2* CD)

Rhapsody was composed in 1964. The piece was recorded for François's second disc for Philips and later dedicated to Ted Botsford, bassist with the Los Angeles Philharmonic. François composed this expansive piece to show the expressive capacities of the bass and to fulfill the need for more solo bass repertoire. The opening of the piece is taken from *La guerre et la paix*, but then is developed in new directions.

Samir (1968; *Nouvelle technique*, vol. 5)

"Samir is my nephew. He was the youngest to attain the rank of capitan of Singapore Airlines at age thirty-eight. When he was a baby, he had asthma. I bought him a small toy and he began to exercise with the toy and the asthma begin to go away. He loved to dance every time I played the bass. *Samir* was used in the movie *Salut à l'aventure*."

Sete-quate (1967; *Live around the World* CD, *Solos for the Double Bassist*)

"The name of this piece is a pun. In French, *Sete-quate* looks like $\frac{7}{4}$, but also sounds like 'seven cats.' It is not exactly in $\frac{7}{4}$, but I like to say it is a complicated confusion. This piece was used in the film *Salut à l'aventure*."

Siciliennes 1–4 (2012; *Nouvelle technique*, vol. 4)

"You can play all four of these short pieces together, individually, or paired—as you wish. When I was performing these years ago, my accompanist, Alain Bernard, said to me, 'These pieces are Sicilienne!'"

Souviens-toi des douze peupliers (1969; *Nouvelle technique*, vol. 5)

Dedicated to Cielito de Jesus, a bass teacher in Los Angeles, the piece is about twelve different types of the poplar tree, like the aspen. It is a very melodic song and was used for the movie soundtrack of *Le bateau sur l'herbe*.

Supremum vale (1965; *François Rabbath No. 2* CD)

"It is a modern piece. I describe the heart, when the heart beats irregularly, and the anxiety of the person who has the irregular beat. For two basses, one pizzicato and one arco, with percussion."

Sylvain (2012; *Nouvelle technique*, vol. 4)

"I describe my son Sylvain. When he was a baby and I yelled at him once, he would cry but couldn't breathe clearly. The piece describes a kind of crying with a hiccup. The middle section is Sylvain's crying. The fast runs are him running around like a crazy boy with lots of energy."

Thanatos (1984; *Nouvelle technique*, vol. 3)

Written for François's father-in-law. The opening in bariolage describes the progress of a cancer as the cells degenerate. The dissonance represents the illness.

Thyossane (1968; *Multi-basse* CD)

For two basses and percussion. Used in the film *Vaudou*, the piece features very fast tremolo.

Timbre phrasé (2012; *Nouvelle technique*, vol. 4)

"The piece is to demonstrate how a phrase changes when you play the same idea on different strings. You use the different colors of the strings to shape the music. I created the piece to show how each string can be used as a different voice—don't just play on one string."

Trombes d'eau (2017; *Trombes d'eau*, Leduc)

"This piece was composed for the ISB 2017 competition. The main theme describes three water funnels which I saw rise up out of the sea into the sky.

"The piece consists of five themes and their variations:

> First variation: the use of differing double strings.
> Second variation: a phrase repeated over several octaves and on different strings.
> Third variation: the use of different bow strokes.
> Fourth variation: play the full length of the key.
> Fifth variation: using artificial harmonics on the four chords."

Variations sur trois cordes (1965; *Nouvelle technique*, vol. 4; *François Rabbath No. 2* CD)

The piece is a set of pizzicato variations across three strings. The piece is dedicated to the great jazz bassist Lynn Seaton.

Variation sur un accord (1977; *Nouvelle technique*, vol. 4)

Dedicated to Ali Yazdanfar, principal bassist, Montreal Symphony, this piece is an homage to Bottesini. It is a set of variations on one of the arpeggios taken from the Bottesini *Gran duo concertante* for bass and violin.

Vera (1966; *Nouvelle technique*, vol. 5)

"*Vera* was music I composed for a short film, about a beautiful young woman with long blond hair running across a wheat field, by Francis Morane. For bass and harp, the piece is dedicated to Madeleine Crouch, executive director of the ISB."

Violette and Arthur (2012; *Nouvelle technique*, vol. 4)

"Violette and Arthur are my grandchildren. I wrote this to show how the bow can be used many different ways. It is dedicated to Los Angeles bass professor David Young."

Voyage (1984; *Nouvelle technique*, vol. 3)

"It is a trip that came to me. There are two different aspects of the bow and left hand. It features the rhythm of the train. You must know that each note can have a harmonic under the fingered pitch. I imagine in this train a kind of yodeling. You travel through different countries and landscapes."

Walpurgis (1963; *The Sound of a Bass* CD)

This piece depicts the night of vampires, very scary.

Western à la Breughel (1963; *The Sound of a Bass* CD)

The piece was inspired by classic Western movies, but as if the movie were instead a painting by the artist Breughel.

Publications and Awards

Original compositions listed in SACEM.

Film Scores

Vera (Francis Morane, 1966)
La cage de Pierre (1967)
Ballade pour un chien (Gérard Vergez, 1967)
Ténèbres (Claude Loubarie, 1969)
Le bateau sur l'herbe (Gérard Brach, 1970)
Vaudou (Jean-Luc Magneron, 1973)
Vanda Teres (Jean-Marie Vincent, 1975)
Vincent mit l'âne dans un pré et s'en vint dans l'autre (Pierre Zucca, 1975–76)
Une femme au bout de la nuit (1979)
Bad Timing (Nicolas Roeg, 1980)
Ana non (Jean Prat, 1985)
Eureka (Nicolas Roeg, 1989)
La goutte d'or (Marcel Bluwal, 1990)

TV Film Scores

Mme Bontemps et le diable (1968)
Salut à l'aventure (1968)
Le roman de Renart (1969)
France Québec (1969)
Le diable de Buridan (1969)
Brueghel (1970)
On n'épouse pas le diable (1970)
Omer Pacha (1971)
La lumière noire (1972)
Rue de Buci (1972)
Des lauriers pour lilas (1974)
Héritage (1996)

Theater Scores

Corneille, *La toison d'or* (Jean Serge, 1963)
Molière, *L'avare* (Claude Piéplu, 1967)
Ionesco, *Le tableau* (Pierre Peyrou, 1968)
Arnold Wesker, *Les quatre saisons* (1968–69, reprised 1972, 1984)
Serge Ganzl, *Le Quichotte, chevalier d'errance* (1973–74)

Solo Recordings

The Sound of a Bass (Philips, 1963)
François Rabbath No. 2 (Philips, 1965)
Collection: *La pensée universelle, No. 2 : Jésus-Christ amour – Revolte*
    (PES, 1971)
François Rabbath au Palais des Sports de Paris (Emen, 1971)
Multi-basse (Emen, 1973)
Sazmorphosis (Emen, 1978)
Toulaï et François Rabbath (Arion, 1980)
Rabbath Plays Bach (QCA Red Mark/Liben, 1982)
Hommage à Nazim Hikmet (Arion, 1982)
60 (Emen, 1990)
70 (Emen, 1990)
Dialogues and Meditations (Emen, 1990)
Live around the World (Emen, 1990)
Bach, Vivaldi, Bizet, Rabbath (Emen, 1995)
Carmen (QCA Red Mark/Liben, 1995)
François Rabbath en concert: Contrebasse & orchestre (Emen, 1995)
Turkey: The Song of Poets (Arion, 1998)
François Rabbath: In a Sentimental Mood (King Records, 2004)
Bach: Suites pour violoncelle seul à la contrebasse (Solstice, 2012)
Paganini (QCA Red Mark/Liben, 2013)
Rabbath and Friends (in production)

Pedagogical Multimedia

CD-ROM: *François Rabbath, la contrebasse: La nouvelle technique; Un
    maître, un instrument* (Label Image,1998)
DVDs: *Art of the Bow* (Avant Bass, 2005)
        Art of the Left Hand (Avant Bass, 2010)

Music Publications

Nouvelle technique de la contrebasse, 5 vols. (Alphonse Leduc, 1977–2015)
Solos for the Double Bassist (Liben, 1979, rev. 1995)
Concerto No. 3 (Liben, 1987)
Two Miniatures (Liben, 1992)
Trombes d'eau (Leduc, 2017)

Awards

ASTA 2006 Isaac Stern International Award (nominated by Gerald Fischbach)

The Isaac Stern International Award has only been given a total of fourteen times since 1964, when the first one was given to the founder of the famed Suzuki Violin School, Shinichi Suzuki. In 2006, Rabbath became the only bassist to have won the honor. Other award winners include such luminaries as violinists Nathan Milstein, Henryk Szeryng, and Itzhak Perlman and cellists Mstislav Rostropovich and Janos Starker.

ISB 1999 Performer Award
ISB 2001 Classical Performance
ISB 2003 Distinguished Achievement Award
ISB 2005 Composition
ISB 2009 Teaching
ISB 2021 Humanitarian Award

Solo Concert History

oncert dates were taken from François's date books. Given the length of history, it was not possible to verify the majority of dates from additional sources except for those events for which a concert review or program exists. There were several discrepancies, including the 1985 touring for Action Artistique to Asia and the 2000 premieres for Proto's *Nine Variants*, which Frank Proto confirmed took place in 2001. There are most certainly others.

1963	France	Paris, Théâtre de l'Ambigu, February 2
		Paris, Théâtre des Capucines, October 8
1964	Belgium	Brussels, Théâtre 140, February 19–23 (Barbara Mouloudji)
	France	Paris, Television: *Mi figue mi raisin*, October 12
1965	France	Paris, Television: *En passant par Paris*, March 19 (Impalas)
		Paris, Television: *Bienvenue chez Guy Béart*, November 2
1967	France	Paris, Television: *Bienvenue chez Guy Béart*, January 27
		Paris, Television: *Samedi et compagnie*, April 28
		Paris, Musée d'Art Moderne, October 7
1968	France	Paris, Château de Maisons-Laffite, Ecole Française des Attachés de Presse, March 19 (festival concert featuring Moody Blues)
		Paris, Television: *Bienvenue chez Guy Béart*, April 12 (Ivry Gitlis)

**Tour of Paris suburbs: Dutronc and Ballet
Béjart, December 4–22)**

Fontenay aux Roses
Puteaux
Rosny joue Bois
Aubervillier
Montrouge
Maison Alfort
Vittry
Cachan
Champigny
Asnières-sur-Seine
Bonneuil-sur-Marne
Épinay-sur-Seine
Ivry-sur-Seine
Tremblay-lès-Gonesse

Paris, Television: *Le nouveau dimanche*, May 5
(*Sete-quate*, *Kobolds*)

1969 France   Paris, Television: *Samedi et compagnie*, October 4

1971 France   Paris, Palais des Sports, June 1–3

Paris, Television: Cognacq-Jay Museum, June 6

Arles, June 27

Vaison la Romaine, June 30

Tropez, Musée de l'Annonciade, September 4

Nantes, September 25

Arcachon, October 15

Montbéliard, October 16

Paris, Paris Cité Universitaire, October 17

Vallauris, October 24 (Picasso celebration with
Neruda, Ibáñez, Duclos)

Paris, Palais des Sports (Picasso celebration),
October 25

Paris, Television: *Samedi pour vous*, October 30
(*Poucha-dass*)

	South American tour with Paco Ibáñez
Chile	Santiago, Estadio Nacional (Allende anniversary), November 4
Argentina	Buenos Aires, Teatro Gran Rex, November 11
	La Plata, Club Atenas, November 13
	Rosario, Auditorio Fundación Astengo, November 14–15
	Santa Fé, Teatro Cine Ideal, November 17
	Cordoba, Gran Teatro de Cordoba, November 18
Peru	Lima, Teatro Municipal, December 7
Colombia	Bogotá, Teatro de Cristóbal Colón, December 15
	Medellín, Teatro Pablo Tobón Uribe, December 17
	Cali, Teatro Municipal Enrique Buenaventura, December 18
1972 **France**	Paris, Radio: ORTF* *Samedi France culture d'une guerre*, January 15–16

	Tour of France with Paco Ibáñez
	Orleans, February 1, 9
	Nancy, February 17
	Clermont-Ferrand, February 23
	Paris, Television: *Télé-midi*, February 28
	Strasbourg, RTL Television, February 29
	Besançon, March 1
	Paris (Denise Glaser), March 4
	Amiens, March 10–11
	Neuchâtel, Cité Universitaire, March 16
Switzerland	Genève, March 18
France	Paris, Théâtre de la Cité Internationale, March 19
	Morlaix, Théâtre de la Culture, March 22
	Brest, Maison de la Culture, March 23
	Nevers, March 25
	Paris, Television: *Un ton au-dessus*, March 28

---

* Office de Radiodiffusion-Télévision Française, national French radio

Belgium	Brussels, Théâtre 140, April 19–23 (with Paco Ibáñez)
France	Mulhouse, April 24
	Orly, Le Gymnase, May 6
	Paris, ORTF, May, 7 (solo recital and dialogue about Picasso, *La guerre et la paix*)
	Paris, Marcadet, May 9
	Metz, May 20
	Paris, Television: CNIT, Salon International Radio Television, June 4
	Paris, Radio: *Directe de chez moi*, June 8
	Paris, Radio: ORTF Studio 140, France Culture au Théâtre, July 11 (live broadcast solo concert with two percussionists, organ)
	Paris, Ecole Normale, June 19
	La Courneuve, Fête de l'Humanité, September 10
	Rennes, October 15
Argentina	Buenos Aires, Teatro Opera, October 30 (two percussionists, organ)
France	Paris, Théâtre du Ranelagh, November 15–21
	Le Havre, Maison des Jeunes et de la Culture, December 1–9 (Discover the Double Bass concert series)
	Reims, Maison de la Culture André Malraux, December 19
1973 **France**	Toulouse, March 20
	Colombes, March 27
	Lyon, Palais d'Hiver, April 7
	Paris, Television, April 12–13
	Paris, Palais des Sports, 6 Heures pour l'Espagne, April 14 (fundraiser for Spain with Arrabel, Ibáñez)
	Hérouville, April 26
	Le Mans, Théâtre Municipal du Mans, May 4 (with Paco Ibáñez)

Paris, Radio: ORTF Studio 105, May 14–15 (the evening François met Martine)

Villepreux, Val de Gally, May 26

Toulon, August 2

Ollioules, Châteauvallon, August 3

Paris, Sainte-Chapelle, Eighth Paris Summer Festival, August 7 (all-Bach program, two recitals, 6 p.m. and 8 p.m.)

Paris, Television: *Bienvenue chez Guy Béart*, August 21 (with Ivry Gitlis)

Paris, Television: Buttes-Chaumont, September 5

Bagneux, September 22

Châteaubriant, October 21

Paris, Fréquence Protestante, *L'antènne est a vous*, October 24

Paris, Bobino, October 30–November 18 (small group)

Nanterre, Television, December 9

1974 Belgium   Brussels, Radio-Télévision Belge, national radio/television network, January 29

France   Aulnay-sous-Bois, Centre Culturel à Aulnay sous Bois, February 1

Paris, 44 rue de Rennes, February 12

Niort, Les Deux Seves, February 15

Corbeil-Essonnes, March 2

Le Péage-de-Roussillon, Salle des Fêtes, March 8

Saint Médard en Jalles, Centre Culturel, April 11

Paris, Théâtre National de l'Est Parisien, April 19–20 (solo bass with two percussionists)

Paris, Palais des Sports, 6 Heures pour l'Espagne, April 27 (Béart, Gréco, Ibáñez)

Italy   Milan, Castello Sforzesco, July 22–23 (with Ibáñez)

	France	Paris, L'Olympia, Hootenanny, November 29 (with Ivry Gitlis, Michel Legrand, Paco Ibáñez)
		Évreux, December 6
		Montrognon, December 7
1975	**USA**	New York, Carnegie Hall, March 13 (New York debut with Coleman, Ibáñez, Yakim, Stone, Legrand)
		Boston, Harvard, Cabot Hall, March 24 (with Antonio Membrado, guitar)
	France	Reims, March 6
		Lyon, September 4
		Saint-Étienne, September 5
		Paris, Salle Gaveau, October 12 (world premiere of Laurent Petitgirard Concerto for Double Bass, Violoncello Concertante, and String Orchestra)
		Bagneux, October 16
		Paris, Carré Thorigny, November 20
1976	**France**	Paris, Petit TEP, January 6 (voices, bass, Turkish flute)
		Paris, Carré Thorigny, February 26
		Chateauvallon, June 27
		Saint-Rémy-de-Provence, August 3
		Villeneuve-lés-Avignon, Chartreuse, July 29–August 8 (based on Middle Eastern poems, with voice, piano, bass, and actors)
		Paris, Grand Théâtre, Cité International Universitaire, November 5 (Indian flute, sitar, double bass/saz)
		Paris, Salle Pleyel, November 21–23 (solo recitals featuring Bach Suites, Vivaldi, and originals)
1977	**France**	Paris, Église des Billettes, February 3 (Vivaldi, improvisation)
		Paris, Television: *Drôle de dessin*, April 2

	England	London, Wigmore Hall, May 14 (London debut, with Jean-Pierre Jumez, guitar)
	France	Rennes, Maison de la Culture, May 20
		Paris, Centre Américain, June 25
		Paris, Television: *Métro mélodie*, September 5 (*Breiz*)
	Spain	Madrid, Feria del Campo, October 15–16
	France	Vaudreuil, Association d'Animation Culturelle Vaudreuil-Soulanges, December 8
1978	**France**	Paris, Television: *Les clés de la musique* Le Contrebasse, March 22 Le Saz, April 19
		Paris, Palais des Arts, May 17–20
	Germany	Berlin, French Institute of Berlin, May 27
	USA	Cincinnati, Ohio, ISB summer course, June 26–July 23
	Luxembourg	Luxembourg, Royal Juillet Musical Saint-Hubert l'Oréal Recogne, July 23
	France	Paris, Television: *Ciné musique, Lalo Schiffrin*, October 2
		Paris, Galeries La Fayette, Exposition France, October 9
		Paris, Palais des Arts, November 6 (saz and double bass with vocalists)
		Paris, Television: *Ciné musique, Nina Rota*, December 4
1979	**Denmark**	Sorø, Sorø Klosterkirke, 10th International Organ Festival, July 4 (with Ilse Maria Reich, organ)
		Dronninglund, Dronninglund Kunstcenter, Vendsyssel Festival July 10–11
	USA	Cincinnati, Ohio, ISB summer course, June 25–July 22
	Spain	Barcelona, Plaça del Rei, La Mercé Festival, September 21–24 (with Pi de la Serra, guitar)

	France	Béziers, Théâtre Municipal, December 5
		Pau, Centre Culturel Le Parvis, December 6
		Paris, Television: *Noël dans la lumière de l'abbaye de Bec-Hellouin*, December 24
1980	France	Aubervilliers, Théâtre La Commune, June 13
	USA	Cincinnati, Ohio, ISB summer course, July 12–August 8
	England	London, Royal College, October 9 (Rodney Slatford)
		London, Wigmore Hall, October 10
1981	Denmark	Copenhagen, Tivoli Koncertsal, July 18 (Proto Concerto No. 2 with Tivoli Symfoniorkester, Frans Rasmussen, conductor)
	Spain	Ordis, Plaça de l'Església, August 22 (Jordi Sabatés, piano)
	USA	Cincinnati, Ohio, Music Hall, November 20–21 (Proto Concerto No. 2 with Cincinnati Symphony Orchestra, David Stahl, conductor)
1982	Philippines	Manila, Little Theater, Cultural Center of the Philippines, March 1
	Taiwan	Taipei, Sun Yat-sen Memorial Hall, Third International Arts Festival, February 22
	France	Paris, Auditorium du FNAC Forum, February 29
1983	France	Paris, Foyer du Théâtre de Paris, May 11 (with Bridgette Vandôme, piano)
		Paris, Opéra Comique, Salle Favart, June 1 (televised recital, Bach Suite No. 1, Bottesini *Gran duo concertante*, Schubert "Trout")
		Paris, Église Saint-Eustache, June 12 (with Alain Bernard, piano)
	Denmark	Svendborg, Valdemars Slot, Musikfestival, August 8 (with Frans Rasmussen, piano)
		Copenhagen, Tivoli Koncertsal, August 9 (with Frans Rasmussen, piano, and Johnny Sølvberg, continuo)

	USA	Houston, Texas, Jones Hall, October 8–9 (world premiere Proto *Carmen Fantasy* with Houston Symphony Orchestra, Sergio Comissiona, conductor)
		Houston, Texas, Sheppard School of Music, Rice University, October 12 (with Katherine Collier, piano)
1984	**Sénégal**	Dakar, Centre Culturel Français, April 23
	France	Laudun-l'Ardoise, Château de Lascour, August 5–12
1985	**Australia**	Canberra, March 12
		Melbourne, no date given
		Brisbane, no date given
	France	Paris, Théâtre de Paris, January 14 (Laurent Petitgirard, conductor/composer)
	Nigeria	Lagos April 13
	Bénin	Lomé, no date given
	Côté d'Ivoire	Abidjan, no date given
	Sierra Leone	Freetown, April 16
	Sénégal	Dakar, April 20 (where François composed *Reitba*)
	Mauritania	Nouakchott, April 25
1986	**France**	Parthenay, March 6
	England	London, Wigmore Hall, April 27 (Susan Bradshaw, piano)
	Czech	Prague, French Embassy, June 11
	Spain	Barcelona, Plaça del Rei, June 27–29
	France	Paris, Église Saint-Louis en l'Ile, July 21–25
		Rennes, Maison de la Culture, November 20 (Proto *Carmen Fantasy* with Orchestre Métropolitain de Rennes, conductor, Claude Schnitzler)

1987 **France**   Rouanne, April 2

Paris, Théâtre des Champs-Élysées, May 11

Paris, Espace Cardin, June 6 (improvisation with Pandit Hariprasad Chourasia)

Prades, International Double Bass Festival, July 6–18

Bécherel, Église de Longaulnay, Premier Festival du Pays du Bécherel, July 21

Bécherel, Église Saint-Ouen (Les Iffs), Premier Festival du Pays du Bécherel, July 22

Paris, Sainte-Chapelle, August 23, 25

Canada   Quebec, Domaine Forget, August 7

France   Paris, Sainte-Chapelle, August 23–26

1988 **Portugal**   Lisbon, Radio, June 21

Lisbon, Institut Français du Portugaise, June 22

France   Bourges, Salle du Duc Jean de Berry, April 7

Rennes, Radio: FR3, July 2 (with Orchestre Métropolitain de Rennes)

Bécherel, Église Saint-Pierre de Miniac-sous-Bécherel, Festival du Pays, July 16

Bécherel, Église Saint-Thomas, July 24

Flaine, Festival de Musique, August 13

Paris, Auditorium des Halles, September 27 (Proto *Carmen Fantasy* with Orchestre Métropolitain de Rennes, Claude Schnitzler, conductor)

USA   Los Angeles, UCLA, August 27

Spain   Madrid, Alcalá de Henares, November 2–6

1989 **France**   Paris, Salle Gaveau, January 22

Paris, Théâtre Mogador, April 10

Paris, Television: TV5Monde, Le Grand Échiquier: *Les printemps de Béjart*, April 24 (with Paco Ibáñez)

	Australia	Perth, July 9
		Adelaide, July 12
		Melbourne, July 19
		Canberra, July 30
		Sydney, Radio: ABC3, August 8
		Sydney, Sydney Conservatorium, Joseph Post Auditorium, August 10
		Sydney, Radio: Radio 2 MBS-FM, August 24
		Brisbane, Queensland Conservatory, August 24
		Tewantin, Noussa Art Gallery, September 1
		Brisbane, ABC Music Center, September 6 (Proto *Carmen Fantasy* with Queensland Symphony Orchestra, Werner Andreas Albert, conductor)
1990	**USA**	Cincinnati, Ohio, International Rabbath Institute, July 3 (solo recital)
		Jackson Hole, Wyoming, Grand Teton Music Festival, July 19 (joint recital with Paul Ellison)
		Jackson Hole, Wyoming, Grand Teton Music Festival, July 27–28
		Proto *Carmen Fantasy* with Grand Teton Music Festival Orchestra, Ling Tung, conductor)
	France	Paris, Théâtre Athene, October 20–27
1991	**Germany**	Mittenwald, International Double Bass Festival, May 29
	USA	Cincinnati, Ohio, International Rabbath Institute, June 29–July 11
		Washington, DC (no dates given for Rabbath Institute); recital, Ellington Auditorium, July 15
	Canada	Quebec, Quebec, Église de Sainte-Pétronille, August 1 (with Claude Soury, piano)
		Winnipeg, Muriel Richardson Auditorium, August 13 (with Barbara Riske, piano)

1992	**France**	Paris, Les Alligators, February 17–18 (with Pierre Yves Sorin)
		Tarbes, Théâtre des Variété, April 30
	USA	Cincinnati, Ohio, Colbert Auditorium, International Rabbath Institute, July 12 (solo recital)
		Washington, DC, July 24 (no dates given for Rabbath Institute)
	Canada	Quebec, Église de Sainte-Pétronille, August 6
	France	Flaine, Festival de Musique, August 23
		Villejuif, Théâtre Romain Rolland, October 3
		Toulouse, November 3 (Proto *Carmen Fantasy* with Toulouse Chamber Orchestra)
1993	**France**	Tarbes, Théâtre des Variété, February 5
	USA	Chicago, March 20 (Proto *Carmen Fantasy* with the Illinois Philharmonic, Carmon DeLeone, conductor)
		Austin, Texas, University of Texas–Austin, March 25 (Proto *Carmen Fantasy* with the University of Texas Philharmonic)
		Tucson, Arizona, Proscenium Theater, March 29 (Proto *Carmen Fantasy* with the ADBS Festival Orchestra)
		Charleston, Gaillard Municipal Auditorium, April 3 (Proto *Carmen Fantasy* with Charleston Symphony, David Stahl, conductor)
	France	Villejuif, Théâtre Romain Roland, October 11 (with Guy Béart)
		Paris, UNESCO, October 12 (*La guerre et la paix*)
	Germany	Heidelberg, October 29, 31
1994	**Australia**	Hobart, Tasmania, March 19 (Proto *Carmen Fantasy* with Tasmanian Symphony Orchestra, Max McBride, conductor)
		Brisbane, Queensland Conservatory, March 24
	Taiwan	Taipei, National Concert Hall, April 7

	France	Cannes, Palais du Festival, July 7 (with Michel Legrand and Nina Simone)
		Lyon, Hôtel de Ville, July 17
		Avignon, Palais des Papes, European Bass Festival, August 5 (Proto *Carmen Fantasy* with Orchestre Régional Avignon-Provence, Xavier Bilger, conductor)
		Apt, Orchestre Régional Avignon-Provence, August 6
		Flaine, Festival de Musique, August 20
1995	**USA**	Cincinnati, Ohio, Cincinnati Conservatory, June 18
		Michigan, June 25–29
		Washington, DC, Rabbath Institute (no dates given); recital, Baltimore, Maryland, French Embassy, July 6
	Scotland	Glasgow, International String Workshop, July 15–29; recital, July 27 (Gerald Fischbach)
	France	Flaine, Festival de Musique, August 18 (Proto *Carmen Fantasy* with Orchestra Symphonique Français)
1996	**Australia**	Melbourne, Geelong Grammar School, January 5, 7
		Melbourne, Radio: Bob Holmes, February 9
	France	Paris, Salle Cortot, April 14 (Proto *Carmen Fantasy* with Orchestra "Lili Boulanger," Michel Cosson, conductor)
	Austria	Graz, International String Workshop, July 23–31
	USA	Washington, DC, Rabbath Institute, August 19–23
		San Francisco, Rabbath Institute, August 27–September 5
	Poland	Wrocław, Zamek (Castle) Wojnowice, World Bass Festival, November 9
	Finland	Helsinki, November 18–23

Canada   Quebec, Orchestre Symphonique de Quebec, December 6–10 (Proto *Carmen Fantasy*; Legrand *Contrebande pour contrebasse*, Boris Brott, conductor)

1997 Denmark   Copenhagen, Garrisons Kirke, January 31 (Proto *Carmen Fantasy*; Legrand *Contrebande pour contrebasse*, Danmarks Radios Underholdnings-Orkester, Frans Rasmussen, conductor, with Niels Henning Ørsted Pedersen)

France   Paris, Theatre Moliere, February 23

USA   Houston, Texas, ISB Convention, June 3–7, concert, June 7 (Proto *Four Scenes after Picasso* with Shepherd School Symphony Orchestra, Larry Rachleff, conductor)

San Francisco, Rabbath Institute, June 9–21

Washington, DC, Rabbath Institute, June 22–30

Norway   Stavanger, International String Workshop, July 18–31

France   Pont Saint-Esprit, Collégiale, August 11–23 (with Ivry Gitlis, August 6; solo recital, August 17; Schubert "Trout," August 18; student recital, August 22 with Min Chung)

1998 France   Morsang-sur-Orge, Château de Morsang-sur Orge, February 3 (Bridgette Vandôme, piano)

USA   CD-ROM promotional tour

Los Angeles, March 29
San Francisco, March 31
Los Angeles, April 5

San Francisco, Dominican College of San Rafael, Golden Gate Bass Camp, June 9–21

Washington, DC, Rabbath Institute, June 22–30

France   Biarritz, International String Workshop, July 7

	Canada	Quebec, Domaine Forget, July 25 (no dates given for workshop)
1999	Italy	Venice, Palazzo Zenobio, Rabbath International Institute, April 21
	USA	Washington, DC, June 24 (no dates given for Rabbath Institute) (Larsson *Concertino for Double Bass*)
		San Francisco, Dominican College of San Rafael, Golden Gate Bass Camp, July 14
	Canada	Quebec, Domaine Forget, July 13–August 1 (Proto *Carmen Fantasy* with Orchestre de l'Estuaire, August 1)
	France	Pont-Saint-Esprit, August 12
2000	USA	Honolulu, Hawaiian Bass Festival, March 21–April 13 (George Wellington)
		Washington, DC, Rabbath International Institute (no dates given) (world premiere Proto *Nine Variants*)
	Australia	Adelaide, Bassworks Workshop, June 9–13
	Austria	Graz, International String Workshop, July 24–August 6 (recital, Proto *Carmen Fantasy*, *Nine Variants*)
	Japan	Tokyo, Tokyo Philharmonic Orchestra, late August–early September (Proto *Carmen Fantasy*)
2001	USA	Washington, DC, Rabbath Institute, June 24–29; recital, June 26
	Australia	Brisbane, July 3–15; recital, July 5 (with Tony Caramea, jazz piano and Diana Beer, piano)
	Canada	Quebec, Domaine Forget, July 23–August 8; recital, August 2 (with Suzannne Goyette, piano)
	France	Pont-Saint-Esprit, August 13–25; recital, August 13 (with Bridgette Vandôme, piano)

2002 USA   Honolulu, Hawaiian Bass Workshop, March 21–April 3 (premiere of Proto *Nine Variants* with Honolulu Symphony Orchestra, Samuel Wong, conductor, March 31, April 2)

Muncie, Indiana, Ball State University, April 4–9; recital, April 7 (with Frank Puzzullo, jazz piano, and Patricia Sweger, piano)

Cincinnati, Ohio, Rabbath International Institute, April 10–17

Washington, DC, Rabbath Institute, June 22–30

Norway   Stavanger, International String Workshop, July 6–19; recital, July 8 (Schubert "Arpeggione," Proto *Nine Variants* with orchestra)

France   Lille, Lille Théâtre, November 15 (concert was filmed for *Carte Blanche* DVD, with Lille Chamber Orchestra, Frank Proto, conductor)

2003 Australia   Adelaide, Eder Hall, April 8–16; recital, April 12

Canberra, April 19–20

Canada   Quebec City, Quebec, May 3–8

France   Biarritz, July 2–13

Canada   Quebec, Domaine Forget, July 16–26

USA   Washington, DC, Rabbath Institute, July 27–August 1

2004 USA   Honolulu, Hawaiian Bass Workshop, March 21–28

Austria   Graz, International String Workshop, July 18–23

Canada   Quebec, Domaine Forget, July 25–August 8

USA   Washington, DC, Rabbath Institute, August 9–14

Poland   Wrocław, World Bass Festival, August 14–22

England   London, Menuhin School, August 31–September 3, September 7–8 (Caroline Emery, organizer)

2005*	**Canada**	Quebec, Domaine Forget (no dates given)
	USA	Kalamazoo, ISB Convention, June 6–11
		Washington, DC, Rabbath Institute, August 5–12
2006	**Canada**	Quebec, Domaine Forget (no dates given)
		Washington, DC, Rabbath Institute, August 1–5
2007	**USA**	Ithaca, New York, Ithaca Theatre, June 20
		Chicago, DePaul University, April 3
		Washington, DC, Rabbath Institute (no dates given)
2008	**USA**	Stony Brook, New York, February 27
		New York, New York, David Gage Bass Shop, Michael's Masterclass Videos, March 3
	Germany	Blankenburg, Michaelstein Abbey, March 7–15 (Silvo Dalla Torre, organizer)
		Berlin, Hochschule für Musik, March 16 (Stephen Petzold, organizer)
	USA	Washington, DC, Rabbath Institute, July 3–12
	Canada	Quebec, Domaine Forget, July 3–28 (Basil Dragon with Cyril Rabbath, juggler)
	Poland	Wrocław World Bass Festival, August 3–9

Tour of the Middle East with Kinan Azmeh, clarinet; Sylvain Rabbath, piano

	Syria	Aleppo, October 13
		Damascus, October 15
	Lebanon	Beirut, October 18
2009	**England**	London, Menuhin School, March 4–8 (Caroline Emery, organizer)
	Germany	Blankenburg, Michaelstein Abbey, March 21–29 (Silvo Dalla Torre, organizer)
		Köthen, March 30
	France	Cluny, April 4

---

* For 2005–07, François's calendar is incomplete.

	Spain	Madrid, National Conservatory, April 24–26 masterclass (with Cyril Rabbath, juggler)
	France	Paris, IRCAM, high-speed internet masterclass and recital to Miami, Florida, April 27 (masterclass to bass section of New World Symphony, Paul Ellison)
	Morocco	Rabat, May 19–25
	Syria	Damascus, May 25–27 (with Kinan Azmeh, clarinet)
		Damascus Syrian National Symphony Orchestra, June 3 (Proto *Nine Variants*)
	Canada	Quebec, Domaine Forget, July 11–27
	France	Paris, Temple d'Otheuill, October 11 (benefit for musician pension fund)
2010	USA	Honolulu, Hawaiian Bass Workshop, March 21–28
		Doris Duke Theater, March 22, Shangri La, March 27
		Washington, DC, Rabbath Institute, July 6–10 (last time in DC)
	Canada	Quebec, Domaine Forget, July 12–25
	Spain	Madrid, Madrid National Conservatory, September 22–23
2011	Korea	Seoul, May, 17–27 (two recitals, press recital, television, La Compagne recital)
	Canada	Quebec, Domaine Forget, July 9–23
	England	London, Menuhin School, August 20–28 (Caroline Emery, organizer)
	USA	Hattiesburg, Mississippi, University of Southern Mississippi, September 21–October 9 (solo recital, Proto *Nine Variants* with USM Symphony)
2012	USA	Honolulu, Hawaiian Bass Workshop, March 15–April 1
		Honolulu Museum of Art, March 30, Shangri La, March 31

Minneapolis, Minnesota, McNally Smith College, McPhail Center for Music, April 13–15: recital, April 14; masterclass April 13, 15

South American tour, Proto *Nine Variants* with orchestra

Brazil	Bagé, FIMP Festival, Rio Grande do Sul, July 22–27
Uruguay	Montevideo, Teatro Solis, July 31–August 1
	Caxias do Sul, televised August 8
	Porto Alegre, August 9
	São Paulo, Casa de Cultura Recital, August 13
France	Paris, Maison de la Radio, November 22–23
	Paris, Théâtre de l'Athénée, November 26 (Bach CD promotion)
Spain	Barcelona, December 28 (with Paco Ibáñez)
2013 **France**	Paris, Thèâtre du Châtelet, January 30 (with Paco Ibáñez)
USA	Lincoln, Nebraska, Meadowlark Music Festival, July 2–6; recital, July 5
	Kansas City, Kansas City Bass Workshop, July 8–14; recital, July 11
Canada	Quebec, Domaine Forget, July 14–23; recital, July 19
France	Capbreton, August 18–25; recital, August 21
	Varacieux, Laborie Atelier, November 30
2014 **USA**	Honolulu, Hawaiian Bass Workshop, March 24–28
	Kansas City, Kansas City Bass Workshop, June 24–July 4
	Minneapolis, Minnesota, Twin Cities Bass Camp, July 5–August 1
Canada	Quebec, Domaine Forget, July 16–24 (no recital)

	France	Paris, Les Pavillons-sous-Bois, November 9
		Paris, Théâtre des Champs-Élysées, November 10 (with Paco Ibáñez)
	Spain	Séville, Séville Théâtre, November 20 (with Paco Ibáñez)
2015	**USA**	Kansas City, Kansas City Bass Workshop, June 19–23
		Saint Paul, Minnesota, Twin Cities Bass Camp, June 27–July 1
		Cleveland, Ohio, Cleveland Institute of Music, July 4–7
		Lincoln, Nebraska, Meadowlark Music Festival, July 9–10
		Austin, Texas, Austin Bass Workshop, July 13–15
		Albuquerque, New Mexico, Albuquerque Bass Workshop, July 17–20
	Canada	Quebec, Domaine Forget, July 23–31; recital, July 31
2016	**France**	**Tour with Philippe Dubreil**
		Les Pavillons-sous-Bois, Conservatoire Hector Berlioz, January 9–10 (two concerts with Sinfonietta Paris)
		Paris, ESRA International Film School, February 7 (with Sylvain Rabbath, piano)
		Longueau, Centre Culturel Picasso, February 13 (with orchestra)
		Saint-Georges-sur-Cher, February 18 (with Sylvain Rabbath, piano)
		Paris, Crémaillère Studio, April 7 (with Sylvain Rabbath, piano)
		Apt, Église Saint-Saturnin d'Apt, May 20 (with Sylvain Rabbath, piano)
		Varacieux, Laborie Atelier, May 22 (with Sylvain Rabbath, piano)

	USA	Tour to four cities, performances with chamber orchestras

> Washington, DC, July 6
> New York, July 12
> Kansas City, Kansas City Bass Workshop, July 15–19
> St. Paul, Twin Cities Bass Camp, July 22–26; Minneapolis, performance

	Canada	Quebec, Domaine Forget, August 1–6; recital, August 5
	Australia	Brisbane, September 8
		Sydney, Blue Mountains, September 11
		Adelaide, September 14
		Hobart, September 18
		Brisbane, September 23
2017	**France**	Alba la Romaine, February 18
		Menneville, May 28 (with Sylvain Rabbath, piano)
	USA	Ithaca, New York, ISB Convention, June 6–10 (Concerto No. 3 for Gary Karr, in attendance)
		Kansas City, Kansas City Bass Workshop, June 14–18; recital, June 15
		Los Angeles, Rabbath Institute, June 22–28
	France	Paris, La Sorbonne, October 6 (with Paco Ibáñez)
		Paris, Opéra Comique, October 10
2018	**Canada**	Quebec, Domaine Forget, July 16–21; recital July 20
	Germany	Mühldorf, Bavarian Bass Days, October 27–29 (Claus Freudenstein)
2019	**Canada**	Quebec, Domaine Forget, July 29–August 3; recital, August 2
2021	**France**	Live-streamed recital from Paris to ISB Convention, June 9
		Apt, Église Saint-Saturnin d'Apt, August 11 (premiere of two movements of François's Concerto No. 4)

Index